THE TERMS
of
THE GAME

Frank Tyson
THE TERMS *of* THE GAME

A DICTIONARY OF CRICKET

Houghton Mifflin Australia

Houghton Mifflin Australia Pty Ltd
PO Box 289, Ferntree Gully, Victoria 3156
112 Lewis Rd, Knoxfield, Victoria 3180, Australia

First published 1990

National Library of Australia
Cataloguing-in-Publication entry:

Tyson, Frank.
    The terms of the game.

    ISBN 0 86770 123 4.
    ISBN 0 86770 112 9 (pbk.).

    1. Cricket — Dictionaries. I. Title.

796.35803

Edited by Alex Skovron
Designed by Peter Yates
Illustrated by Bill Farr
Typeset in Plantin by Abb-typesetting Pty Ltd
Printed in Australia by Australian Print Group

For Lyall Frederick George Miels,
the best of fathers-in-law.

To a man who loved cricket
from a cricketer who loved him.

Contents

List of diagrams

Introduction

'The game is played between two sides, one out in the field and one in. The side that's in goes in, and the side that's out in the field goes out and tries to get the side coming in out. Each man in the side that's in goes in until he's out, when the next man goes in. When each man in the side that's in has been in and out, the side that was out in the field then goes in and the side that was in goes out into the field and tries to get the team then coming in out. When both teams have been in and out, including the not-outs, that ends the game.'

Cricket is a closed book to many people. Spectators reared on a fast-food sporting diet of immediate thrills and physical contact find it hard to enthuse over cricket's unexciting lacunae when few boundaries are hit and no wickets fall. They have little empathy with the languid ambience and the fine technicalities of the game. It is a different story for the participant. A bowler gets a real buzz out of beating a batsman with swing or spin — even if he does not send the stumps rocketing out of the ground or entice his opponent into giving a catch. And a batsman gains a tremendous satisfaction from mere survival — unproductive though it may be — on a green seaming pitch which is helping the fast-bowler. In such situations Test players may exhibit superb bowling and batting skills; but without the icing of stylish boundaries, spectacular catches and flying stumps, the spectator finds the cake unappetizing.

Whole nations find the subtleties of cricket incomprehensible. The sedate pace and cerebral machinations of a five-day Test leave even the most excitable Frenchman cold; he cannot believe that a day of lounging around a field, and sometimes hitting, throwing or chasing a ball, constitutes either amusement or entertainment. He believes that the English were — and probably still are — so irreligious that they invented cricket to give themselves some idea of eternity! When British colonists introduced the sport into Australia, it was said that the mystified Aborigines regarded a game of cricket as a rainmaking ceremony: every time the newcomers produced their clubs, sticks and ball, the heavens opened! During one of his visits to England, the American comedian Groucho Marx was taken to see a cricket match at Lord's. For two hours he watched a placid county game, before he finally turned to his host and remarked, 'Say, when are those guys going to stop warming up and start this game?'

This book is an attempt to conduct even gallic Groucho Marxes into a better appreciation of the beauties of cricket. It seeks to sharpen the innocent observer's palate to some of the tasty nuances of cricket enjoyed by the player, while introducing and illuminating the technical knowledge and language which radio and television commentators often and erroneously presume their audiences to share. The language of cricket is, after all, prone to a manner of ellipsis that can shorten expressions almost to cryptic incomprehensibility. Thus, a bowler who is 'slashed through the gully' does not suffer partial decapitation, but rather has one of his deliveries struck hard behind the wicket on the off-side of the third-slip position. By the same token, the exclamation 'He's hooked him!' refers neither to a punch nor to a manoeuvre with a fishing-line; it tells us simply that the subject has struck the object's delivery with a hook shot.

Understandably, the game's idiom renders it extremely difficult to reproduce in a foreign language. In French, for example, to dismiss a batsman lbw is rendered as 'mettre un batteur hors du jeu à cause du pied obstructif'. The point fieldsman becomes 'le chasseur, à droite du batteur dans le prolongement du guichet'. So much for ellipsis!

Television has revolutionized cricket, by bringing, into the living-room, Tests and limited-over games contested by the best cricketers in the world. Without going out through the front door, home viewers now have an excellent vantage over a first-class sporting spectacle from the best and most comfortable seat available — their own armchair, immediately in line with the pitch. If the game they are watching is a one-day match, they are virtually assured of an exciting result and a good deal of entertaining action within a predetermined time-frame. Cricket's shift into the world of TV entertainment, however, has not radically transformed the game's use of the English language. It is true that graphic new expressions have crept into the lexicon of terms used by the media in talking and writing about limited-over cricket: such terms as *circle*, *go for ten runs an over* and *strike-rate*. But cricketing terminology remains largely based on the traditional vernacular that has evolved over a thousand years of playing the game. This book expounds on both the new and the old dialects, dovetailing the ancient with the modern; it explains both antique and newly-arisen terms to converts to televised cricket, while adding, it is hoped, to the knowledge of veteran aficionados.

I intend this book to be more than a comprehensive cricket dictionary, to go beyond the mere explanation of cricketing terms, expanding and enriching the reader's knowledge of every aspect of the game. It illustrates by examples, explains the components of the skills, and traces historical developments. It adds Attic salt to the factual dish with occasional anecdotes and observations. I have never lost sight of the fact that cricket is a game played by real people with human foibles, personal failings and amusing traits. Human nature can transform cricketing technicalities into funny incidents that sometimes illustrate an explanation better than a thousand words. The text seeks to be impersonally authoritative, to be sure, but also to present some of my own views on the issues and incidents that have made my life in cricket so interesting and rewarding. It seeks to entertain as well as to inform.

No publication of this kind can be all-embracing. Space limitations do not permit the inclusion of too many statistical records, the mention of every Test ground or the explanation of every law. But in performing a balanced factual duty, the book does yield up a kind of database: record team scores, outstanding achievements with bat and ball, unusual feats, large crowds, the names of the world's main Test grounds, and the notable deeds of famous cricketers, past and present (though of course, no individual players can be given their own entries). The statistically minded, however, seeking the minutiae of the game, should use this book in conjunction with the *Wisden Cricketers' Almanack* and its allied publications.

Cross-references to other entries are given, in italics, when the information in those entries extends or impinges directly on the facts provided in the item at hand. Thus, a glance at the entry *edge* and its cross-references reveals that there are many surprising slants on the definition of a simple deflection. According to the part of the bat which makes contact with the ball, the unintentional stroke can be described as an *inside, outside, bottom* or *top edge*, a *thin* or *thick edge*; a shot can come off the *middle of the edge*; and one deliberately steered through the slips is given an intelligence of its own and called an *educated edge*.

Whilst I have exercised an editorial discretion in determining what should be omitted, I have always sought to include items that titillate the reader's curiosity — often with intriguing details whose importance may be small in the broader context of the game, but whose interest is great. An entry rarely exists in splendid isolation; it is usually part of a grander plan to help the inquisitive to venture into previously unknown byways of the game. Whether adhering to or turning off the freeways of cricketing jargon, the reader never knows where his or her curiosity might lead. The entry *fast-bowler*, for instance, might be a starting-point for a journey whose sequence of interlinked stations includes *swing, outswinger, bowl from wide on the crease, return crease, no-ball, intimidatory bowling, short-pitched delivery, hook, back and across, inside the line of the ball, outside the off-stump, off-side, playing area, boundary, sightscreen* — and so on. An alternative route from *fast-bowler* might lead through *seam, work on the ball, shine, ball, out, run-out, runner, square-leg, umpires, short run, ground one's bat, batting crease, mankadding, back up, non-striker's end, leg-byes* — again the pathways could be extended indefinitely, as individual entries fan out in multiple directions. The ramifications proliferate richly as the exploration proceeds.

The overlap and repetition of information are inevitable if related entries are to be covered fully. The restating of information, however, is confined to explanations and definitions which would be either confusing or incomplete — and therefore incorrect — without it. Thus, it is imperative to reiterate descriptions of identical foot-movements in outlining the technique involved in playing those two very different shots, the *front-foot drive* and the *front-foot defensive stroke*; without these details the portrayals of the shots would be incomplete and the reader's appreciation of them confused. But it is not necessary to restate the theory of swing in the entries *outswinger* and *inswinger*; that principle is adequately dealt with in the cross-referenced entry *swing* and is not essential to the understanding of how outswing or inswing is bowled. Nor is it necessary to cross-reference constantly repeated terms such as 'ball', 'bat', 'pitch' and 'wicket' each time they occur.

In consulting this book, the reader should adopt a flexible approach. A cross-reference is sometimes stated using an ending or grammatical form slightly different from that under which the term in question appears. It should also be noted that there are no cross-references to the diagrams that have been scattered throughout the book. A list of these illustrations will be found on the Contents page.

In outlining the game's skills, I have resorted to a majority position and presumed the player to be right-handed. Descriptions of field placements and of the movements involved in the execution of a skill are therefore generally based on this premise, with the words 'right' and 'left' usually avoided. Also, and without meaning to be sexist, I have consistently used the terms 'batsman' and 'fieldsman' — having discovered that most women who play cricket prefer the traditional terminology to 'batter', 'batsperson' or 'fieldsperson'. Accordingly I have uniformly employed the masculine pronouns 'he' and 'him', and the male possessive 'his'. Key measurements are often stated in both imperial and metric units; in view of the fact that some of the dimensions were originally in Saxon and other pre-imperial measures, I could do no less.

I sincerely hope that this book adds to your enjoyment of a wonderful game.

Frank Tyson

Cricket: a historical outline

In 1787 the English Society of Antiquarians discovered an entry in the royal wardrobe accounts of Edward I for March 1300, allocating £6 to Master John de Leek, Prince Edward's chaplain, for the Prince's 'playing at creag and other sports at Westminster and Newenton'. While it is very likely that this ledger record is the first written reference to the game of cricket, it seems certain that the sport was played by Saxon Englishmen on the Sussex weald long before the Norman Conquest.

Indeed it is generally accepted that the game is of Anglo-Saxon origin. The implement which gave the game its name is defined by Dr Johnson in his dictionary as: '*cryce*, Saxon, a stick'. Nor is it a coincidence that the length of a cricket pitch remains to this day 66 feet: the exact width of a Saxon farmer's strip-holding under the medieval agricultural system. The Saxon verb *wican* means 'to yield or offer a way through' and was employed by the wealden shepherds to denote the wicket gate that closed the entrance to a sheep-pen, and subsequently the 'wicket' which, together with the 'stumps' of trees, served as the bowler's target when they whiled away the weary watches playing cricket. The first wickets used in cricket were like the sheep-pen gates, long and low, without a centre stump. Similarly, early cricket bats were, like shepherd's crooks, curved at the bottom — a feature that greatly helped the batsman to dig out the 'grubbers' or 'sneaks' which were the speciality of the early underarm bowlers.

Before the English Civil War, cricket remained the pastime of children and villagers. It was introduced into France in 1540 by the Roman Catholic Stoney Hurst School, which was forced to flee to Rouen to avoid the religious persecution of Henry VIII's Reformation. Significantly the French added a term to the language of cricket: *non pair* — the 'odd man' or umpire called in to settle differences between teams. In 1617 it was recorded that the future Lord Protector, Oliver Cromwell, gained for himself the name of 'a royster' by going to London and indulging in football, cricket, cudgelling and wrestling: behaviour hardly appropriate for a man whose government later decreed the burning of all cricket bats in Ireland by the public hangman!

The defeat of the Royalists in the Civil War led to the banishment of the royal house of Stuart, the abolition of the court and the exclusion of the nobility from government. Earls and peers such as the Sackvilles and Richmonds retired to their country estates, where they observed the peasantry playing cricket. Out of boredom they joined in and, when

Charles II was restored to the throne in 1660 and the nobility to favour, they brought their new recreation back to London and the court. Devotees of the game included the Earls of Middlesex, Sandwich and Tankerville, the Duke of Dorset, and even the 'First Gentleman of Europe', Frederick Louis, the Prince of Wales. Sums as large as £20 000 were wagered on matches; to win them, patrons recruited star players from the ranks of villagers and employed them as huntsmen, whippers-in, bailiffs — and as professional cricketers! Laws to govern a game that had become financially significant became important and in 1744 the existing orally defined regulations were set down in the first written code of laws. In 1771 a Reigate batsman, 'Shock' White, defied dismissal by batting with a bat that was wider than the wicket; thereafter bats were restricted to a width of 10.8 cm. In 1774 the laws were revised, and one year later a third stump was added to the wicket to prevent batsmen such as John Small escaping being bowled when bowlers like 'Lumpy' Stevens continually sent the ball through the stumps!

From 1756 to 1787 the premier club in England was the Hambledon, whose home was on the 'Cradle of Cricket', Broad Halfpenny Down, just outside Winchester. Hambledon could call upon the services of star players such as 'Silver Billy' Beldham, Tom Sueter, David Harris, the Nyrens, William Fenex and John Small, and on its day was capable of beating county sides. In 1787 the Earl of Winchelsea and the future Duke of Richmond, Charles Lennox, both members of the White Conduit Club, commissioned an employee, Yorkshire-born Thomas Lord, to establish a cricket ground on Dorset Square in London. The ground was subsequently moved to Regent's Park and then Marylebone, where Lord's still remains: the headquarters of the Marylebone Cricket Club. The MCC took over the mantle of the Hambledon Club, assumed the responsibilities of making and revising the laws, and in 1903 became the body sponsoring England sides that toured overseas.

Cricket was being played regularly in Australia on Sydney's Domain in 1803, between teams from the military and civilian populations. It took root in Melbourne in 1838 with the establishment of the Melbourne Cricket Club. At the same time, representative county teams were springing up in England. Sussex, Nottinghamshire, Surrey, Yorkshire, Middlesex, Gloucestershire and Lancashire all took to the field between 1835 and 1870. The expansion of the railways enabled teams to travel far afield to show off their skills to spectators. National sides were formed. In 1846, Nottinghamshire-born William Clarke, the architect of the Trent Bridge ground, founded his professional All-England Eleven and processed through the country with talents such as those of George Parr, Fuller Pilch, Alfred Mynn, John Jackson, Richard Daft, John Wisden and 'Felix'. Other professional elevens were formed, including the United All-England and the United South of England.

It was only a small step from national to international cricket. An England eleven visited America and Canada in 1859, and two years later the Surrey professional H.H. Stephenson led the first England team to visit the Australian colonies. The visit of Stephenson's side was underwritten by the Melbourne catering firm of Spiers and Pond and substituted for a cancelled lecture tour by the author Charles Dickens. In 1868 Australia sent its first touring side to England: an Aboriginal eleven managed and trained in Victoria's Western District by visiting English professional Charles Lawrence. In 1877, encouraged by earlier successes against English teams, a combined side from New South Wales and Victoria met James Lillywhite's Englishmen on an equal footing at the Melbourne Cricket Ground. The home side won by 45 runs what has become recognized as the inaugural Test match, and the following year a cock-a-hoop Australia sent its first official touring party to England under the captaincy of David Gregory. Since 1878 England and Australia have exchanged touring teams and contested Test series on a regular basis. During the 1891/92 tour of Australia, the patron of the England side, Lord Sheffield, donated the money that purchased the shield named after him, which became the trophy of the annual first-class competition played between the states.

More than 1000 Tests have been played since the inaugural game of 1877. The club of Test-playing nations was expanded in 1905 by the addition of South Africa, followed in 1928 by the West Indies, in 1929 by New Zealand, in 1932 by India, in 1952 by Pakistan and in 1982 by Sri Lanka. To regulate the game, national and international governing bodies have proliferated. In 1898 the English Board of Control (renamed the Test and County Cricket Board in 1968) was set up, and seven years later its Australian counterpart was established. Cricket followed the English to every corner of their empire and soon the pupils were turning the tables on their former masters, showing themselves adept enough at the game to play at the highest level. The Imperial Cricket Conference, subsequently known as the International Cricket Conference, was established in 1909 by England, Australia and South Africa to oversee Test matches. Its membership was swollen as other countries took up the Test cudgels, and was depleted when South Africa left the Commonwealth in 1961.

The tapestry of Test cricket since its inception has been colourful and variegated. It has been adorned by great players: W.G. Grace, the man who invented modern batting technique, bringing it out of the middle ages of the game; Fred Spofforth, the 'Demon' bowler; Victor Trumper, the personification of batting elegance; Jack Hobbs, the 'Master' batting technician; Wilfred Rhodes, the complete all-rounder; Don Bradman, the batting phenomenon; George Headley, the Black Bradman from the West Indies; Harold Larwood, the Nottinghamshire express bowler and the victim of the Bodyline controversy; Len Hutton, the breaker of Bradman's record Test score of 334 and the compiler of 364 runs in 13 hours; the three 'W's, Frank Worrell, Everton Weekes and Clyde Walcott, the great triumvirate of West Indian batsmen; Gary Sobers, the holder of the record Test score; Sunil Gavaskar, the little Indian opener who out-Bradmanned the prolific centurian; lightning-fast bowlers such as West Indians Wes Hall, Andy Roberts, Michael Holding and Malcolm Marshall, and Australians Keith Miller, Ray Lindwall, Jeff Thomson and Dennis Lillee; master craftsmen of seam and swing such as Englishmen Maurice Tate, Alec Bedser, Brian Statham, Fred Trueman and Ian Botham, Pakistanis Fazal Mahmood and Imran Khan, Indian Kapil Dev and New Zealander Richard Hadlee. The list of talents swells beyond the possibility of comprehensiveness when one considers other individual claims on greatness: Australians Neil Harvey, Arthur Morris, Norm O'Neill, the Chappell brothers, Doug Walters, Bill Lawry, Bob Simpson; Englishmen Ken Barrington, Peter May, Colin Cowdrey, Geoff Boycott; West Indians Sonny Ramadhin, Alf Valentine, Viv Richards, Gordon Greenidge, Desmond Haynes, Clive Lloyd; South Africans Barry Richards and Graeme Pollock; Indian spinners such as Bishen Bedi, B.S. Chandrasekhar and E.A.S. Prasanna; New Zealander Martin Crowe; and Sri Lankan Aravinda de Silva.

The history of cricket has also been studded with great sides, and momentous issues and events. Have there ever been better Test teams than Darling's 1902 Australian tourists, F.S. Jackson's 1905 England combination, Warwick Armstrong's side of 1920/21, Bradman's 1948 eleven, or Clive Lloyd's West Indian juggernaut of the 1980s? Have there been more contentious developments, more exciting moments or more engrossing episodes in the annals of sport than the Australian wins over England in the 'Ashes' Test of 1882 and at Old Trafford in 1902, the Bodyline tour of 1932/33, the tied Australia–West Indies Test in Brisbane in 1960/61, the introduction of limited-over cricket at first-class and international level, and the 'Packer Revolution' of 1977?

Cricket began as a rustic game, played by peasants who bowled underarm and used primitive equipment. Passing through eras that produced roundarm and then overarm bowling, a scientific approach to batting methods, improved pitches and grounds, better equipment, more efficient organization and professional players, it has evolved into a subtle and highly complex sport which is both a popular pastime and a popular entertainment. It has spread to most countries in the British Commonwealth, and beyond, and has come to occupy a quasi-religious position in the English culture.

Abbreviations used in scoring and reporting

av, avge	average (runs per innings or per wicket)	LB	leg-bye
		lbw	leg before wicket
b	bowled	M	maiden over
B	bye	NB	no-ball
BLSP	bad light stopped play	n.o., NO	not out
		R	runs
(c)	captain	r.o.	run out
c, ct	caught	ret	retired
c & b	caught and bowled	RSP	rain stopped play
dec	declared	O	over
DNB	did not bat	st	stumped
FOW	fall of wicket	ump	umpire
HS	highest score	(vc)	vice-captain
inns, I	innings	W	wide; wicket

A DICTIONARY OF CRICKET

a

across the line. The batsman who attempts to strike a straight ball at an angle across the line of its approach is said to be hitting across the line of the ball. Perfect timing is needed to hit the ball, since the only possible point of contact is where the flight of the ball and the path of the bat intersect. Hitting across the line or flight of the ball is regarded as a major batting fault — one that greatly reduces the chances of making contact with a delivery. (See also *play straight*)

action replays. Instant videotape reruns, usually in slowmotion, of interesting, instructive or contentious moments in a game, shown to television viewers, and to spectators at grounds that have electronic *scoreboards* with videoscreens. Action replays permit even the inexpert viewer to gain a precise appreciation of vital incidents, such as dismissals and run-outs. When an umpire gives a wrong decision, however, he suffers by seeing his mistake immediately and repeatedly shown to the world at large. Batsmen, indignant at the rough justice handed out by the umpire, can now glare back at the replay on the electronic scoreboard — and sometimes see their indignation justified! On the other hand, the replay has been a godsend to radio and television commentators. The TV monitors that are now essential equipment in every broadcasting box have endowed them with the qualities of hindsight and retrospective expertise that some may have lacked in the past. (See also *photo-finish*)

adjournments. See *intervals*.

administration. General term applied to the various governing bodies and secretariats of cricket: organizations responsible for the efficient running of the game at all levels. In Australia, the administration of international, first-class, grade, country and all junior cricket is centralized in the hands of the Australian Cricket Board (ACB) and its affiliated state associations. The ACB is made up of delegates from each of the states. In England there is more devolution. The Test and County Cricket Board (TCCB) and county committees administer Tests, official tours and first-class competitions, but responsibility for junior cricket is delegated to the National Cricket Association (NCA) and autonomous league committees. The TCCB comprises representatives from the 17 first-class counties, the MCC, the Minor Counties Cricket

1

Association, the Oxford and Cambridge Cricket Clubs, and the Irish and Scottish Cricket Unions. The Cricket Council (CC) is the umbrella governing body for cricket in the British Isles, comprising a chairman, a vice-chairman, and representatives from the TCCB, the NCA, the MCC, the Minor Counties Cricket Association, and the Irish and Scottish Cricket Unions.

The International Cricket Council (ICC), formerly the International Cricket Conference, is the supreme governing body of international cricket. It is made up of representatives from 2 foundation member nations (England and Australia), 5 full Test-playing member nations (India, New Zealand, West Indies, Pakistan and Sri Lanka), 18 Associate member nations, and 5 Affiliate member nations. The various national boards of control oversee the game in their respective countries. (See also *MCC*)

aggregate. The total number of runs scored or wickets taken by a player in the course of an innings, a match, a season, a tour or a career at a specified level of cricket — e.g. a first-class run aggregate, a career aggregate of Test wickets, and so on. (See also *batting average*; *bowling average*)

aggro. Abbreviation for 'aggression' provocatively combined with 'aggravation': a characteristic deemed by many commentators to be an essential part of a competitive cricketer's make-up. Nonetheless, it is a quality that leads to many instances of *sledging*, bad language and angry confrontations on the cricket field — and situations that are simply '*not cricket*'.

agricultural stroke. A rough-and-ready, unscientific stroke, usually a wild looping swing of the bat, similar to the swing of a scythe; also called a slog. The chances of such a stroke making contact with the ball are remote since the semicircular path of the swinging bat rarely crosses the straight line of the approaching ball. However, when a *slogger* does make contact with the ball, he can hit it 'out of sight'. A useful if risky stroke, when quick runs are needed.

In the mid-1930s, Robert Menzies, cricket buff and future prime minister of Australia, was watching a New South Wales game from the delegates' room of the Sydney Cricket Ground. The young Don Bradman was batting, when one of the many experts found in such places passed the opinion that the Don's strokes were very agricultural. 'Perhaps,' answered Menzies, 'but certainly very fruitful.'

all out. See *dismiss a side*.

all-rounder. A player who is adept at both batting and bowling; usually a bowler who can bat adequately. The all-rounder generally bats at number 6, 7 or 8 in the *batting order*. Number 6 was the favourite position of Gary Sobers, one of the most remarkable and versatile players ever to grace Test cricket. By the end of his international career he had scored 8032 runs, taken 235 wickets and caught 109 batsmen in 93 Tests. The astonishing thing about these figures was that to achieve them he batted at almost every position from 1 to 10, bowled in three different styles (fast-medium, finger-spin and wrist-spin), and was equally adept in every position and style! Australia has produced such all-round stars as Richie Benaud (2201 runs and 248 wickets), Alan Davidson (1328 runs and 186 wickets) and Keith Miller (2958 runs and 170 wickets). Outstanding modern international all-rounders include Ian Botham (England), Richard Hadlee (New Zealand), Imran Khan (Pakistan) and Malcolm Marshall (West Indies).

But perhaps the greatest all-rounder of them all was the Lancashire League player Ebbut Thewles. Of him it was said that 'he could bat a bit, bowl and field a bit, keep wicket, give a song and clog dance on the dressing-room table after the game, and pay his round of drinks more often than others'.

appeal. To ask the *umpire* if the batsman is *out*. Any member of the fielding side may appeal to the umpire for his decision. The question 'How's that?' or 'Owzat?' asks if the batsman is out, and this appeal applies to any of the ten possible ways of being given out in cricket.

approach. See *run-up*.

arm ball. A disguised delivery of the *finger-spinner*, which does not turn but maintains its original direction or 'goes with the arm'. Thus a right-handed *off-spinner*'s arm ball goes with the arm or *drifts* towards the slips, so that the batsman who plays for the spin might edge a catch to the wicketkeeper or slip fieldsman. A left-handed *leg-spinner*'s arm ball comes back from the batsman's off-side and often finds the 'gate' between bat and pad to hit the stumps. To bowl the off-spin arm ball, the bowler uses the off-spinner's grip but holds the seam vertically, angling it towards the slips. At release the hand slips around the ball rather than spinning it and the seam maintains its angle towards the slips — as in the case of the outswinger.

around the wicket. In bowling around the wicket, the bowling arm is on the side of the body further from the bowler's wicket. A right-arm bowler going around the wicket therefore bowls from the right of the stumps; left-hand around-the-wicket means bowling left-handed from the left side of the stumps. (See also *over the wicket*)

Ashes. The trophy awarded to the winner of an England–Australia Test series: a small, simple, unbaked-clay urn, containing ashes of doubtful origin. The Ashes legend began with the Test played at the Kennington Oval in August 1882. For the first time on English soil, an Australian team, led by Billy Murdoch, lowered the colours of a full-strength England side, by 7 runs. English sporting pride was humbled, and on the day after the national defeat an obituary appeared in the 'Pink 'un' edition of the *Sporting Times*:

In Affectionate Remembrance
of
ENGLISH CRICKET,
Which died at the Oval
on
29th August 1882.
Deeply lamented by a large circle of
Sorrowing Friends and Acquaintances.
R.I.P.

N.B.—The body will be cremated, and the
ashes taken to Australia.

The following English winter of 1882/83 saw the Honourable Ivo Bligh, later Lord Darnley, in Australia with an English team, whose avowed intention, according to a speech by their captain in the Adelaide Town Hall, was that of returning the ashes of English cricket to Lord's. After Bligh's men clinched a series 2–1 victory in the Third Test in Sydney, a group of Melbourne ladies — amongst whom was Bligh's future wife, Miss Frances Morphy — presented the English captain with a tiny clay urn containing the symbolic Ashes. Some say that the ashes were those of the bails used in the Melbourne Test of 1882/83; others that they were those of a cricket ball used in a social game played by the England team on the estate of Sir William Clarke at Ruperts-wood, Sunbury, over Christmas 1882. Modern-day iconoclasts maintain that the ashes are now those from the hearth of Lord Darnley's country house in Kent, swept into the urn by a maid who upset and spilt the precious cinders in the course of her cleaning duties.

Whatever their origins and composition, the Ashes now repose in their urn in the Memorial Gallery at Lord's, where they have stood since Lord Darnley bequeathed them to the MCC in 1928. They have left the gallery only once — on the occasion of their journeying to Australia, in the custody of the Prince of Wales, for the Australian Bicentenary celebrations of 1988.

ask the question. To *appeal* to the umpire for the dismissal of a batsman: i.e. to ask the umpire the all-important question.

asking rate. The average number of runs per over which the side batting last must score in order to win a game — i.e. the number of runs per over which the bowling side 'asks' its opponents to score to emerge victorious. Note that the asking rate will vary as the innings progresses: if the side batting last scores quickly at the outset of its innings, the asking rate will decrease as the tempo of scoring increases. On the other hand, if the side's scoring rate is slow in the early stages of the innings, the asking rate will increase. The term is sometimes applied in respect of the team batting last in a two-innings game, but it is more often used in *limited-over* competitions. (See also *run-rate*)

at full stretch. A batsman who plays at full stretch plays forward to the full extent of his reach; he is deemed to be extremely unlucky if he is adjudged *lbw* at full stretch, since his front pad is a long way from his wicket, reducing to a mere guess any assessment about the ball hitting the stumps. A fieldsman at full stretch reaches or dives as far as he can to take a catch or stop a ball.

attack the ball. To run in from a fielding position to stop, collect and throw to the keeper, in the shortest possible time, the ball hit by the batsman. Attacking the ball is an integral part of the *fieldsman*'s technique when attempting to *run out* a batsman. From his station, the fielder sprints in, stoops and, while still running, collects the ball in his throwing hand, just in front of the foot on the natural side of his body. He steps towards his target wicket and returns the ball with an appropriate *throw*, according to his distance from the target.

Time-saving is the essence of attacking the ball. A close fieldsman should not stand to return the ball, because merely to rise from a stooped position takes one-tenth of a second. In that time an Olympic sprinter can cover one metre; a running batsman probably half that distance. Thus, standing up to throw from cover or mid-wicket can be the difference between not running out a batsman and finding him half a metre out of his crease!

attacking field. The placement of fieldsmen in such a way as to increase the probability of their taking *catches* and dismissing the batsman. Such a field usually has the majority of fieldsmen placed close to the bat, though it can also embrace strategically placed outfielders. For the faster bowler, it might consist of four *slips*, a *gully*, a *silly mid-off* and *silly mid-on*, a *leg-slip* and a *cover* fieldsman — all but one man in wicket-taking or *catching positions*.

Auld Enemy. A term used by Australian and English Test teams to describe each other: inveterate and implacable opponents who have met regularly on the Test field since 1877.

awards and prizes. See *International Cricketer of the Year*; *Man of the Match*; *Player of the Series*.

away-swinger. See *outswinger*.

b

back and across. Initial movement of the batsman which shifts the rear foot back towards the stumps and across towards the off-side, enough to ensure that the rear leg is just alongside the line of the approaching ball with no gap between it and the descending bat. The movement also takes the batsman's head and eyes to a position directly behind the line of the ball, enabling him to follow its every movement through the air and off the pitch. This retreating shift of weight is common to both back-foot and front-foot strokes, since a movement onto the back foot provides the batsman with the launching-pad of a weighted foot from which to play forward; or enables him to continue the backward movement if he decides to play off the back foot.

When he plays a *hook*, or ducks a bouncer, the movement of the back foot takes the batsman's body and head *inside the line* (i.e. to the off-side) of the ball. (See *move inside the line of the ball*)

back away. The player who is afraid of the bowling — particularly when it is fast — betrays his fear of being hit and injured by edging away from the stumps towards square-leg. In so doing, he exposes his wicket and is more likely to be bowled by the full-length straight ball. Ironically, he is also more liable to be hit and injured. Backing away from the wicket means backing away from the *line of the ball* and being unaware of its direction; this causes misjudgment, which may lead to the batsman being hit by the ball that 'follows' him. The batsman who backs away is often teased with accusations of 'treading on the square-leg umpire's corns', or of going so far towards square-leg that 'it looks as if he's going on his holidays'.

back up. To initiate a run at the *non-striker's end* as the bowler takes the last stride of his run-up and begins his bowling action. The non-striking batsman walks up with the bowler in the final phases of the latter's approach, gaining forward momentum and a flying start to the run. He takes care, however, to drag his bat behind him, keeping it in the batting crease until the bowler releases the ball. The batsman who strays out of his ground when backing up can be *'mankadded'* and run out, if the bowler suddenly stops and puts down his wicket. (See also *back-up a fieldsman*)

back-foot defensive stroke. A stroke intended to prevent a ball that pitches just *short of a length* from hitting the wicket or being lofted for a catch. The batsman steps *back and across* in front of his stumps, positioning his rear leg alongside the line of the approaching ball and pointing his front elbow, shoulder, side and leg towards it. The toes of the rear foot point towards *point*. The front elbow is bent, pointing upwards, as the vertical bat is lifted to become *dead* and make contact with the ball alongside the top of the front pad. He pushes the ball to ground by advancing the top of the bat blade ahead of the bottom.

In popular parlance, the term 'on the back foot' denotes any defensive posture or demeanour.

back-foot drive. An attacking stroke that hits a straight, *short-of-a-length* ball for runs. It is a *straight-bat stroke*, played alongside the pads, combining defence of the stumps with attack and leaving no *gate* through which the ball may pass. The batsman steps back from his crease across the wicket. His head and eyes are behind the line of the ball. He points his front elbow, shoulder, side and leg towards the approaching delivery, bending the elbow upwards to raise the bat to a point of contact with the ball level with the top of his pads. His toes point towards *point*. Rocking his shoulders towards the ball, he hits first with the top and then the bottom hand, throwing them after it and angling the bat blade towards the ground to keep the ball on the carpet. Back-foot drives are classified according to the direction in which the ball is struck: e.g. back-foot *off-drive*, back-foot *straight-drive*, etc.

back-of-the-hand. Term used to describe a slow *wrist-spin* bowler. Precisely applied, it describes the delivery of a *wrong'un*, which is released with the back of the hand facing the ground and with the ball spinning over the top of the fingers.

back-up a fieldsman. To move behind a fellow fieldsman when the ball is struck or thrown towards him. Thus, if the ball eludes his grasp, there is still a fieldsman in reserve to stop the ball and prevent the scoring of further runs. Backing-up is essential when the ball is returned to the keeper, a fielder or the bowler poised over the stumps at the bowler's end, ready to effect a run-out. (See also *back up*)

backhand flip. A short *throw* which returns the ball to a fieldsman or the wicketkeeper standing in line with the thrower, a few metres to his left or right. The fieldsman advances towards the ball, stopping it in front of the body and picking it up with the hand of the arm closer to the target. To throw, he draws this arm away from the target across his body, bending the elbow and pointing it back towards the ball's destination. The back of the throwing hand faces away from the target before it pushes the ball with a straightening of the arm and wrist towards its goal. The hand follows through after releasing the ball.

backlift. The initial movement or 'take-away' of the bat prefatory to playing a stroke. The batsman must lift the bat back towards the stumps to dispel inertia, before he can swing it forward. If he is to *play straight* at the line of an approaching delivery, he must first swing the bat straight back towards the middle- and off-stumps. *Cross-bat strokes* involve a backlift which in its later stages raises the bat horizontally behind the batsman's head. (See also *stance*)

backlift towards fine-leg. A faulty *backlift* which starts the bat moving back not straight, as recommended, but towards the leg-side and *fine-leg*. This backlift, initially angled towards the batsman's left, produces a stroke whose downswing is to the right, slightly *across the line* of the delivery and towards *mid-off*. Thus, the batsman's chances of hitting the ball are reduced, and he becomes vulnerable to the ball that pitches in line with the leg-stump: a delivery that cannot be reached without playing across the front of the leading pad. A backlift towards fine-leg is the outcome of a closed *stance*.

backlift towards third slip. A faulty *backlift* which starts the bat moving back not straight, as recommended, but towards the off-side and third *slip*. This backlift, initially angled towards the batsman's right, produces a stroke whose downswing is to the left, slightly *across the line* of the ball and towards *mid-on*. The odds of this shot hitting the ball are reduced; if contact is made, it is often with the outside edge and produces a catch behind the wicket. A backlift towards third slip is usually the outcome of an open *stance*, or of the strong domination of the *bottom hand* on the handle in the execution of a stroke.

backspin. See *flipper*; *undercut*.

backward short-leg. Leg-side fieldsman placed a few metres from the bat just to the left and behind the batsman, so positioned to take the catch deflected by the batsman off his toes. He is sometimes known as leg-gully.

bad light. When dark clouds or the approaching evening make it difficult for the batsmen to see the ball clearly, the *umpires* have the power to suspend the match until close of play or until the light improves. Umpires are equipped with light-meters to measure the acceptability of the light. On some Test grounds there are large light-meters, similar to clocks and attached to stands in the same way, visible to the spectators. When a light-meter registers an unacceptable level of visibility, the umpires 'offer the light to the batsmen', who may come off the field or (if it is to their tactical advantage) continue to bat. If they bat on and lose wickets, they cannot subsequently change their minds and come off, unless the light becomes worse. A suspension owing to bad light is noted in the scorebook and the media as BLSP (bad light stopped play). (See also *rain*)

bag a pair. To bag a pair of *ducks*, or score nought in each innings of a two-innings match. A batsman dismissed for a duck in the first innings and about to face his first ball in the second innings is said to be 'on a pair'. (See also *king pair*)

baggage man. Now a virtually vanished institution, the baggage man of a touring Test team was responsible for transporting the players' personal and cricketing luggage, initially from the home country to the host country and subsequently from playing venue to playing venue, city to city, and hotel to hotel. With as many as 20 persons in a touring party — a number sometimes augmented by journalists wanting luggage service — his duties became quite involved, faced as he was with moving more than 120 pieces of luggage, sometimes every second day, and ensuring that each piece arrived at its appropriate hotel or ground; he often required luggage to be placed outside each player's hotel-room door on the eve of departure. The baggage man frequently doubled as the *scorer*.

In modern times, airline baggage services have largely replaced the old baggage man. It is a loss to the game, since he was often a former player who had much cricketing wisdom to contribute to a touring team's fortunes. Such a one, in my time, was the former England keeper George 'The Admiral' Duckworth.

bags. Valises used by cricketers to transport their equipment and clothes from match to match. The early bags of professional players were solidly made of cowhide. In these days of air-travel, international cricketers opt for lightweight fibre cricket bags, rectangular in shape and colloquially called 'coffins'. Club cricketers usually use only small canvas bags.

bail-trimmer. An extremely good delivery which beats and bowls the batsman, just clipping the bails from the top of the wicket without disturbing the stumps.

bails. Short, shaped and rounded pieces of wood, 11.1 cm long, two of which are placed in the grooves at the top of and across the three *stumps* to complete the *wicket*. When in their grooves, the bails must not protrude more than 1.3 cm above the stumps. The wicket is down when one bail is dislodged completely from the top of the stumps. Special heavy bails are used in windy weather, whilst in stormy conditions bails may be dispensed with altogether.

The umpires are the guardians of the bails. They place them on top of the stumps to begin play; and when they remove them ('take off the bails' or 'lift the bails') this automatically denotes the cessation of hostilities: the close of play at an interval or at the end of the day.

ball. The spherical object bowled by the bowler and struck by the batsman in cricket. The bowler tries to hit the batsman's wicket with the ball, and dismiss him by any of the ten means outlined in the laws of cricket (see *out*). The batsman defends his wicket against the ball, and tries to strike it to the boundary or into the field of play so that he and his partner will have time to run between the wickets to score runs. The ball is made up of many layers of twine wound around a cork core, and encased in a red leather shell painted with lacquer to give it a sheen. The external casing is made of either two or four symmetrical pieces of leather sewn together. 'Four-piece' balls are used in most senior cricket; 'two-piecers' are used in junior cricket. Six protruding rows of coarse stitching encircle and hold the two halves of the ball together. These stitches are called the *seam* and control or assist the *swing*, *cut* and *spin* of the ball. (See also *shine*)

The ball is most commonly red, but other colours — usually yellow or white — may be used in night games, against the background of a black sightscreen. The ball is hard and must not weigh less than 155.9 grams or more than 163 grams. Its circumference must not exceed 22.9 cm or be less than 22.4 cm, though these measurements and weights may vary in the case of *women's cricket* and junior cricket. Balls shall be approved by the umpires and captains before a game. The umpires measure the ball against two gauges, one of which is just too small and the other just too large. A new ball is generally used in each innings of a game, and in first-class and international cricket the ball may be replaced after 85 overs have been bowled with it. It may also be replaced by the umpires if it is damaged or goes out of shape in the course of a game.

In junior matches, balls made of moulded plastic or synthetic material may be used at the discretion of the authority controlling the game. (See also *helmet*)

ball in play. The ball is in play when, at the start of each innings and each day's play, and on the resumption of play after any interval or interruption, the umpire at the bowler's end calls 'play'. The ball is in play from the moment the bowler begins his run-up, and it remains 'live' until the umpire judges it 'dead' and signals accordingly. (See also *dead ball*)

banners. Cloth or paper placards, posters and flags, which bear amusing comments or encouraging messages and are displayed by *spectators*. An exercise carried out largely for the benefit of television cameras, banner creation has been put to some unusual uses and produced some unexpected results. Spectators at a telecast England–Australia Test in England used a banner to relay back to Sydney the message 'Send more money mum!'. Supportive remarks such as 'Top Shot' are common. Witticisms have included 'Marshy Swamps Them Every Time' and 'Hogg'll Bring Home The Bacon'. Perhaps the most illuminating demonstration of Banner Power came from the determined efforts of a band of Doug Walters supporters. Every time Walters appeared on the Sydney Cricket Ground they put up a banner at the crest of the Hill, proclaiming it to be the 'Doug Walters Stand'. Responding to this prompting, the SCG Trust erected a concrete stand, bearing the batsman's name, on the site of the former cloth construction!

barndoor. A term used to describe the technique of a defensive batsman — as in a persistent blocker's 'barndoor tactics'. (See also *stonewall*)

barrack. The *Shorter Oxford English Dictionary* tells us that 'barrack' is an alternative form of the Australian Aboriginal word *borak*, meaning 'fun'. Thus to 'poke borak' in a cricket game involved shouting derisively so as to disconcert the opposing players. In modern usage 'barrack for' denotes encouragement and support of a team. In the Australian *outer*, however, the barracker is often still the heckler who harasses the opponents of the team he supports.

One immortal barracker, a denizen of the 'Hill' at the Sydney Cricket Ground, was Stephen Harold Gascoigne, better known by his professional name 'Yabba' — a corruption of 'Rabbo', the call of the rabbit-seller which he was in the 1920s and '30s in Balmain. At the beginning of every major game at the SCG, Yabba took up his position on the fence beneath the scoreboard surrounded by an admiring audience. The penetration of his voice was such that his comments could be heard over the radio and his remarks became legendary. On one occasion when the umpire held up his arm to help the batsman line up the sightscreen, Yabba called out, 'It's no use, umpire, you'll have to wait until playtime like the rest of us!'

11

My first encounter with an Australian barracker was at the Melbourne Cricket Ground. I was bowling at the Victorian batsman Neil Harvey, who continually played at and missed the ball, when a voice from the outer called, 'Tyson, why don't yer bowl 'im down a piano? P'raps he can play that!'

bat. Implement used by the batsman to defend his wicket and hit the ball. Originally this was a shepherd's staff. Early bats were curved at the bottom like a crook to scoop grubbers or *shooters* off the pitch. Modern bats consist of a handle and a hitting surface or *blade*. The blade is flat-faced for striking the ball, and to give the bat weight it is curved at the back or spine where it has been fashioned from a wedge-shaped cleft of *willow*. The rounded handle is turned from long strips of cane, glued together and made more resilient by the insertion of thin strips of rubber or sprung steel (see *springs*). It is wedged into the top of the blade at the *splice*.

The bat must be made of wood and cannot be longer than 96.5 cm or wider than 10.8 cm. The blade is open-barked willow. In the 1970s Australian fast-bowler Dennis Lillee tried to introduce an aluminium bat into a Test match in Perth, but this bat was condemned because it damaged the ball. Willow is the most suitable material for bat-making because of its resilience and durability. In junior cricket, plastic bats are permitted and used.

The blade is grained. The wider the grain, the softer the wood but the better its hitting qualities. A narrow-grained bat lasts longer. The ideal number of grains in the face of a bat blade is about eight. The blade should be free of blemishes such as *watermarks*, *knots*, or brown and brittle *heartwood*. Such flaws are difficult to detect because modern bats are bleached white. Often manufacturers lengthen the life of a bat by coating the blade with a plastic varnish or similar material; these coating materials must not be thicker than 1.56 mm. Until a few years ago the face of a bat blade was waterproofed and hardened by being coated with raw linseed oil and 'played in' gradually against slow bowling or by being beaten with a hand-held ball. Modern bats do not need such treatment since their blades are pre-hardened by rolling.

Formerly all bats were crafted and balanced by hand. Now they are turned by machine and only finished and balanced by hand. The balance and *pick-up* of a bat are more important than its weight: manageability depends on balance. Weights vary between 1 and 1½ kg. Heavier bats have been popularized by players such as former West Indian skipper Clive Lloyd, the premise being that one can hit a ball harder with a bigger bat. Heavier bats, however, strike the ball harder only if the hitting surface is moving quickly at the point of impact.

Basic equipment
and the pitch

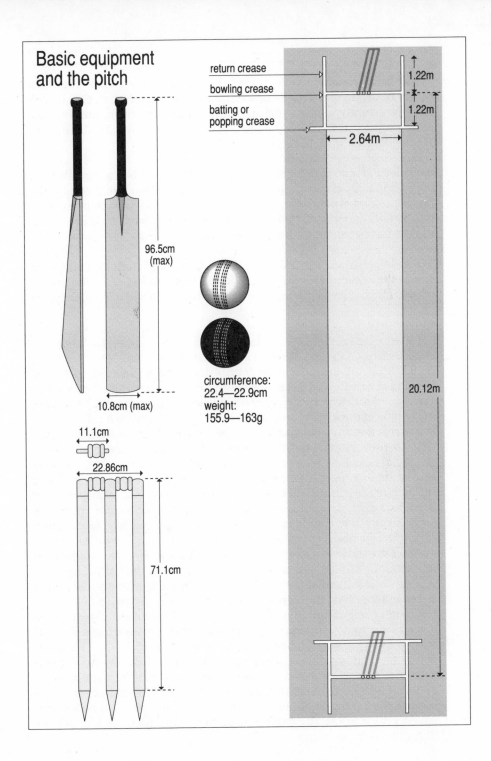

return crease

bowling crease

batting or
popping crease

1.22m

1.22m

2.64m

96.5cm
(max)

10.8cm (max)

circumference:
22.4—22.9cm
weight:
155.9—163g

11.1cm

22.86cm

71.1cm

20.12m

The handle is attached to the blade by the splice joint, and is bound by a layer of strong thread and encased in a rubber grip to enable the bat to be held securely. The grip absorbs the shock of the ball, and for this reason some batsmen sheathe the bat in as many as five grips. (See also *edge*; *shoulders*; *springs*; *toe*)

bat twice. To go to the wicket and take strike in both innings of a two-innings match. Batsmen and teams usually bat twice in two-innings games, except when their side totals enough runs in one innings to outscore its opponents' two knocks. When a team bats twice in succession, it has been compelled to *follow on*.

bat-pad fieldsman. A *close-to-the-bat fieldsman*, in front and on either side of the wicket. He is the man who snaps up catches deflected off the edge of the bat on to the pad and thence briefly into the air for about a metre.

batsman. A member of the batting side. To begin their team's *innings*, two batsmen go to the wicket and hit the ball with their *bats*, defending their stumps against a series of 6 balls delivered alternately from both bowling creases by different opposition *bowlers*. The batsmen seek to avoid dismissal, which may be effected in any of the ten ways prescribed in the laws of cricket (see *out*); at the same time they try to hit the ball out of the reach of the fieldsmen or across the *boundary* to give themselves time to run between the wickets and score or be awarded *runs*. If a batsman is dismissed, he is replaced by the next batsman in his team's *batting order*, waiting his turn in the *pavilion* or dressing-room. When all the men in the batting team have been to the wicket and 10 players have been dismissed, the innings of that team is over. The number of runs it scores in one or two innings is the total that its opponents have to surpass to win the game.
  A right-handed batsman holds the bat handle with the right hand lower on the handle and stands on the left side of the bat to make his strokes. A left-handed batsman holds the handle with the left hand lower and stands on the right side of the bat. Many people think that the left-hander enjoys an advantage over the right-handed player. Most bowlers are right-arm and aim to bowl at the opposing right-handed batsman's *off-stump*. When the batsman is left-handed, they have difficulty in changing their direction, or line; they therefore bowl many deliveries on the left-hander's *leg-stump*, providing him with an ideal opportunity to hit the ball on the leg-side with little danger of being bowled and no threat of *lbw*. On the other hand, the left-hander does have a problem with the *rough* dug up by the right-arm bowler outside his vulnerable off-stump.

A batsman who begins an innings is termed an *opening batsman*, an opener, or a number 1 or 2. Subsequent batsmen are described by the number in the batting order which they occupy or by the number of wickets lost by their team when they go in to bat. Thus, the number 3 batsman is also termed the first-wicket-down batsman. Batsmen who bat early in their side's innings are described as early-order batsmen, those in the middle of the batting order as middle-order batsmen, and those coming in last as the *tail-enders*. (See also *bottom-handed* and *top-handed player*; *drive*; *stroke*)

To date, the most prolific batsman in Test history is India's Sunil Gavaskar, who in the course of accumulating 10 122 runs compiled a record 34 centuries. Garfield Sobers of the West Indies is the holder of the world record Test score of 365 not out, against Pakistan in Jamaica in 1957/58. Don Bradman's remarkable claim to fame (among others) is that in a career of 52 Tests he averaged 99.94 in compiling 6996 runs and 29 centuries. The most prolific run-scorer in first-class cricket was Surrey's J.B. Hobbs, who in a 29-year career scored 61 237 runs. The highest score made in first-class cricket was Hanif Mohammad's 499 for Karachi against Bahawalpur in 1958/59: Pakistan's 'Little Master' was run out going for the fifth run which would have brought him his 500!

batsmen had not crossed. A phrase indicating that the batsmen had only just started running, or had just turned for another run, when an event — usually disastrous — took place. A stupid *run-out*, for instance, can result from an error in judgment or a call which is so bad that the bails are removed before the batsmen have run far enough to pass each other on the pitch.

batting average. The mean number of runs scored by a batsman per innings. A player's batting average is calculated by dividing his run *aggregate* from all his innings by the number of times he has been dismissed.

batting crease. Also known as the *popping crease*. A line marked 1.22 metres in front of the centre of the *stumps* and parallel to the *bowling crease* — a measure equivalent to an arrow's length, or a cloth-yard, in Norman England. Like the bowling crease, it was originally scratched in the turf, and it is on this crease that the batsman *takes guard* and adopts his *stance* to face the bowler. The batsman is deemed to be in his ground, and safe from dismissal by stumping or run-out, if any part of his body or bat touches down behind the crease. The batsman at the non-striker's end must stay behind his batting crease until the bowler has released the ball, otherwise he may be *run out* — or *mankadded*.

To make bowlers deliver over a uniform distance, cricket laws dictate that the bowler must have some part of his front foot behind the rear edge of the popping crease at the moment he releases the ball; otherwise the delivery is deemed a *no-ball*.

batting depth.   The composite batting strength of a team. The batsmen of a side usually go in to bat in descending order of ability, the competent players occupying the early order and the weaker ones fetching up the *tail*. If, however, a side has batsmen capable of scoring useful runs as deep in the *batting order* as (say) number 8, it is said to have batting depth.

batting order.   The order in which the eleven players of a team go to the wicket to bat. The captain of the side notifies his men — either by a written list on the pavilion notice-board or verbally — of the sequence from 1 to 11 in which he would like them to bat. Certain players are specialists in particular positions. For example, numbers 1 and 2 are the *opening batsmen* or openers whose special task is to prevent the opposing fast-bowlers from taking wickets at the beginning of the innings when the ball is new and swinging in the air. Number 3 is also a responsible position, especially if a wicket falls early. Batsmen number 4 to 7 are the *middle order* and theirs is the aggressive role of scoring quickly as the ball becomes old, bounces less and comes off the pitch more slowly, and as the bowlers tire. Numbers 6 to 11 are the *all-rounders*, and the *tail-enders* or 'rabbits'. The all-rounders can both bat and bowl; the rabbits are usually bowlers and the least accomplished with the bat.
A batsman's position in the batting order is also identified by the number of wickets down when he goes in. The number 3 batsman, for instance, goes in to bat when one wicket has fallen and is thus described as batting at 'first wicket down'; number 4 goes in 'second wicket down'; and so on.

batting wicket.   A playing surface or pitch conducive to batting: a good wicket from which the ball comes quickly and truly on to the bat, at a uniform height and with no deviation. Such a pitch enables the batsman to play his strokes with a minimum of effort and risk.

beamer.   A fast head-high *full-toss* which follows the batsman, making it extremely hard for him to avoid being struck. It is said that the delivery was patented by a Cambridge University fast-bowler who, fed up with the slow, placid pitches at his home ground of Fenners, decided to upset the complacency of the opposing batsmen with this threat to their personal safety. At Fenners it was very difficult to detect the ball in flight since it bored in at the batsman out of a dark background of trees!

bean ball. A delivery directed at the head or 'bean'; it may be a *bouncer* or a head-high *full-toss*. (See also *beamer*)

beat the bat. When a delivery, by its movement through the air or off the wicket, or by its speed or flight, gets past the bat and the batsman's proffered stroke, it is said to have beaten the bat.

bend the back. In fast-bowling, to try hard and bowl as quickly and tenaciously as possible.

benefit of doubt. See *leg before wicket*; *too far forward*; *too high*.

blade. The flat-faced hitting surface of the *bat*, shaped from a *willow* cleft. The bat itself is sometimes referred to as the 'blade'.

blazer. Uniform jacket originally worn by the sailors of HMS *Blazer* to distinguish them from other naval crews. This type of coat was adopted by 18th-century cricket teams such as the Hambledon eleven, who wore sky-blue coats with black velvet collars and buttons engraved with the letters C.C. Naturally these coats were discarded when the cricketers were at play.
 Present-day teams wear such jackets to identify them off the field. The Australian team is distinguished by its green blazer with the national coat-of-arms embroidered on the breast pocket. The Marylebone Cricket Club blazer is tailored of a light-blue material with a representation on the pocket of St George slaying the dragon. New Zealand's representatives wear a black blazer with a silver fernleaf emblazoned on the breast. Each country has its own distinctive colours and badge.

blind spot. A spot in one's field of view where the ball is momentarily lost from sight. A batsman's blind spot is usually on his *leg-stump*.

block. To defend the wicket, refusing to swing at the ball, but simply using the bat to block the ball's passage towards the stumps. A block is a *front-foot* or *back-foot defensive stroke* with a *dead bat*. Sometimes it is taken to excess: by the negative batsman who occupies the crease for long periods of time without advancing the game. (See also *stonewall*)

blockhole. A hole or mark made by the batsman on or behind the *batting crease* when he *takes guard* or block. Thus, when a bowler delivers a ball 'right in the blockhole', he has pitched it on the batting crease and bowled a *yorker*.

17

Bodyline. Term invented by a New Zealand journalist to describe the 'fast leg theory' tactic employed by England captain Douglas Jardine and his fast-bowlers, Harold Larwood, Bill Voce and Bill Bowes, against the Australian batsmen, and Don Bradman in particular, during the Ashes series in Australia in 1932/33. Bradman was the great batting success of the Australian tour of England in 1930, scoring 974 runs in seven innings. It was said, however, that in the course of recording 232 in the Oval Test, Bradman had flinched when a delivery from Larwood reared towards his chest.

Concentrating on this theoretical Achilles' Heel, Jardine and his men planned an attack in which Larwood and Voce in particular directed fast short-pitched balls at the body of the batsman, who was surrounded by a ring of leg-side fieldsmen. Amateur fast-bowler G.O. Allen refused to adopt the dangerous tactic, but professionals Larwood and Voce followed the instructions of their amateur captain to perfection. They were well suited to their task, for they were extremely fast and accurate. If the batsmen defended their bodies against the short, rearing deliveries, they were caught by the fieldsmen close to the wicket; if they tried to hook their way out of trouble, they were caught by one of the three fieldsmen waiting on the boundary. The ploy was highly successful: England won the series 4–1 (they had lost the previous rubber 2–1). Larwood himself was the key bowler in England's triumph, taking 33 wickets, whilst Bradman was restricted to the almost-human average of just over 50.

The real importance of Bodyline, however, did not lie in figures but in the blitzkrieg philosophy it introduced into cricket: human considerations were ignored and winning became the only criterion for dubious tactics. Batsmen, such as Bill Woodfull and Bert Oldfield, were injured, and the Australian Cricket Board of Control was sufficiently angered to cable the Marylebone Cricket Club condemning Bodyline as 'unsportsmanlike'. The English club, far from the scene of action, bridled at this accusation and offered to cancel the tour and the series. At one stage the Secretary for the Dominions, J.H. Thomas, was called in and political relations between England and Australia were strained.

The storm passed, but the problem of Bodyline remained. It was not until the following county season in England, when Larwood and Voce employed the tactic for Nottinghamshire, that the MCC awoke to its physical danger. It branded short-pitched bowling at the batsman standing clear of his wicket as intimidatory. Since 1934, however, 'mini-Bodyline' has periodically raised its head, particularly when Test sides have been well endowed with fast-bowlers able to mount such an assault. The problem still lies in defining just what constitutes *intimidatory bowling* — and in finding umpires strong enough to condemn bowlers who employ the tactic. (See also *leg theory*)

bonus balls. In *limited-over* cricket, extra balls received by the batting side in the form of *no-balls* and *wides* sent down by the opposing bowlers. In a game of 50 overs, such deliveries can be of vital importance: 12 no-balls and wides represent two supplementary overs and thus a dozen additional scoring opportunities in a game that might be decided by a handful of runs.

boots. Cricket boots are made of white leather or buckskin, with leather or rubber soles. The earliest cricket footwear was ordinary shoes, studded with nails, and sometimes decorated with buckles peculiar to the wearer's team. Later came white buckskin boots worn above the ankle; they gave support to the bowler when bowling into worn footholds. Today's boots are low-cut and the ankle is supported by strapping. Boots may be laced or secured by velcro. The soles are cushioned and fabricated out of rippled rubber into which eight or nine *spikes* may be screwed or set to provide a better grip on the turf. The heels are raised so that the player's weight does not fall back, making him tired. The toes, which used to be hard to provide protection against the ball when batting, are now often soft so that toenails are not endangered through constant pushing against a stiffened *toecap* when bowling. (The usual practice is to use different boots for batting and for bowling.) When boots were constructed entirely of buckskin and leather, they were heavy. England fast-bowler Harold Larwood, for instance, needed to protect his feet with boots that weighed almost a kilogram each — in spite of which he still broke a bone in his foot while bowling in his last Test in Australia! Today's boots, however, combine lightness with strength.

Modern boot technology is still not universally accepted by cricket authorities. John Benaud, the New South Wales batsman and brother of former Australian captain Richie Benaud, was once dropped by his state selectors because they did not support his non-supportive, low-cut footwear. Some *curators* still do not condone ripple soles, which they maintain create friction and burn grass off their wickets.

bosie. Another name for the *wrong'un* or *googly*. It is a term used almost exclusively by Australians, who named the delivery after its inventor, Englishman B.J.T. Bosanquet. This tall, athletic young man, who threw the hammer for Oxford, discovered the googly while playing a game of 'twisty-grab' late one night on a common-room billiard table. The idea of this game was to defeat the 'grab' of the opponent by the amount of 'twist' one put on the billiard ball in rolling it from one end of the table to the other. Bosanquet found that if a ball was spun vigorously from right to left, and released out of the back of the hand, it would turn from left to right. Having begun his cricket career as a rather ordinary medium-pace bowler, he transformed his mundane skills by switching to *wrist-spin* and employing his bosie brainchild. He tried out his new artform at Lord's in the varsity game of 1900, claiming his first victim, Coe, with a ball that bounced four times! He twice made his mark on Test cricket with the delivery, taking 6/51 in one Australian innings of the Sydney Test in 1904, and 8/107 at Nottingham in 1905.

Botany Bay Lad. Early nickname for an Australian cricketer; derived from Australia's original convict settlers, transported to Botany Bay in 1788.

bottom edge. The *inside edge* of the bat, when the batsman plays a *cross-bat stroke*; so called because the inside edge in that posture is the bottom edge of the bat, being the edge closer to the ground. Catches rarely result from the ball hitting the bottom edge of the bat, since the ball usually flies immediately to ground. Occasionally, however, batsmen *play on* off the bottom edge while attempting to cut, pull or hook.

bottom-handed player. A batsman whose bottom or stronger hand controls the swing of the bat. This produces more power in the stroke, which is usually played slightly *across the line* of the ball towards the leg-side. In professional players sure of their skills, the bottom hand is often referred to as the 'guide and master' when it is used to place the ball into the gaps between the fieldsmen.

bounce. See *pitch (bounce).*

bouncer. A *short-pitched*, fast delivery which rises or bounces abruptly from the pitch to chest-level or higher; also known as a bumper. One of the purposes of such a ball is the totally illegal — and unacknowledged — intention of intimidating the batsman. (The bowler would prefer to interpret his motive as one of forcing the batsman, who automatically plays forward on a good non-bouncing wicket, onto the back foot.) The bowler also seeks to tempt the batsman into playing the injudicious *hook* or a back-foot defensive stroke. A batsman who tries to hook a bouncer which is too high or too far outside the off-stump runs the risk of lofting the ball to fieldsmen behind the wicket, on either side. Alternatively, if he can be cramped into a hurried defensive shot, there is a good chance that he will pop up a catch to *short-leg*. The batsman should always be on the qui vive for the sudden acceleration in the bowler's run which might indicate a quicker delivery — especially a quicker and shorter one such as the bouncer. (See also *intimidatory bowling*)

boundary. The outer extent of the *playing area*. It is indicated by a white line, a rope, a fence, flags or markers. Its distance from the pitch varies from ground to ground, though efforts have been made over the years to standardize it at about 60 metres. The boundary is agreed upon by the opposing captains and the umpires before the game begins. Objects such as trees, *sightscreens* or rollers which lie within the playing area may be designated as boundaries. If the ball is struck, is carried or rolls across a boundary, 4 runs are awarded to the batting side and the batsman who struck the ball. If the ball crosses the boundary without bouncing after being struck, carried or bowled, 6 runs are awarded. The *umpire* calls and signals boundaries to the *scorers*. The greater the number of boundaries in an innings, the faster and more exciting the tempo of the batting.

Whilst 4 and 6 runs are the common awards, other amounts may be agreed upon by the captains and umpires in consultation, particularly where boundaries are at abnormal distances from the pitch. If a batsman strikes the ball over the boundary, he is said to have scored or hit a boundary — a four or a six. *Extras* may go for boundaries.

boundary rider. Synonym for *sweeper*: a fast-moving fieldsman who patrols the boundary and whose role is to cut off strokes that are headed there.

bowl close to the batsman. To deliver the ball on a line close to the batsman's body, so as to deny him room to employ a full swing of the bat and execute a free stroke. (See also *following the batsman*)

bowl from over the top of middle-stump. To deliver the ball *over the wicket* from close to the bowler's stumps. Consequently, at the moment of release the bowling arm is directly over the top of the bowler's wicket, and if the ball is accurate its flight takes it from middle-stump at the bowler's end to middle-stump at the batsman's end. Such a ball gains maximum advantage of *swing* and *spin,* because, if the batsman defends on the line of his middle-stump, the ball has only to move sideways by half of the bat's width (i.e. by 5.4 cm) to pass it. Contrast an *outswinger* delivered from close to the bowler's wicket with one bowled from near the *return crease*. The latter is first angled in towards the batsman's wicket before it can begin to move out. The sideways movement described by such a ball must, to defeat the bat, be much greater than that of a delivery bowled from close to the stumps; it is hence a more difficult and less effective ball.

bowl from wide on the crease. To deliver the ball from near the extremity of the *bowling crease*, far from the stumps and next to the *return*

21

crease; the antithesis of bowling 'middle-stump to middle-stump'. Bowlers deliver from wide on the crease, either over or around the wicket, to
increase or change the angle of their attack. Because the ball is slanted
across the face of the batsman's stumps, there is little chance of an lbw
decision unless the ball pitches in line with the wicket, straightens, and
would have hit it. Moreover, the bowler has to swing, cut and spin the
ball far more to *beat the bat.*

bowl into the rough. To deliver the ball so that it bounces in the area of
the pitch which has been damaged by the bowler's boots in his follow-
through. A ball that is spun or cut will grip and turn more readily from
these roughened spots. It also slows up minimally, or 'stops' on the
batsman, making it more difficult to time drives and increasing the
chance of lofting a catch. Legally, the rough can occur only outside the
danger area; thus the damage done to the wicket by a right-arm over-
the-wicket bowler usually lies outside the right-hand batsman's leg-
stump. This means that the batsman can use his pads to defend his
stumps against a delivery turning from this rough, since he cannot be
given out lbw to a ball pitching outside leg-stump. A left-handed batsman, however, is more at risk since the most common patch of rough
lies outside his off-stump, inhibiting his off-side driving and placing
him in considerable danger from the ball turning into him from the off.
A left-handed over-the-wicket bowler creates similar problems for the
right-handed batsman. (See also *running on the pitch*)

bowl off the wrong foot. The orthodox bowler releases the ball as he
steps down the pitch towards the batsman and his weight passes over the
braced front leg. The unorthodox bowler who bowls off the wrong foot
releases the ball while his weight is still on the back foot and then steps
down the pitch with the front foot. He hops on the rear foot twice in the
delivery stride and gives the impression of being ungainly and uncoor-
dinated. Bowlers of this type are said to have an open action and to be
front-on or chest-on. They have a great capacity to bowl the *inswinger*
and *leg-cutter*, and often cause batsmen, accustomed to an orthodox
bowling stride and action, to mistime their strokes. On the other hand,
they are less effective when it comes to speed, spin and outswing. Successful wrong-foot bowlers have included India's Lala Amarnath, Australia's Max Walker and New Zealand's Lance Cairns.

bowl to one side of the wicket. To aim the direction of one's bowling
to one side of the batsman's stumps, so as to facilitate the setting of a
field. Obviously, if a bowler consistently pitches on the off-stump or just
outside it, he would be wise to station most of his fieldsmen on the off-
side. Similarly, if he aims at the leg-side, he needs a strong leg-side

cordon. A bowler poses problems for his skipper when he is not consistent in his line, and bowls half of the over down the leg-side and the other half down the off. The fielding captain then has to divide his resources between the two sides, thus increasing the batsman's opportunities of scoring (see *split field*). If, however, the bowler's direction is consistent, his skipper can *pack* one side of the field with run-savers and make the batsman's job all the more difficult.

The former England bowler Brian Statham offered the following aphorism about the advisability of directing a bowling attack at one side of the wicket: 'If tha' bowls at off-stump, tha' needs all of thi' men on th' off side. An' if tha' bowls at leg-stump, like as not, tha' needs all thi' men on th' leg-side. But if tha' bowls straight, like me, tha' doesn't need any fieldsmen!'

bowl to one's field. To direct one's deliveries in such a way that the batsman hits the ball to positions in the field where fieldsmen have been placed. This serves the double purpose of saving runs and increasing the chances of the batsman giving a catch. Thus a bowler who bowls outswingers at the off-stump requires a strong slip-and-gully cordon to take the catches, with men at cover and mid-off to save runs when the overpitched ball is driven. Conversely, an inswing bowler needs a strong on-side fielding formation.

bowl up/down the hill. Some grounds slope slightly from wicket to wicket, from one set of stumps to the other. On such grounds, one bowler has the easy job of running down the slope to bowl, but his opposite number has the more arduous task of 'coming up the hill' in his approach. The faster bowlers are usually given the advantage of bowling down the hill in the hope that they will gain extra pace; if there is a breeze they are also afforded its benefit at their back, for the same reason. In such a situation, bowling at the other end, up the hill and into the breeze, is very hard work. It is usually reserved for the 'workhorse' bowlers; and even they are not expected to bowl long spells from the disadvantaged end. (See also *move the ball up/down the hill*)

bowled. Method of dismissal in which the batsman's *wicket* is put down directly by a ball delivered by the bowler. A batsman is *out* 'bowled' when a delivery dislodges a *bail* from the top of the wicket. He may also be bowled by a ball deflected from his bat, his equipment or his person. (See also *hit wicket*; *play on*)

bowler. A member of the fielding side who, on the umpire's call of 'play', begins the game of cricket by bowling the ball from either of the two *bowling creases* and attempts to prevent the batsman from scoring runs, and to dismiss him *bowled, caught, stumped, hit wicket,* or *lbw.* Bowlers are either specialists or, if they can also bat, *all-rounders.* The bowler delivers the ball by running to the wicket and projecting the ball with a straight arm and with some part of his front foot behind the *batting crease.* If he *throws* the ball or places his front foot over the batting crease, the delivery is illegal and is called a *no-ball.* The fielding captain may direct any of his team to bowl; he changes his bowlers according to his assessment of the tactical situation, the perceived weaknesses of a batsman, the state of the pitch and the condition of the bowlers. Any member of the fielding side may bowl any number of *overs* in a standard game; in *limited-over* games the number of overs allowed any one bowler is restricted. Different bowlers bowl alternate overs, from both ends of the pitch.

Bowlers are described by the methods they employ. They are called right-arm or left-arm according to the hand with which they bowl, and are designated by the speed at which they deliver the ball: *fast, medium-paced* or *slow.* Express bowlers have been recorded bowling at 160 km/h, but an average medium-pacer bowls at about 120 km/h. The quicker bowlers seek to defeat the batsman by pace, *swing,* movement off the *seam,* or cut off the pitch (see *cutter*); they are therefore sometimes called swing-bowlers, seam-bowlers, leg-cutters or off-cutters. *Spin-bowlers* try to bamboozle the opposition by imparting twist to the ball to make it change direction after it bounces. The slow-bowlers who are more accurate and faster through the air use only their fingers to spin the ball and are classified as *finger-spinners*; the slower, bigger spinners of the ball gain their greater degree of turn by using their wrists and fingers and are termed *wrist-spinners* or over-the-wrist spinners. If a slow-bowler spins the ball from the off, he is an *off-spinner*; turn from leg is the stamp of a *leg-spinner.* Bowlers are also described according to the position of the bowling hand at the moment of release: if they release the ball above the wicket, they are *over-the-wicket* bowlers; if it is on the side of the body away from the stumps, they are bowling *around the wicket.* Formerly bowlers bowled with the bowling hand below or at shoulder-level: *underarm* (lob) or *roundarm* bowling. These styles are not used in modern cricket and are illegal in the limited-over game. (See also *bowling action*)

Certain bowlers have enjoyed phenomenal success in Tests. In 1990, New Zealand's fast-bowler Richard Hadlee became the first wicket-taker with more than 400 victims to his name. Australian speedster Dennis Lillee overthrew 355 batsmen in his Test career. England's off-spinner Jim Laker took 19 of the 20 Australian wickets to fall in the Manchester Test of 1956. The best-ever bowling analysis in a single innings in first-class cricket was Hedley Verity's 10 for 10 clean-sweep for Yorkshire in a game against Nottinghamshire in 1932.

bowler's end.   The end or wicket from which the bowler is operating; the *non-striker's end*.

bowling action.   The movement of the bowler's body and arms in the delivery stride, and the body-action with which he delivers the ball. The orthodox closed or *side-on* action endows the bowler with maximum speed, *flight, swing, curve, cut* and *spin*. At the end of his *run-up* and one pace behind the *bowling crease*, the bowler jumps off his left foot, about 35 cm into the air, twisting as he does to execute a feet-astride jump facing the stumps at the non-striker's end. He lands on his right foot, reaching up as high as possible with his leading arm, looking from behind it at the batsman. The front arm levers the bowler's body back like a sapling bending in a high wind, before it is flung forward and upwards toward the batsman as the bowler steps down the pitch with his front foot. The left arm is then folded and the left elbow digs into the leading side of the body, dragging the bowling arm over in a windmill delivery swing which brushes the side of the head. The bowler releases the ball as the bowling arm reaches the top of its arc and his weight passes over his braced left leg. After the release, the left arm swings behind the body and the bowling arm across it, absorbing the energy of the action. The bowler's rear leg swings forward, brushing the knee of the left leg as he follows through down the wicket for two steps before veering to the off-side to avoid the *danger area*. At all times the bowling action maintains the movement of the body-weight towards the target of the batsman's wicket. (See also *falling away; high action*)

bowling analysis.   The statistical summary of a bowler's performance in an innings or match, as recorded in the scorebook and the media. This summary enumerates the *overs* or balls bowled, the overs off which no runs were scored (*maiden overs*), the *runs* scored by the opposing batsmen off the bowler, the *wickets* taken, the *no-balls* and *wides* bowled, and the average number of runs conceded per wicket taken.

bowling average.   The mean number of runs conceded by a bowler for each wicket he takes. A player's bowling average is calculated by dividing the number of runs conceded by the number of wickets taken. (See also *aggregate*)

bowling containment.   Tactics of a team to bowl and field in a way designed to restrict or contain the scoring of the batting side. The prime consideration is to bowl a *line and length* that forces the batsman to hit the ball to a part of the field where fieldsmen have been placed. A bowler may opt to *bowl to one side of the wicket* — say, exclusively at off-stump, or at leg-stump. The off-side attack demands a strong cordon of fieldsmen on that side of the wicket; similarly, concentration on the leg-stump entails the placement of a predominantly on-side field. A bowler can contain a batsman by directing his attack close to the striker's body and not giving him room to play shots. To contain successfully, he must pitch the ball well up, so that the striker has to hit straight and safely into the arc between the mid-off and mid-on fieldsmen, or risk being bowled or trapped lbw in hitting across the line of the delivery. Bowling *short of a length* 'opens up the angles for the batsman'.

bowling crease. A line, 2.64 metres long, lying within the two *return creases*, and marking the extremity of the pitch at each end. The *stumps* making up the *wicket* are pitched in the centre of the bowling crease. Originally bowlers delivered the ball with both feet behind the bowling crease; subsequently the bowler needed to have only some part of one foot behind the bowling crease when he released the ball. With the advent of the front-foot *no-ball* law, the bowling crease ceased to play a part in the determination of a no-ball and served only to mark the length of the pitch.

bowling flat. Possessing no *flight*; employed to describe negative or miserly slow-bowlers who, by bowling the ball with a flatter trajectory than is usual for slow-bowlers, refuse to tempt batsmen into misjudgments of length. Flat slow-bowlers are not big spinners of the ball, are quicker through the air and very accurate, and generally deny the batsman the opportunity of using his feet to reach the pitch of the ball. On a good wicket their aim is to contain and prevent the scoring of runs; but on 'sticky dogs' or turning wickets they can be match-winners, since they are fast through the air and spin the ball enough to bamboozle the batsman. In the 1960s and 1970s the predilection of the Lancashire off-spinner Jack Simmons for *pushing the ball through* earned him the parsimonious nickname 'Flat Jack'.

bowling restrictions (limited-over game). Restrictions placed on the bowling side in *limited-over* games, preventing the overuse of a team's economical bowling experts. The restrictions ensure that the bowling responsibilities in an innings will be shared equitably amongst the proficient and the less proficient, and thus increase the batsmen's scoring opportunities: rules designed to maximize the entertainment, crowd-pulling and money-making attributes of the limited-over game.

The most common bowling limitation restricts any one bowler to one-fifth of the overs allocated to an innings. Other restrictions are placed on bowlers in the various limited-over competitions. Some of them allow the fast-bowler to send down one *bouncer* per over; others forbid its use, on pain of it being deemed a no-ball or a wide. In the

English Sunday League, the game is speeded up by the restriction of the bowler's *run-ups* to 15 yards (13.7 metres). All competitions banned *underarm bowling* in the aftermath of a World Series Cup game between Australia and New Zealand in Melbourne in February 1981. (See also *over-rate penalties*)

box. Abdominal protector worn by batsmen and wicketkeepers over the genitalia. The box may be strapped on, or slipped into the pouch of the *jockstrap*. Being hit in the groin area is very painful and sometimes occasions wry comments such as 'I'll bet that made your eyes water!' or 'Don't rub them, count them!'. Woman cricketer Rachel Heyhoe Flint once described the women's equivalent of the box as the 'manhole cover'.

break. To make a ball turn or change direction after it bounces on the pitch, by imparting *spin* or twist to it with the wrist and fingers of the bowling hand. A delivery that deviates from the off-side of the wicket towards the leg-side is termed an off-break or *off-spinner*; the person who delivers such a ball is called an off-break bowler, an off-spin bowler or an off-spinner. A ball that breaks from the leg-side towards the off-side is called a leg-break or *leg-spinner*; its exponent is known as a leg-break bowler, a leg-spin bowler or a leg-spinner. Bowlers who break or turn the ball do so at slow speed.

break the wicket. To put down the *wicket*, dislodging at least one *bail* — or, if the bails are off, knocking one stump out of the ground — with the ball, or the hand or arm holding the ball. The keeper or a member of the fielding side must break the wicket in order to *stump* a batsman or have him *run out*. (See also *bowled*; *wicket is down*)

break-back. A fast or medium-pace delivery which bounces outside the line of the off-stump and, because of the cut imparted to it, or because it lands on the *seam*, does not continue in its original direction but breaks or cuts back in towards the batsman's wicket. It is also known as nip-backer, or as a ball that 'jags back'.

In the late 19th century, when only one ball was available to the bowling side throughout the longest innings, *swinging* the ball was out of the question after 30 overs. Consequently, the break-back was the quick-bowler's strike-weapon. The England and Surrey bowler Tom Richardson made it an artform: he could produce his famous break-back on the hardest, most unyielding pitches.

bump-ball. An illusory catch which the batsman appears to drive into the hands of a fieldsman. The striker seems to loft a *half-volley* to the catcher — though in fact he has first hit the ball hard into the ground immediately after contact, making it 'bump' up to the fieldsman.

bumper. Another term for a *bouncer*.

bunny. See *rabbit*.

byes. Runs scored off a ball which is not struck by a batsman or deflected off his person or equipment and which the wicketkeeper fails to gather, giving the batsmen time to change ends and score one or more runs. If such a ball subsequently reaches the boundary, 4 byes are scored. The *umpire* at the bowler's end signals the award of byes and boundaries, which are recorded as *extras* in the appropriate box on the scoresheet.

C

call for a catch. When a *catch* is about to fall between two fieldsmen, there is often confusion in their minds about who should go for the ball. In these circumstances, one of the fieldsmen — usually the one who is running forward to take the ball — should call for the catch and take it. Failure to carry out this simple drill can cause disastrously funny situations.

call for a run. A batsman's indication to his batting partner that he wants a *run*. This is done by calling 'Yes'. If a batsman is certain that he does not want a run, he will call 'No'. Should he be uncertain, the call is 'Wait'. It is batting protocol to call after each ball or stroke, and to use only these three calls, for fear of being misheard or misunderstood. (A call of 'Go', for instance, could be confused with 'No'.) A batsman may also call for more than one run, telling his partner of his intentions as they *cross* in the centre of the pitch.

In the etiquette of *running between the wickets*, the batsman with the clearer view of the ball calls for the runs to be taken. It is his call; he calls his partner through. Generally this means that the striker calls the runs when he hits the ball in front of the wicket; whilst the non-striker calls when the ball is deflected behind the batsman's wicket and thus behind his back. Indecisive or bad calling inevitably leads to confusion in running between the wickets and sometimes to a *run-out*.

caps and hats. Headgear worn to shield the eyes and neck from the adverse effects of the sun. Early cricketers wore billycock hats, with hard crowns and stiff brims. In hot countries a softer felt version found favour. Both styles, however, were adorned by bands whose colour proclaimed the wearer's team and frequently his identity.

Modern caps fit close to the skull and have a protruding peak to shade the eyes. The underside of the peak is often covered with a green material to soften the sun's reflection off hard, white wickets. Caps are usually made of coloured materials that identify the wearer's club; the club's insignia or badge is embroidered on the front above the peak. In tropical countries, wide-brimmed white washing-hats are popular, since their brims not only protect the eyes from glare but shield the back of the neck. These hats are also adorned with team badges.

English county clubs award caps only to players who, by their performances, command a regular place in the first eleven (i.e. 'win their caps'). They are deemed to deserve a capped player's salary. In other countries, at all levels, cap status is not tied to salary: players are usually awarded caps on their first appearance for a side.

The hat was a prized possession of the 19th-century player. So much so that if a bowler captured three wickets with consecutive deliveries, he was rewarded with the presentation of a hat; hence the *hat-trick*.

captain. The leader of a team. His responsibilities include: tossing for choice of innings and deciding whether to bat or bowl; directing his bowlers and the order in which they will bowl; placing the fieldsmen; choosing the order in which his batsmen will go to the wicket; implementing the tactics of his side; overseeing his players' conduct, and reporting to the appropriate authorities on the conduct of his team and of the other participants in the game. Sometimes the captain of a team is one of the men who select it — and sometimes the only selector. In the higher echelons of the game, he is regarded as the side's figurehead, public representative, public-relations man and spokesman.

card. An abbreviation for 'scorecard': a shortened visual résumé of a match displayed on television or printed in a newspaper, to summarize the state of a game. At its fullest, the card displays the names of the two teams, the date and venue of the match, the winner of the toss, the names of the members of the batting side in the order of going in, the runs scored by individual batsmen, the methods of their dismissal, the extras, and the team total. In limited-over games the number of balls faced by each batsman is also given, to enable the viewer to gain an appreciation of his *strike-rate*. In extended games, the time the batsman has been at the crease is displayed to facilitate an estimate of his scoring rate. Bowling cards are shown separately: they give the name of each bowler, the number of overs he has bowled, the number of wickets he has taken, the number of wides and no-balls in those overs, and the runs he has conceded.

The term 'card' originated in England, where scorecards were, and still are, printed by portable presses at every first-class and Test match, usually after each session of play. The state of the game is detailed on the card, and space is left for the spectator to write in the further developments in the day's play. Vendors of these cards move amongst the spectators with cries of 'Card', and the enthusiast may purchase one for a small sum.

carpet. Colloquialism for the ground or turf. A stroke hit 'along the carpet' is hit along the ground, not lofted above it.

carry. As a verb applied to a ball that has been struck: to travel through the air over a certain distance without bouncing. A catch that does not carry to a fielder or to the wicketkeeper does not reach him before bouncing. As a noun, the carry of a ball is the distance it covers while it is in the air.

carry one's bat. To remain *not out* at the conclusion of an innings. (See also next entry)

carry one's bat through an innings. The achievement of an opening batsman who bats throughout an innings and remains *not out* after all ten of his teammates have been dismissed. A.B. Tancred was the first to perform this feat in Test cricket, playing for South Africa against England at Cape Town in 1888/89. He was followed one year later by Australia's Dr J.E. Barrett at Lord's. Only some 30 batsmen have achieved the distinction in international cricket.

castle. The batsman's *wicket*, which he, the king, must defend like a castle. When he is bowled, he is said to have been castled — not, as in chess, placed in a less vulnerable position, but rather swept off the board!

catch. The act of gathering the ball after it is hit by the bat and before it touches the ground. The taking of a catch by a member of the fielding side dismisses the batsman, who is deemed *caught*. Correct catching technique involves the fieldsman positioning himself in the path of or underneath the ball, with the palms and fingers of one or both hands (preferably both) facing it, above or below eye-level; to cushion the ball's impact, the hands are allowed to 'give', as though catching a fragile object (see *soft hands*).

catching positions. Posts allocated to the fieldsmen close to the batsman so that they have an optimum chance of catching and dismissing him. Catching positions are allocated by the captain, normally within 20 metres of the striker. Catching fieldsmen include *wicketkeeper, slips, gully, point, silly point, silly mid-off, silly mid-on, short-leg* and *leg-slip*. Tactically stationed attacking fieldsmen outside a 20-metre radius may also be designated as catching positions.

In some formats of *limited-over* cricket, regulations state that two fieldsmen must remain in catching positions, no more than 15 metres from the batsman, for the first 15 overs of an innings. (See also *circle; field restrictions*)

caught. The batsman is *out* 'caught' if the ball touches his bat, or his hand or glove (the one holding the bat) below the wrist, and is subsequently held by a fieldsman before it touches the ground. A *catch* is considered fair only if the fieldsman remains within the field of play throughout the act of making the catch. It may be hugged to the body or may accidentally lodge in a fieldsman's dress or equipment. A catch is also fair if the hand holding it touches the ground — provided the ball does not. It is not a fair catch if the ball lodges accidentally in the protective helmet worn by a close fieldsman.

caught and bowled. Mode of dismissal in which the bowler takes a catch hit to him off his own delivery. A *return catch*.

caught behind. Short for 'caught behind the wicket': a term describing the demise of a batsman who is *caught* by the wicketkeeper.

caught on the fence. Dismissed by a *catch* taken, off a big hit, by a fieldsman positioned on the edge of the playing area, close to the boundary fence.

century. A score of between 100 and 199 runs in a single innings. It is the next important scoring ambition of a batsman who has attained a *half-century* and is still at the crease. A maiden century is a batsman's first hundred at a given level — e.g. a maiden first-class century.

chance. An opportunity to catch, stump or run out a batsman. A 'sharp chance' is one which, travelling fast and over a short distance, demands very sharp reflexes on the part of the fieldsman. Often a batsman gives several chances in his innings before he is finally dismissed. Commentators enumerate these chances, pinpointing the score at which the batsman offered them.

chance the arm.   To take a risk and hit out, or *slog*, in the execution of a stroke; to attack the bowling.

change hands with the bat.   To switch the bat from one hand to the other, so that, in *grounding his bat* while turning for a second or further run, the batsman can face the ball and the man fielding it, and thus see any developments that could spell danger for him. (See also *turn blind*)

chase the leather.   To field, continually chasing and retrieving the ball while the batsmen are punishing the bowling and scoring heavily.

chest protector.   Shaped pad of plastic, rubber or stuffed material which is strapped or attached around the leading side of the batsman's chest to prevent bruising caused by fast, rising bouncers that strike his ribs. Towels were used by Australian batsmen in 1932/33 to protect their chests against the *Bodyline* tactics of English skipper Douglas Jardine and his two fast-bowlers, Larwood and Voce.

chest-on.   See *square up*.

chinaman.   The left-handed *wrist-spinner*'s delivery which turns into the right-handed batsman from outside the off-stump. Contrary to popular belief, it is not a left-handed spin-bowler's *wrong'un* — which turns away from the right-handed batsman. The term originated in the West Indies in 1929/30, where the England and Middlesex batsman 'Patsy' Hendren reeled off a succession of enormous scores for a touring MCC team led by F.S.G. Calthorpe. Amongst the suffering West Indian bowlers in the Trinidad Test was Ellis Achong, an orthodox left-handed spinner of Chinese ancestry. Desperate to penetrate Hendren's defences, Achong threw in a wrist-spinner — and bowled him! Hendren, disgusted by his dismissal, returned to the pavilion commenting, 'Fancy being bowled by a bloody Chinaman!'

Chinese cut.   See *French cut*.

chip/loft the ball over the infield.   To loft the ball deliberately and delicately — in the manner of playing an approach shot in golf — over the heads of the fieldsmen stationed within 30 metres of the pitch, and into the safe and vacant spaces between the *boundary riders* and the fieldsmen placed around the wicket to save the single. The tactic is often used by early batsmen in some forms of *limited-over* cricket, at the stage when all but two fieldsmen must be positioned within 30 yards (27.4 metres) of the bat for the first 15 overs of an innings. In this situation it is a logical, safe and run-rewarding ploy. (See also *over the top*)

chucking. See *throwing or chucking.*

cipher. An alternative expression for a *duck.*

circle. A marking employed in *limited-over* games to restrict defensive field placements. The term is a misnomer, since the marking is, in reality, two semicircles, each with a radius of 30 yards (27.4 metres), drawn with the middle-stump at each end as their centres. The two semicircles are joined by straight lines, each the length of the pitch, in the *cover* and *mid-wicket* areas. The 'circle' is marked by white lines or dots on the playing surface.

In some limited-over formats, such as the World Series Cup, the fielding side is forbidden from positioning more than two fieldsmen outside the circle in the first 15 overs of the match; it is thus prevented from going prematurely on the defensive. It is further stipulated that, of the seven fieldsmen who must remain within the circle in this early stage, two must be in *catching positions.* Even after the elapse of 15 overs, the bowling team must retain at least four men (in addition to the bowler and wicketkeeper) inside the circle. Again the purpose is to prevent the fielding side from placing all of its men in the *outfield* to curtail the scoring of boundaries. If these regulations are violated, the delivery is deemed a *no-ball.* (See also *field restrictions*)

classic catch. A spectacular or difficult catch, well taken. The expression originated in a television competition in which viewers were invited to nominate, from a selected shortlist and in order of merit, the best catches of the games telecast by the station in the course of one season.

clean-bowled. The fate of a batsman whose wicket is put down directly by a bowler's delivery, without any deflection off the bat, equipment or person.

clock. The match clock on the cricket ground is in full view of players, umpires and spectators, and is the clock from which the umpires take their times for start of play, *intervals* and cessation of play. Although this clock is often not set to (say) Greenwich or Australian time, it is nonetheless the official timepiece for the game.

close-to-the-bat fieldsman. Fielder positioned within a few metres of the batsman and his wicket, with a view to taking catches. *Slips, gully, point, silly point, silly mid-off, silly mid-on*, backward and forward *short-leg* and the *leg-slip* positions are all close-to-the-wicket fieldsmen. (See also *bat-pad fieldsman*)

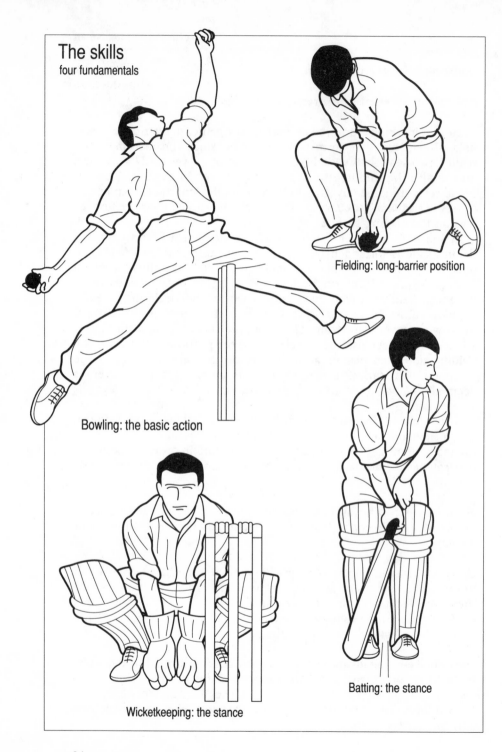

The skills
four fundamentals

Bowling: the basic action

Fielding: long-barrier position

Wicketkeeping: the stance

Batting: the stance

cloth-yard. Also, ell. An old lineal yard of 45 inches (1143 mm) by which cloth was measured. A cloth-yard was divided into four quarters and sixteen 'nails', and once equalled the distance from the batsman's *stumps* to the back edge of his *batting crease*.

clothing and equipment, misuse of The laws of cricket forbid the misuse of clothing and equipment. The fieldsman who stops the ball with an item of clothing such as a *cap* is penalized 5 runs. The same penalty applies when a fieldsman's *helmet* or *sweater*, lying on the ground, impedes the progress of the ball towards the boundary; hence the reason why fielders secrete their protective helmets in *water points* or place them directly behind the wicketkeeper.

The batsman who prevents the ball from hitting his stumps by deliberately padding the ball away may be given out *lbw*, even though the ball strikes his pads outside the line of the off-stump. The player who punches the ball away with a batting *glove* which is not gripping the bat may be dismissed *handled ball*. But a batsman may not be caught off the helmet of a fieldsman. Nor may he be caught out if one of his hits lodges in his own *pads* or clothing, or in the coat of the *umpire*. (See also *caught*)

coat of varnish. Commentators frequently describe a delivery that has almost *bowled* the batsman as having 'missed by a coat of varnish' — i.e. very narrowly. Had the stump concerned been painted with just one more coat of varnish, the ball would have hit it.

collapse. Sudden and unexpected loss of wickets in an innings. A side that finds itself 5 wickets down for 100 after starting with an opening *stand* of 95 can safely be said to have collapsed.

collapsed front knee. If the front leg collapses or bends at the knee in the bowling stride, the height from which the bowler delivers the ball is reduced. He then releases it from less than his maximum reach; he obtains less bounce from the pitch; and, since the distance from the front foot to the delivery hand at the point of release, and the arc of the bowling arm, are both shortened, the speed of the arm and hence of the delivery is correspondingly diminished.

come in. To come in to the wicket to bat, at the beginning of an innings, at the fall of a wicket or on the retirement of a batsman. The term 'go in' is sometimes synonymously used.

come on. To come on to the field; or to come on to bowl at the beginning of a new *spell*.

commentary-box end.   The end of the ground or wicket at which the broadcasting box, housing the commentators, is to be found. At Lord's the boxes are on the top deck of the *pavilion*. In Melbourne they are situated in the *members'* stand; whilst in Sydney the commentators are posted in the Bradman and Brewongle stands. With television cameras covering the match action from both ends of the wicket, it is not easy for viewers to identify the commentators' vantage-point. To clarify this, the callers will often state that a bowler is operating from the commentary-box end — or that he is 'running away from us'.

composition of sides.   Matches are played between two sides, each of eleven men, one of whom is the *captain*. In the absence of the captain, a deputy or *vice-captain* acts for him. Before the *toss* for the choice of *innings*, the captain nominates his side, which cannot thereafter be changed without the consent of the opposing skipper. By agreement, matches may be played between teams of more or less than eleven participants, but only eleven men may field.

concede.   To give away — usually applied to the concession of runs that could have been avoided. Thus, wicketkeepers can be said to concede a certain number of *byes* in an innings, and bowlers to concede a tally of runs in a spell of bowling.

Cornstalks.   Nickname given to early Australian cricketers: the agricultural products of the colonies.

country, in the.   A familiar term used by cricketers to refer to the *outfield*. Synonymous with 'in the deep'.

cover.   Fielding position to the off-side and slightly in front of the batsman, at an angle of 45° to him, level with the midpoint of the pitch and some 25 to 30 metres from it. The term comes from the fact that the man in that position moves behind *point* to cover him, in case point should miss or fumble the ball.

cover a lot of ground.   A nimble *wicketkeeper* whose agility and footwork enable him to range a long way to the left and right of the batsman's wicket, to stop a delivery or take a catch, 'covers of a lot of ground'. Such a keeper allows the *slip* and *leg-slip* fieldsmen to stand wider of the stumps, thereby increasing the angle and area covered by the slip cordon and thus its chances of taking catches. The phrase is also applied to fleet-footed fieldsmen who patrol larger-than-normal areas and effectively prevent runs.

cover-drive. A front-foot or back-foot *drive* struck towards the *cover* position in the field. It is a slightly risky shot which involves hitting *across the line* of the ball towards the off-side.

cover-point. See *cover*.

covers. Tarpaulins or specially constructed temporary and mobile roofing placed over the *pitch* and *square* to protect them from rain and bad weather. Covers prevent atmospheric *moisture* from affecting the playing surface, or minimize its effects, reducing the time lost to the elements and hastening the resumption of play after an interruption. A sodden playing area delays a game because bowlers and batsmen are denied a firm foothold; nor does the ball bounce or go through to the keeper on such a pitch.

In Australia and other countries affected by heavy rain, *curators* peg tarpaulins close to the ground so that no rain will affect the wicket. This is particularly important in hot climates where any rain falling on clay pitches or getting under the covers, followed by hot sun, can create a *sticky wicket*, making batting difficult. But close covering of the pitch causes condensation or sweating under the tarpaulin, which greens up the pitch and helps the quicker bowlers to *move the ball* off the seam when play resumes. To prevent this, hessian strips are first laid under the tarpaulin to absorb the condensation. At Edgbaston, Birmingham, machinery drags the aptly named tarpaulin 'Brumbella' into position, greatly reducing the delay normally encountered in laying these types of covers.

In England, where wet loamy pitches are often slow but good batting surfaces, miniature roofed frameworks are sometimes deemed sufficient to protect the pitch from the worst of the rain. Raised off the ground on wheels, they are easily manoeuvred into position and, because of their elevation, eliminate the danger of sweating. Gutterings and drainpipes carry the water off the covers and the wicket area to prevent it forming pools. A recent English innovation is the air-bubble cover: a diminutive, condensation-free air-hall stored in a permanent pit alongside the square and inflated in minutes over it.

To hit a ball 'into the covers' is to propel it in the direction of the *cover* fieldsmen, not into tarpaulins left lying around.

cracked wicket. Initially the pitch should be a smooth, unblemished surface containing the amount of *moisture* necessary to bind it into a good *batting wicket* for the game's duration. Because of the pitch's exposure to a hot sun, however, the moisture sometimes evaporates too quickly and the surface soil contracts, causing fissures. As the match progresses (in Test matches, over five days), the cracks can widen to as much as 10 mm, and every time the ball bounces on the side of one of these cracks it behaves in an unpredictable manner, creating problems for batsmen. Each time it hits the pitch, it crushes a section of it into dust, leaving a hole. On such a cracked wicket, the side batting first enjoys the better batting conditions and should win the match. Cracked wickets occur on clay pitches in warm climates.

cramping the batsman.   See *bowl close to the batsman*; *following the batsman*; *make room for a stroke*.

creases.   Painted white lines on the *pitch* marking its length and width, the placement of the *stumps*, the areas from which the bowler may legally deliver the ball, and those in which the batsman may safely stand to hit it and run without incurring the risk of being stumped or run out. Creases are deemed to have no thickness, the extent of the areas they mark lying within their back and inside edges. (See *batting crease*; *bowling crease*; *popping crease*; *return crease*)

Originally creases were scratches in the ground. Later they were cut into the turf — a method of marking which survived until the time of W.G. Grace, when painted white lines were introduced. The roles of the bowling and batting creases have changed through the years with the modification of the *no-ball* law.

creeper.   See *shooter or creeper*.

cricket.   A concise overview of the origins and history of the game will be found at the front of the book, on pages xiii–xvi.

cross.   When two batsmen pass each other in the middle of the pitch while running between the wickets, they are said to cross. (See also *batsmen had not crossed*; *run-out*; *short run*)

cross-bat strokes.   Strokes played mainly off the back foot with a horizontal bat. Cross-bat strokes are attacking shots and should be played only when, because of the bounce and direction of the delivery, there is no chance of the batsman being bowled. Bats swung horizontally defend very little — only about 240 square cm — of the area of the wicket (see *straight-bat strokes*). The main danger of dismissal in cross-bat strokes lies in lofting the ball as a catch. Consequently batsmen aim to swing such strokes down on the ball to hit it immediately to ground. Cross-bat strokes include the *cuts*, the *pull* and the *hook*.

crowd catch.   An optical illusion created by the swiftness of a fielding incident: a hit which results in what the spectators believe to be a fair *catch* and therefore the dismissal of a batsman. They clap and cheer accordingly — only to find that the supposed catch is disallowed by the umpires, either because the batsman did not hit the ball or because he hit it into the ground before it was caught.

crumbling (dusty) wicket. A dry pitch which, in the course of a game, breaks up into a dusty surface because of hot conditions and a lack of grass. Spin-bowlers make the ball grip and turn in the dust and loosened earth. The slowness of *wrist-spinners* through the air handicaps them on slow *turning* pitches; but on dry, dusty wickets they come into their own, making the ball bounce, turn and go through quickly to the keeper.

curator. Name given in Australia to the person who in England and other countries is known as the groundsman. It is his responsibility to care for the cricket ground and its amenities. He waters, cuts, rolls and marks the *pitches* in preparation for matches; he ensures that pitches are covered against rain, if bad weather prevails before or during a game; and if rain affects the pitch during a game, he and his helpers dry the playing area so that the match can be resumed as soon as possible. He also mends pitches damaged during games.

His duties are multifarious. He tends the *square* from which the pitches are prepared, fertilizing, scarifying, top-dressing and cross-rolling in the off-season and at the beginning of each new season; top-dresses, weeds, rolls and cuts the *outfield*; prepares practice wickets; cleans, repairs and paints sightscreens, seating, scoreboards and pavilions. He is jack-of-all-cricketing-trades, and master of them as well. (See also *maintenance of playing area*)

curve. The uniform lateral movement of the ball in the air before it bounces. The delivery which curves from leg to off is called outcurve; that which curves from off to leg is called incurve. Curve differs from *swing*. Curve begins from the moment the hand releases the ball; swing occurs in varying degrees at about the optimum speed of 90 km/h, is aerodynamically induced and can take place either early or late in the ball's flight. Curve is produced by the *spin* imparted to the ball; swing depends on the various air-pressures created around the ball by its *seam* and *shine*. A bowler can curve an old ball; swing depends on the raised seam and the sheen of the new ball.

Off-spin and *off-cut* result in outcurves that spin or cut back into the wicket from the off-side. *Leg-spin* and *leg-cut* produce incurves that deviate off the pitch from leg to off. It is interesting to note that a baseball pitcher curves the ball by spinning it in much the same way as a medium-paced off-cutter is produced in cricket. (See also *drift*)

cut. In batting, to cut means to *deflect* or 'slip' the ball away on the off-side, between the *point* and wicketkeeping positions. The cut strokes that produce such deflections may hit the ball at right-angles to the pitch — *square-cuts* — or glance them just wide of the wicketkeeper — *late-cuts*. The cut is predominantly a back-foot stroke, though on wickets with little bounce it can sometimes be played off the front foot.

An unintentional deflection is derisively called a *French cut* (or Chinese cut, or Surrey cut).

cut (in bowling). See *cutter*.

cut loose. A vivid term that denotes the tactics of a batsman who, after a period of defensive play, moves on to the attack.

cut-off relay return. Baseball fielding technique sometimes used in cricket to speed up *returns* from the outfield. The tactic involves two fieldsmen, one chasing and retrieving the ball and the other positioning himself midway between the point of retrieval and the wicket. The chaser picks up the ball and throws it to the cut-off man, who then relays it to the wicketkeeper or bowler (whichever is in the better position to effect a run-out). The cut-off relay return is speedy because it allows the fieldsmen to use fast *flat throws* over short distances. It also gives the cut-off man the choice of which wicket to throw to, and thus a better chance of a run-out.

cutter. A delivery bowled by medium or medium-fast bowlers. The first two fingers of the bowling hand grip the ball on top of the *seam*, which points in the direction of the intended cut. They are pulled quickly down the left or right side of the ball at the moment of release, imparting fast spin in the direction of either second slip or fine-leg and causing the ball to deviate on bouncing. Drawing the fingers down the left side of the ball and rotating the seam towards slip produces the *leg-cutter*; drawing them down the right side and spinning the seam towards fine-leg produces the *off-cutter*. Cutters are suited to wet pitches that provide only sluggish turn for the spinners. They are percentage balls which do not grip and cut every time they are bowled. The bowler has to be careful not to pull the ball down on to a short length with the downward motion of the bowling hand at the moment of release.

cutting the wicket. See *mower*.

d

dance down the wicket. To advance, moving with the twinkling toes of a ballroom dancer, down the wicket to *get to the pitch of the ball* in order to play an aggressive stroke.

danger area. That area of the pitch which lies immediately in front of the batsman, up to 1.22 metres in front of the *batting crease* and 30.48 cm either side of middle-stump. If a bowler runs on this area while bowling, he roughens the turf in front of the stumps. If the bowler from the opposite end then pitches his deliveries in this 'rough', he gains unfair advantage by being better able to spin and cut the ball on the damaged surface. (See *bowl into the rough*; *running on the pitch*)

danger end. The end or wicket to which a batsman, completing one or more runs, is running, and to which the ball is being returned, thus occasioning the danger of a *run-out*. In the code that governs running between the wickets, it is always the batsman running to the danger end who makes the final decision about the advisability of the last run.

dasher. A batsman who 'dashes' at the task of batting, scoring runs quickly by means of risky and spectacular strokes. Australian and Victorian opening batsman Paul Hibbert earned himself the ironic sobriquet of 'Dasher' by scoring a century against the Indian team touring Australia in 1977 — an innings so enterprising that it did not contain a single boundary!

day match. A game which is played entirely in daylight conditions. All Test and *first-class* games are day matches. Some international and representative *limited-over* games played at weekends, during spectators' leisure hours, are day matches, as are similar limited-over contests played on grounds not equipped with floodlights.

day/night match. Representative *limited-over* game which begins in the afternoon in daylight conditions and ends at night under lights. Strict regulations govern the times at which the floodlights are turned on to reproduce daytime conditions. This format is aimed at maximizing spectator attendances in after-work hours. (See also *light towers*)

dead ball. When the ball is dead, the game stops. No runs are scored and no dismissals effected. A ball is dead when:

- it finally settles in the hands of the wicketkeeper or bowler, such that no further development in the game is possible at that point;
- it reaches the boundary;
- it lodges in the clothing or equipment of a batsman or umpire;
- it lodges in the protective helmet of a fielder;
- it is lost;
- it is deliberately stopped by a fielder with his equipment or clothing;
- a batsman is out;
- the umpire calls 'over' or 'time';
- the umpire intervenes because of unfair play;
- a player or umpire is seriously injured;
- the umpire judges a batsman as unready to receive a ball and making no attempt to play it;
- the bowler accidentally drops the ball or fails to deliver it;
- one or both bails fall from the batsman's wicket before the ball is delivered;
- the umpire leaves his position to consult with his colleague;
- the umpire disallows leg-byes because the batsman has made no attempt to play the ball.

dead bat. A motionless and limp bat. Dead-bat strokes are the *front-foot* and *back-foot defensive strokes*. In both of these the forward movement of the bat is arrested alongside the pads, with the angled bat directing the ball to ground and preventing a catch. The grip of the bottom hand is relaxed at the moment of contact, with the result that no power is imparted to a stroke — the ball drops stone-dead at the feet of the batsman.

dead wicket. A pitch that gives no evidence of life, such as bounce, pace and movement — and thus no encouragement to the bowler. The ball comes off the playing surface sluggishly, with no movement off the *seam* for faster bowlers, little or no bounce, and no evidence of *spin* for slow-bowlers. The pitch may be a slow wet English wicket or a dry grassless Australian strip; both are entirely devoid of animation. Whilst such a surface militates against the dismissal of a batsman, it does not favour strokemaking since the ball does not come on to the bat. Thus it is not a favourite of batsmen because it makes them punch out their strokes — and it is certainly not the darling of the bowler.

death rattle. Heard by a batsman, the deadly sound of the ball hitting the stumps behind his back.

declare. To close the *innings* of one's team by choice. A declaration is the action of the captain of a batting side, who, for tactical reasons, declares to his opposite number that he wants to end his team's innings before all eleven of his batsmen have been dismissed. A skipper declares because he considers that his team has scored enough runs to win; because he wants to give his bowlers enough time to bowl out the opposition; or because he is of the opinion that the condition of the pitch will assist his bowlers to dismiss the opposing batsmen.

The declaration option was introduced into the laws of cricket in 1889, owing to the ludicrous situation which compelled a captain who wished to end his team's innings prematurely to instruct the batsmen at the crease, and those who subsequently went in, to hit down their wickets immediately — which caused much pointless cricket and wastage of time. The extreme form of declaration is contained in the law which now permits a team with a substantial lead in the first innings, but not enough runs on the board to enforce the *follow-on*, to *forfeit* its second innings.

Imaginative captains have written their names into cricket history with daring and sometimes unfortunate closures. Gary Sobers declared the West Indian innings closed in the Fourth Port-of-Spain Test in 1968 against Colin Cowdrey's Englishmen, setting the tourists 215 runs for victory in 165 minutes. The visitors won the run-race with 3 minutes to spare, Cowdrey himself scoring 71 and opener Geoff Boycott 80 not out. The loss was one which Caribbean spectators never allowed the previously popular Sobers to forget.

deep. In the outfield, a long way from the pitch and the batsman. Thus, 'in the deep' describes the position of an outfielder, or the area of the field in which a catch is taken or fielding occurs.

The word is also used as a descriptive prefix for a fielding position. Thus, whilst the *cover* fieldsman is placed only about 30 metres from the batsman, deep cover finds himself close to the boundary.

deep backward square-leg. Leg-side fieldsman positioned on the boundary, just behind the imaginary extension of the batting crease, whose role is to take catches and stop potential boundaries struck to that part of the ground. On faster pitches the position is favoured by captains over deep square-leg, because under those conditions the ball is often deflected finer.

deep extra-cover. Off-side fielding position on the boundary behind *extra-cover,* i.e. to the right and in front of the batsman, and in line with the *batting crease* at the bowler's end. This fieldsman's function is to cut off an *off-drive* that beats extra-cover and is destined for the boundary. Sometimes he is referred to as the off-side *sweeper*: the man who sweeps up the ball when everyone else has failed to stop it.

deep fine-leg. Leg-side fielding position on the boundary behind the batsman's wicket and just a few degrees from the line of the pitch and the wicketkeeper. Essentially a run-saving position, deep fine-leg's function is to retrieve *deflections* behind the wicket on the leg-side, off the bat and the batsman's pads and body. He also acts as a back-up or *long-stop* for the wicketkeeper, should the latter fail to take the ball on the leg-side and allow *byes*. Occasionally he is called upon to catch or stop *hook* shots when the batsman mis-hits a bouncer.

deep forward square-leg. Leg-side fieldsman positioned on the boundary, just in front of the imaginary extension of the batting crease, whose role is to take catches and cut off potential boundaries struck to that part of the ground. On slower wickets the position is favoured by captains over deep square-leg, because under those conditions the ball hit on the leg-side usually travels in front of square.

deep mid-off. Another term for *long-off*.

deep mid-on. Another term for *long-on*.

deep mid-wicket. Leg-side fieldsman, positioned level with the mid-point of the pitch, behind orthodox *mid-wicket* and on the boundary. Predominantly a defensive post, intended to cut off the hard-hit stroke or to catch the lofted drive or pull, deep mid-wicket is sometimes referred to as the on-side *sweeper*.

deep square-leg. Leg-side fieldsman, positioned close to or on the boundary in line with the *batting crease*. This defensive fielder cuts off potential boundaries hit in his direction, and occasionally takes catches unintentionally lofted into the outfield. (See also *square-leg*)

defensive field. Fielding formation set by the captain of the bowling side purely to stop the batting team from scoring runs. These negative tactics entail the removal of fieldsmen from attacking catching positions and their distribution in a circle around the bat to prevent the batsmen from taking singles. Others are liberally spread along the boundaries to stop fours. *Bowling to one side of the wicket* with a preponderance of the fieldsmen stationed on that side is one negative tactic employing a defensive field. A *leg-side field* is also a restrictive tactic, particularly when the bowler bowls close to the batsman's body to cramp his strokes. Defensive fields inevitably produce stagnant, unspectacular cricket in which the batting side scores few runs and the bowlers take few if any wickets.

defensive strokes. See *back-foot defensive stroke; dead bat; front-foot defensive stroke.*

deflect the ball. To score runs by exploiting the pace of the bowler. Instead of hitting the ball, the batsman merely seeks to turn or glide it away from and behind the wicket, using the speed of the delivery to dispatch it into the outfield. This skill involves the use of the *cut* shot or the *leg-glance*, strokes that penetrate the slips or the short-leg cordon, and can require the batsman to make room for himself to play off the line of the stumps.

deflect the ball on to the stumps. To *play on.*

delivery. A ball delivered by a bowler, with the intention of dismissing the batsman.

delivery stride. See *bowling action; run-up.*

Deloittes rating. A computerized grading of the international status of batsmen and bowlers based on performance statistics and sponsored by the Deloittes Computer Company. Much like the ranking procedure in tennis.

demon bowler. A bowler feared by the opposing batsmen. Originally the sobriquet of Fred Spofforth, the Australian 'Demon' who was largely instrumental in Australia winning its first Ashes Test on English soil in 1882.

deviation. See *cut; spin; seam; swing.*

devil's number. A reputedly unlucky point in a team or individual's score: a total at which superstitious batsmen or teams believe that misfortune is more likely to overtake them. English teams fear the *Nelson*, or 111. Australians hate 87, which is a devilishly unlucky 13 runs short of the coveted century mark.

    Australians' antipathy towards 87 gained acceptance in the 1930s when all-rounder Keith Miller and his future Test skipper Ian Johnson were playing club cricket with South Melbourne. They noticed that, in all grades, many batsmen were dismissed with their score on 87. Later, fielding next to one another in the Australian slip cordon in the 1950s, they were again struck by the frequency with which batsmen met their nemesis just 13 short of their hundred. 'Nugget' Miller's fixation on the unlucky 87 had begun in 1931, when he saw his childhood idol Don Bradman, after a spate of hundreds for New South Wales, bowled by the

Victorian fast man Harry 'Bull' Alexander for 87. When he consulted the record books about the game in question, however, he discovered the entry 'Bradman bowled Alexander 89'. Such is the fallacious basis for many superstitions!

dig out a yorker. The *yorker*, a ball that pitches on the *batting crease*, often takes the batsman by surprise and almost slips under his guard. He is forced to come down hard on the ball at the last minute to 'dig it out' and avoid being bowled. (See also *sandshoe crusher*)

dismiss a side. To put *out*, by any of the ten ways outlined in the laws of cricket, ten of the eleven batsmen in a side, thus bringing its *innings* to an end. When ten men of the batting side have been dismissed, the eleventh is not permitted to bat by himself and the team is deemed to be *all out*. If a side *declares* its innings closed, it is not deemed dismissed; nor is it all out.

dismissed. The status of a batsman who is *out* in any of the ten ways described in the laws of cricket. A batsman who suffers dismissal is excluded from further participation in that innings; he is not allowed to continue batting, and is sent from the wicket. (But see also *runner*)

diver. A mediocre *wicketkeeper*, with little or no footwork or anticipation, who consequently has to lunge or dive at the last moment to stop wide deliveries. This diving technique pushes wide catches out of his gloves and has little chance of success. However, keepers who can combine good mobility and footwork with, when necessary, a final dive are able to cover an enormous amount of ground.

diving for the ball. Desperation fielding tactics, used when the *fieldsman* has not enough time to move into position behind the line of a stroke. Instead he literally flings himself at the ball in an attempt to stop it penetrating the field and proceeding to the boundary. This dynamic technique was introduced into the staid sport of cricket when Jackie McGlew's South African side visited England in 1955 and displayed a fielding zest which almost enabled them to share the Test series with England.

Wicketkeepers sometimes have to *dive* to take an edged catch or to stop a ball when they are wrong-footed. Keepers who dive to stop regulation wide balls betray a lack of mobility or faulty footwork.

dolly. An easy catch, a *sitter*. Used in the plural, 'dollies' may mean the stumps or wicket. A bowler who 'knocks over the dollies' bowls a batsman: imagery probably taken from fairground parlance.

donkey drop. A very slow delivery which is lobbed high into the air so that it descends almost vertically on the batsman's wicket. It creates problems about where and how to hit the ball. (See also *Spettigew dropper*)

double-century. A score of between 200 and 299 runs notched in a single innings. In the 1950s the feat yielded the award of a silver tankard and a crate of Double Century Ale from a leading English brewery!

double-ton. A *double-century*, or 200 runs.

drag line. A marker-line scratched in the turf, a metre or more behind and parallel to the *bowling crease*, by a bowler who drags his rear foot in the delivery stride. The bowler aims to land the foot behind this line before he begins to drag it as he delivers the ball. The line is far enough behind the bowling crease to ensure that the bowler's stride will not take his front foot over the *batting crease* and thus make his delivery a *no-ball*.

In the days before the front-foot no-ball law, umpires drew this line for the 'draggers', to prevent them from skating down the wicket and thus bowling over a shorter distance than the non-draggers. They then called a no-ball for every delivery in which the bowler overstepped the drag line. This no-balling method offered the advantage of earlier judgment, giving the umpire more time to raise his head to assess matters at the batsman's end — as well as giving the batsman more time to have a gratuitous and early swing at every delivery deemed illegal.

drag on. See *play on*.

drains. Agricultural drains usually crisscross a first-class ground to expedite the removal of water after rain. Some grounds have inlet points to these drains at the corners of the wicket area, and surface water is swept into them off the *covers* when play is about to resume.

As a matter of interest, the playing area of the Melbourne Cricket Ground is surrounded by an enormous barrel drain. During the rainy spring season the outlet to this drain is closed off, so that a reservoir of water is formed in it. The *curator* uses this water to irrigate the ground in times of water shortages during hot summers!

draw. The result of a match other than an *outright win* or *a tie*: an outcome in which one team does not complete its second innings (or, in one-innings games, its only innings) and fails to overtake the number of runs scored by its opponents. A *first-innings win* is possible in a drawn two-innings game.

draw shot. An antique cricket stroke, in vogue in the 19th century. It was played to an off-side delivery. The batsman lifted his bat towards point and waited until the ball was level with or past him. Then he swung the bat down either behind his body or between his spreadeagled legs, with the blade angled towards the leg-side, deflecting or 'drawing' the ball wide of his leg-stump towards square- or fine-leg. Nowadays the stroke is rarely played intentionally. Sometimes, however, when a batsman jams down hard on a yorker or an overpitched delivery with a closed face of the bat, and accidentally hits the ball between or behind his legs, glancing it wide of the leg-stump to fine-leg or square-leg, commentators describe the inadvertent stroke as a 'draw shot'.

dressing-rooms. Set aside in the *pavilion* for the sole use of each team, the dressing-rooms are where the players change into their cricket togs and put on their equipment; and it is from the dressing-room windows that they often watch the match. During first-class and Test games, ground authorities employ attendants whose duties are to maintain the cleanliness of these rooms, ensure that only those with authority enter them, and cater for the comfort and needs of the players. In English county pavilions, one attendant looks after both dressing-rooms, cleans and restuds players' boots, cleans their pads, and attends to their laundry. He also keeps a small shop, supplying equipment ranging from bats to socks and athletic supports. Test venues provide an attendant for each dressing-room. His role and services remain constant, but much of his time is taken up with policing entry to the dressing-rooms.

drift. Slow sideways movement of the ball in the air before it bounces. Drift is in fact slow *curve*, and is produced by the combination of spin, the bowler's body-movement and the prevailing wind conditions. It is achieved by the slower *spin-bowlers*, who normally make the ball move in the air in one direction before spinning it back the opposite way. Thus an *off-spinner* drifts the ball towards slips before turning it back, and a *leg-spinner* floats the ball from off to leg before spinning it towards the off-side. A breeze blowing from leg to off suits the drift of the off-spinner, whilst a wind in the opposite direction is well suited to the leg-spinner. Drift also increases the effectiveness of the finger-spinner's *arm ball*.

drink trolley. Wheeled tray used to transport *drinks* to the players on the field at the agreed times. It is now a canopied wonder-box containing iced towels, chewing-gum, and various other items for the players' comfort, and is used extensively by sponsors as a colourful advertisement for their products. Formerly drinks were taken out on trays by the *twelfth men* or by dressing-room attendants; nowadays attendants dressed in the sponsors' uniforms are employed.

drinks. On hot days, the captains and umpires agree for cool drinks to be taken by the players on the field. These are prepared and served halfway through a *session* of play, or at the fall of a wicket if within 5 minutes of drinks being due, either by the *twelfth men* or by attendants with their *drink trolley*. On days of extreme heat, the captains may agree to allow two drink intervals per session.

drive. To strike the ball forcibly with a vertical bat in front of the batsman's wicket. Drives are classified according to the direction in which the ball is struck, and often also according to the footwork employed: see *back-foot drive*; *front-foot drive*; *cover-drive*; *lofted drive*; *off-drive*; *on-drive*; *square-drive*; *straight-drive*.

dropped. A player who is dropped from a side is omitted from it. In the other sense of the word, a batsman who has been dropped offered a *catch* which was fumbled or dropped by a fieldsman; the fieldsman is said to have dropped the batsman.

drying the ground. The drying of a cricket ground after heavy rain has been facilitated by mechanical inventions such as the *super-sopper*. Tried and true methods — squeegeeing the water into *drains* and soaking up puddles with mats of absorbent materials or rubber, or with sawdust — are still employed, particularly at club level. In international cricket, however, there have been instances of helicopters being used to whisk away *moisture* with the upward draught of the rotor blades. At the Melbourne Cricket Ground, a subterranean electrical heating system is used, not only to promote the early growth of grass but also to dry the wicket area.

At Kimberley in South Africa in 1956/57, when the first rain in two years swamped the ground, the frustrated organizers of a match between Griqualand West and the touring MCC side dried the ground by the simple expedient of drenching it with petrol and setting it alight! At the Oval in 1968, a thunderstorm flooded the ground on the final afternoon and threatened to deprive England of the certain victory that would square the Test series with Bill Lawry's Australians. The groundsman immediately issued hundreds of spectators with pointed staves which they used to perforate the ground and drain away the surface water, just in time for Cowdrey's England to gain a thrilling but narrow victory. (See also *curator*)

duck. No runs, zero, zilch! A batsman who is *out* for a duck has failed to trouble the scorers and has not recorded a run. The origin of the expression lies in the old description of a batsman who failed to score as having made a 'duck's egg', the shape of which resembles the figure 0. Television has put black humour into the scoring of a duck, by inventing an appropriate cartoon figure: the tear-shedding, dolefully waddling 'Daddles'. In the *action-replay* images on some electronic scoreboards and on home viewers' TV screens, this graphic little character accompanies the unfortunate batsman back to the pavilion. (See also *bag a pair*; *golden duck*)

duck the ball. A batsman avoids being struck by a fast-bowler's bouncer by ducking his head beneath the height of its bounce. This manoeuvre is more effective when the batsman is in a *side-on* position with his chest facing point: he then ducks to the off and under the line of the ball. If he ducks in a chest-on position, he is still in the path of the approaching delivery.

dustbowl / dustheap. Pejorative terms denoting a pitch whose surface is loose and dusty: a pitch which assists the spin-bowler by allowing the ball to grip and turn. (See also *crumbling wicket*)

dusty wicket. See *crumbling wicket*.

e

early-order batsmen. Batsmen who go to the wicket early in the *batting order*, or high on the captain's list designating the sequence in which his men shall bat. The term generally describes batsmen number 1, 2 and 3, who usually have excellent defensive techniques to combat the opposition's opening fast-bowlers and the *new ball*.

easy / comfortable single. A run scored without the batsmen needing to hurry between the wickets, since there is no danger of a run-out. The words 'easy' and 'comfortable' can refer to any number of runs scored without urgency.

edge. The extremity and thinnest part of the *blade* of the bat. Balls hit with the edge are not hit hard; they are 'edged'. Bowlers seek to *find the edge* of the bat, since balls that strike this part of the blade are generally deflected as catches to fieldsmen close to the wicket, either directly from the bat (as in slip-catches) or via the pads. The edge further from the batsman's body and on the off-side is the *outside edge*; that closer to his body and on the leg-side is the *inside edge*. (See also *bottom edge; educated edge; middle of the edge; thick edge; thin edge; top edge*)

educated edge. In attempting to *glance* or run the ball behind the wicket and wide of the stumps, the batsman, not infrequently, hits it with the edge rather than the middle of the bat. The intelligent intent to strike the ball in the direction of its ultimate destination is there; but the perfect middled execution is not. It is an educated edge.

eleven. Alternative term for a team, since a cricket side is usually made up of 11 players. It should be noted, however, that, by agreement between the captains of the opposing teams, the number of players in each side may be varied. In the 19th century, early touring England teams often played matches 'against odds' — games in which eleven English players were pitted against a greater number of opponents. In 1861, it was not unusual that H.H. Stephenson's English eleven matched themselves against an eighteen from Victoria or a twenty-two of Castlemaine.

emergency fieldsman. See *substitute fieldsman; twelfth man.*

ends of a ground. The two opposite extremities of a cricket ground, on a line with the pitch. Ends are frequently called after nearby roads or adjoining suburbs. Thus, in Brisbane a bowler may deliver from the Vulture Street or the Stanley Street end. At Headingley a batsman takes strike at the Kirkstall Lane or the Rugby Ground end; at the Oval the ball is returned to the Vauxhall or Kennington end. In Sydney there are the Paddington and Randwick ends; and in Melbourne the Richmond and Members' Stand ends.

ends of a wicket. The longitudinal extremities of the pitch, 20.12 metres apart where the *wickets* are pitched and the *bowling creases* marked. The end at which the batsman takes strike is known as the striker's end, and that from which the bowler bowls as the bowler's or *non-striker's end*. The batsman who is not taking strike stands at the non-striker's end ready to run when the striker hits the ball.

esky. Large insulated carrying-chest, made of plastic or metal, used by Australian *spectators* to transport food and drink, packed in ice, to cricket matches. Such is the Aussie spectator's thirst for the 'amber fluid' that it was not unusual for two mates to press a capacious dustbin into service as an esky! Increasing drunkenness and hooliganism at cricket matches has prompted authorities to forbid the importation of alcohol into grounds, and the esky is nowadays less in evidence than it used to be. The word originated as a trademark.

expensive. Term applied to a bowler who gives away too many runs, or to a missed opportunity to dismiss a batsman who goes on to make a high score.

experimental laws. Laws not included in the official code but, by common consent of the Test-playing nations, observed in international, first-class and lower ranks on a trial basis — until their value is proved. The front-foot *no-ball* regulation was for many years an experimental law until it was absorbed into the 1980 recodification of the laws. (See also *laws, codification of; umpiring difficulties*)

extra-cover Off-side fielding position in front of the batsman, in line with and about 30 metres from the *batting crease* at the bowler's end. Extra-cover prevents runs by stopping the *off-drive*, and is stationed 30 to 40 metres from the bat.

extras. Runs scored in a team's innings, but not off the bat. These 'extra' runs are *byes, leg-byes, no-balls* and *wides*; they are credited to the batting side's run total, not to that of the individual batsman. The Australian term for extras is 'sundries'. (See also *maiden over*)

f

face up. To *take strike*.

fail. To be unsuccessful with the bat or the ball.

fail to make one's ground. A batsman who moves out of the *batting crease* in making a stroke or taking a run, and fails to return to his own or reach the opposite batting crease before the wicket towards which he is moving is put down, does not make his ground. He is dismissed *stumped* or *run out*. (See also *ground one's bat; out of his ground*)

fail to trouble the scorer. To fail to score a run; to score a *duck*.

fair and unfair bowling. See *danger area; intimidatory bowling; running on the pitch; throwing or chucking*.

falling away. A fault that occurs when a bowler's weight falls away to his left, and the batsman's off-side, as the ball is being delivered. This movement means that the bowler's momentum is no longer directed, as it should be, towards the target of the batsman's wicket. The falling-away may stem from a *run-up* which is angled towards the return crease at the outside extremity of the bowling crease; from the bowler coming too close to the stumps and taking a step to his left to avoid hitting them; from the bowler allowing his head to lean to the left, and subsequently throwing his front arm and stepping with his foot towards the slips; or from the over-arching of the bowler's back. All of these causes have the result of *opening up* the bowler's action, making him fall away.

farm the bowling. The batsman who ensures that he virtually mon-opolizes the bowling, by taking strategic runs at the end of each over he has faced, farms the bowling. The tactic is employed by an accom-plished batsman who survives into the latter part of an innings, and wishes to shield weaker players and thus prevent their wickets from falling while he continues to score.

fast-bowler. A bowler who delivers the ball at speeds of 130–150 km/h, attempting to dismiss batsmen by using *variation in pace*, *swing* and *cut*. Fast-bowlers usually begin or open the bowling for the fielding side. They use the *new ball*, which, because it is hard, shiny and has a pro-nounced *seam*, swings, bounces, seams and comes off the wicket quicker than the old ball, giving the opening bowler his best chance of getting the batsmen out.

feather a catch. To *edge* the ball very thinly, the result being a catch to the wicketkeeper.

featherbed wicket. A pitch that has all the soft, cushioning character-istics of a feather mattress. On such a surface, bowlers have difficulty making the ball bounce stump-high, and fast-bowlers are reduced to two speeds: slow and stop. It is an excellent wicket on which to bat, provided the only consideration is not to be dismissed: the ball is so slow off the wicket and the bounce so minimal that even the least accomplished batsman can survive by playing the forward defensive prod. It is not a pleasant *batting wicket* for strokemakers because the ball does not come on to the bat; consequently every shot has to be punched hard rather than caressed. Generally speaking, featherbed wickets are disliked by batsmen and bowlers alike since they militate against an even contest between the respective abilities of players.

Featherbed pitches are 'doctored' surfaces, produced in one of several ways: (a) leaving a thick cushion of dry grass and root growth on the wicket when it is cut; (b) covering the pitch with marl loam, fertilizer or any light soil which is impossible to compact into a firm hard surface; (c) neglecting to roll or compact the wicket for long periods; (d) scarifying the wicket to remove the grass and make the surface loose. There is the danger in this last process of creating a pitch that *turns* from the first ball of the game.

Excellent examples of featherbed wickets in my playing days were my own home pitch at Northampton and Nottinghamshire's Trent Bridge wicket. At the time when I was bowling for England at speeds close to 150 km/h, my fastest bouncers at Northampton sometimes ran along the ground before reaching the keeper, Keith Andrew, standing 25 metres behind the stumps. There was so much cow dung puddled into the turf that spin-bowlers who rubbed their fingers into the soil and then licked them to gain a better grip of the ball were seen to pull very peculiar faces!

At Trent Bridge in the 1960s, the ground authorities despaired of producing a hard, fast wicket. Finally they called in a council steam-roller to compact the wicket. The enormous juggernaut chugged along the pitch, depressing the turf a full 5 cm under its front roller; but after the rear roller had passed, the grass rose again like the Phoenix. Subsequent exploratory digging revealed 10 cm of turf and root growth, and then an air-pocket of similar depth, before the spade reached soil! The turf had completely separated from the earth. Trent Bridge was not a featherbed — it was an airbed that had to be dug up and relaid.

ferret. A terrible batsman: so poor that he is called after an animal that rabbiters send into the burrows after the *rabbits*!

field restrictions (limited-over game). Regulations that govern the positioning of fieldsmen in *limited-over* games, aimed at preventing the fielding side from adopting an ultra-defensive attitude and playing cricket that is unattractive to the spectators. These rules are essentially designed to make limited-over games an entertainment, a crowd-puller and a money-maker.

The fielding restriction common to most limited-over competitions provides that at the instant of delivery a minimum of four fieldsmen, plus the bowler and wicketkeeper, must be within the *circle* — a marked area bounded by two semicircles centred on each middle-stump and joined by a straight line on each side of the pitch. In some competitions it is also stipulated that no more than two fieldsmen may be outside this circle during the first 15 overs of an innings; in that period, there must also be two fieldsmen in *catching positions*. The number of overs affected may be proportionately reduced in games curtailed by the weather.

field restrictions (standard game). The internationally accepted laws of cricket forbid the placement of more than two leg-side fieldsmen behind the batting crease at the moment the bowler releases the ball. The law is designed to prevent negative, run-saving bowling down the leg-side. The regulations also state that no fieldsman may stand on or have any part of his person over the pitch until the ball has hit or passed the bat or struck the batsman. That rule is intended to prevent a close fieldsman from distracting the batsman.

On penalty of 5 runs plus those already scored at the time of an incident, no fieldsman may stop the ball with any item of equipment or clothing; 5 runs are also added if the ball strikes a fieldsman's *helmet* lying on the ground. Indeed the fieldsman's helmet has provided the legislators with many headaches in recent years. Thus, a batsman may no longer be caught off a deflection from the helmet of a close-in fieldsman; nor can he be deemed caught if his hit lodges in a fieldsman's helmet. (See also *no-ball*; *penalties*)

fielding positions. Positions or places on the cricket field where players of the bowling side are stationed for the express purpose of stopping the ball, saving runs, taking catches and running out the batsmen. (All the principal positions are described under their own entries.)

fieldsman. A member of the team that goes into the field of play and attempts to dismiss members of the batting side and prevent them from scoring runs. A fieldsman assists in putting out batsmen by taking catches or effecting run-outs. He prevents runs by intercepting the ball after it is struck, obstructing its passage to the boundary, and not allowing the batsmen time to run between the wickets.

Fieldsmen whose primary function is to stop hits and prevent runs are termed defensive fieldsmen. They concentrate on stopping and gathering the ball by employing techniques such as the *long-barrier* and *ideal fielding positions*. Defensive fieldsmen usually occupy outfield and midfield positions such as *third man, point, cover, extra-cover, mid-off, mid-on, mid-wicket, square-leg* and *fine-leg*.

Fieldsmen whose main role is to dismiss batsmen are called attacking fieldsmen. They move or position themselves in the path of or underneath a lofted hit, in order to effect a *catch*. Catching/attacking fieldsmen are usually found in positions such as *slips, gully, point, silly point, silly mid-off* and *silly mid-on*, short cover and *extra-cover*, short *mid-wicket, short-leg* (forward, square and backward) and *leg-slip* or leg-gully. Any member of the fielding team assumes the mantle of an attacking fieldsman when he dismisses an opponent with a *catch* or a *run-out*. To run a batsman out, the fielder attacks the ball, gathering it with *soft*

Fielding positions

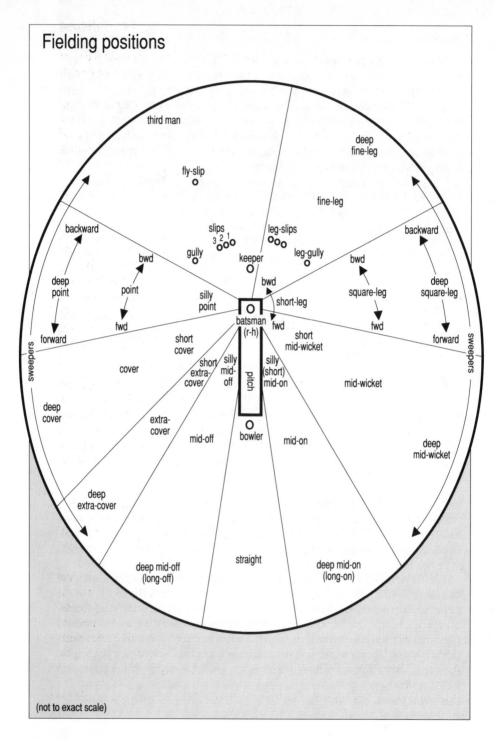

(not to exact scale)

hands in front of his rear foot as he steps forward towards the target of the stumps. He then returns the ball to the keeper's or bowler's end with the fastest possible *throw*.

The fieldsman's role in cricket is of paramount importance. Fielding represents 80 percent of a player's involvement in a game, and a team's proficiency in the field is essential to its success. Well over half of all dismissals are catches, run-outs and *stumpings*. Catches — and fielding skills — win matches. (See also *substitute fieldsman*; *twelfth man*)

find the boundary.   To score a four or a six by hitting the ball across the boundary, either along the ground or in the air.

find the edge.   A bowler finds the *edge* when he swings, cuts, spins or seams the ball enough to make the batsman fail to hit it plumb in the centre of the bat; instead, the ball clips the edge of the blade. This may make the batsman *play on* or edge a catch to the wicketkeeper or a fieldsman behind the wicket. Usually it is the ball that moves away in the air or off the wicket which finds the *outside edge*; to find the *inside edge* the ball moves in to the bat. A delivery that finds the *middle of the edge* strikes the bat slightly off-centre towards either the outside or the inside edge.

find the gap.   The bowler who finds the gap or *gate* between the bat and pad of a batsman and bowls him, usually makes the ball swing, cut, spin or seam back into the batsman from outside the off-stump. The batsman aims his stroke at the original line of the delivery only to find that the ball's movement takes it past the inside edge of the bat and through the gate he has inadvertently left between it and his pad. (See also *find the gaps in the field*)

find the gaps in the field.   To hit the ball for runs through the gaps between the fieldsmen specifically positioned by their captain to save runs. The skilful batsman who finds the gaps in the field 'places the ball' or has 'good placement'. (See also *find the gap*)

fine.   Behind the batsman and his wicket and at an angle of a few degrees to the left or right of the line of the pitch. Balls struck or deflected fine are hit behind the stumps and slightly to the left or right of the wicketkeeper. Fieldsmen who are positioned fine stand behind the batsman's wicket and slightly to the left or right of a line that joins the stumps at both ends. Thus *deep fine-leg* is the fieldsman posted on the boundary, behind the wicketkeeper and slightly to his left.

fine deflection.   A shot that *glances* or *cuts* the ball just wide of the wicket. (See also *deflect the ball*)

fine edge. See *thin edge.*

fine-leg. See *deep fine-leg.*

finger-spin. Sometimes described by Sir Donald Bradman as 'first-finger spin', this is the spin or twist imparted mainly by the index finger of the bowling hand. Finger-spinners are usually right-arm *off-spinners* or left-arm *leg-spinners* (some old Australian schools of thought still inaccurately describe the latter as left-arm off-spinners). In the case of right-arm off-spinners, spin is produced by pushing the first finger from left to right, or from off to leg; the delivery consequently turns from outside the off-stump towards the leg-side. Left-arm leg-spinners thrust the first finger of the bowling hand from right to left, or from leg to off, and turn the ball in the same direction. A right-handed finger-spinner usually makes the ball *curve* in the air towards the slips before spinning back; a left-hander's curve in the air is towards the leg-side.

The finger-spinner relies little on the turn of the wrist to spin the ball, and because he employs fewer 'moving parts', he is more accurate than the *wrist-spinner*; this enables him to bowl very effectively to attacking fields. He is also faster through the air and off the wicket. He is therefore very effective on slower wickets and batsmen find it more difficult to use their feet to get to the pitch of the ball.

The best illustration of the effectiveness of a finger-spinner on a turning wicket is the example of English off-spinner Jim Laker. In 1956, on a dusty Old Trafford wicket, Laker took a record 19 of the 20 Australian wickets to fall in the Manchester Test, at a cost of 90 runs. The most prolific wicket-taker of all time was a finger-spinner, Wilfred Rhodes, whose first-class career (1898-1930) netted him 4187 victims.

first, second, third, fourth slip. See *slips.*

first, second, third change (bowler). The first two bowlers to operate in an innings are designated the 'opening bowlers'. The first bowler to replace either of these is known as the 'first-change bowler', the subsequent substitute is called the 'second-change bowler', and so on.

first, second, third wicket down. See *batting order.*

first-class cricket. Under ICC regulations a first-class game must be of at least three days' duration and be played between two sides of 11 players adjudged first-class. Test matches and games of three days or more contested by touring and local first-class sides are automatically recognized as first-class. Accepted first-class competitions include the English county championship; Australia's Sheffield Shield; the Ranji,

Duleep and Irani trophies in India; the Quaid-e-Azam Trophy, BCCP Patron's Trophy and President's Cup Championship in Pakistan; the inter-island games in the West Indies; the Shell Trophy in New Zealand; and the Currie Cup in South Africa. In England, MCC and varsity games against first-class counties, and the Oxford–Cambridge inter-varsity match, are also classified as first-class.

first-finger spin. See *finger-spin.*

first-innings win. In a two-innings game, when one team does not complete its second innings and fails to overtake the total of runs notched by its opponents, the result is a *draw.* In most league competitions, however, *points* are awarded to the team that scores more runs than its opponents in their first completed innings. This team is deemed to have registered a first-innings win, regardless of the final outcome. (See also *result*)

five-day wicket. A playing surface that deals evenhandedly with the two teams contesting a five-day Test match, and is fair to batsmen and bowlers, fast and slow, within that timespan. The pitch is prepared weeks in advance to last five days. It is well watered two days before a game, and diligently rolled and compacted so that it will not become dry and break up. It is not overexposed to the sun in the days preceding a game, and is covered at night and when rain threatens. Sufficient grass is left on the pitch to hold it together before a game, but this grass is shaved off on the morning of the match.

The ideal pitch provides pace, bounce and a little movement off the *seam* to encourage faster bowlers on the first day. On the second and third days the wicket is drier, has reduced movement off the seam, but still has enough bounce and pace to encourage both the quick bowler and the strokemaker. By the fourth day (if the weather holds) the playing surface is completely dry, a little worn, not entirely trustworthy in bounce, and permits the spin-bowler to evince a little *turn.* By the final day the wicket has deteriorated further and now assists the slow spinner much more, making the survival of the side batting last a chancy affair and giving value to the winning of the *toss* and batting first.

flannels. Long white or off-white trousers worn by cricketers. They evolved from the white knee-breeches of the 18th-century game, and were originally made out of thick warm flannel, eminently suited to the English game and that country's predominantly chilly summer climate. They were also known as 'creams', after the colour of flannel. Modern cricket trousers are made of bleached synthetic material that stretches to the contours of the wearer's body. Flannel was less malleable and was tailored for comfort and ventilation; wicketkeeping trousers, for instance, were roomy in the seat for comfort in the keeping stance. The wide legs of old-fashioned flannels were folded and wrapped around the calves, where they were secured into position by the straps of the *pads*. It was regarded as bad form to tuck the trouser-legs into the socks. Nowadays there is no need to fold and strap the trouser-legs, since they are close-fitting to the calves. In Australia cricket flannels are also known as 'strides' or 'whites'.

flap. Rounded upper part of the *pad* above the *knee-roll*: it protects the front of the thigh and is only loosely strapped around the leg. A wicketkeeper's pads have no flaps, since the keeper is rarely struck in this area; they are therefore lighter and make the keeper more mobile. In limited-over games, keepers have discarded orthodox pads for hockey shin-pads; the extra mobility gained in this way enables a keeper to act as an extra fieldsman.

flash. To attempt an ambitious and showy stroke, usually outside the off-stump, and either miss the ball completely or edge a catch behind the wicket.

flat throw. A low, fast *return* from the midfield or outfield, employing the *sidearm* throw.

flight. The path of a ball through the air, after it is released by the bowler and before it bounces. A fast ball's trajectory is flat, sometimes involves *swing* and demands a swift judgment on the part of the batsman about *line*, *length*, and the appropriate stroke to play. A spin-bowler's flight is slow, high, has a loop which causes the ball to drop on unexpected lengths, and gives the batsman time to vacillate about moving forward to meet the ball or stepping back to play it. It also *curves* or *drifts* in the air according to the direction of the breeze and the type of spin imparted to it. On good batting wickets that do not allow turn, more than half of a spin-bowler's skill lies in his ability to beat the batsman 'in the air'. (See *give the ball air*; *spin*)

flipper. A *wrist-spinner*'s delivery which is 'flipped' or spun backwards at the moment of release. The result of this backspin is a flat trajectory which causes the ball to skid quickly towards the batsman after bouncing. The bowler usually bowls the flipper well *short of a length* to tempt the batsman into trying to pull the ball. When the delivery subsequently comes through fast and low, the batsman often hits above the bounce and is bowled or struck on the pads to be trapped lbw. For the flipper, the bowler grips the ball in the same way as for a leg-spinner, but at the moment of release draws the first three fingers briskly down the back of the ball, pushing the ball out of the front of the hand. It is an extremely difficult ball to pick, because of the rapid movement of the bowling hand.

fly-slip. Fielding position situated behind and to the off-side of the wicketkeeper. Fly-slip stands behind the slip fieldsmen, at a variable point between them and the third-man boundary: an unusual field placement set to catch batsmen who deliberately edge or slice the short deliveries of fast-bowlers safely over the heads of the slip cordon into the no man's land between the close-to-the-wicket fieldsmen and third man. South African opening batsman Eddie Barlow was a master of this stroke.

follow on. When a team, batting second, is dismissed for a total which is 200, 150, 100 or 75 runs less than that of its opponents — according to whether it is a five-day, three- or four-day, two-day or one-day game — it may be asked to take its second innings immediately. This is termed 'following on'. The side that batted first enforces the follow-on and defers its second knock, if one is needed, until the team following on has been dismissed a second time. (See also *forfeit an innings*)

follow-through. That part of the action of bowling, batting or throwing which occurs immediately after the ball has been struck, bowled or thrown. The main function of the follow-through is to absorb the energy expended and so avoid physical injury. The follow-through can also fulfil an important role in the detection of technical faults. For instance, if the bat's follow-through in a vertical stroke, intended as a straight hit, takes it towards the leg-side, the batsman is hitting *across the line* of the ball. If a bowler's follow-through propels him towards his left and the batsman's off-side, the bowler has not maintained his forward momentum towards his target of the batsman's wicket and is *opening up*: a fault that will cause him to direct his deliveries down the leg-side. To throw straight, a fieldsman must step and follow-through towards his target.

Ideally, the follow-through of a bat should be in the direction of the executed stroke. It should also be full, to indicate that at the moment of impact the bat was moving quickly to hit the ball hard. A short follow-through is evidence of the bat slowing up at this important phase of its swing. Similarly, the follow-through of the bowler ought to be full to signify that he maintained his maximum momentum at the moment of release. It should be straight down the wicket, thus ensuring that the delivery is directed at its target. But the bowler must also veer off the pitch after one or two strides of the follow-through, so that he does not trespass on the *danger area*.

61

following the batsman. The skill of bowling to restrict scoring opportunities, both in the one-day and the stretch format of the game, often revolves around the bowler's ability to direct his attack at a point close to the batsman's body. This tactic denies the batsman the room he needs to swing his bat freely to produce strokes. To counter the ploy the striker may ignore the position of his stumps and move away to leg-side or off-side to give himself enough space to operate. To counter this counterploy the bowler also ignores the batsman's stumps and continues to bowl at his body, even though he is standing clear of his wicket. This is called 'following the batsman'.

forearm guard. Small, shaped, rigid plastic guard fitted and strapped around the front of the leading forearm of a batsman, protecting the area between hand and elbow, and the radius and ulna bones, from fracture. It was first popularized by players such as Geoff Boycott and Sunil Gavaskar when playing against the bouncy hostility of the West Indian fast-bowlers of the 1970s and 1980s.

forfeit an innings. When a captain of the team batting first does not have enough of a first-innings run-advantage to enforce the *follow-on*, but thinks that under the prevailing pitch, weather and time conditions he has sufficient runs on the board to win *outright* — or at worst *draw* the game — he may forfeit his second innings. He thereupon asks the captain of the team batting second to go in again immediately it is dismissed in its first innings, notifying him early enough to allow 7 minutes' rolling of the pitch.

forward short-leg. Leg-side fieldsman positioned a few metres from the bat just in front and to the left of the batsman. Placed to pick up chances popped up by the batsman playing defensively on the leg-side, he is sometimes known as the *bat-pad fieldsman* because he catches deflections from the inside edge of the bat on to the pad and into the air.

four. Short for four runs. By previous agreement between the captains of the two competing teams, 4 runs are normally awarded when the ball in play crosses, touches or is carried across the *boundary* after bouncing. Runs exceeding the boundary allowance may be scored by the batsmen running between the wickets, even though the ball subsequently crosses the boundary.

fox the ball. A deception practised by a fieldsman who pursues a ball into the outfield and, by pretending either that he is about to pick it up or that it is still a long way in front of him, attempts (respectively) to prevent the batsmen from taking an extra easy run or to inveigle them into another run leading to a *run-out*.

Frank Worrell Trophy. The trophy awarded to the winners of a Test series between Australia and the West Indies. It was inaugurated and first won by the West Indies in 1964/65 and commemorates Sir Frank Worrell, the former West Indian captain and the first black to captain his side. Worrell led his team in the famous tied Test against Australia in 1960/61, was knighted in 1964 and died tragically of leukaemia in 1967 at the age of 42.

French cut. An attempted *drive* or *defensive stroke* off either the front or the back foot, unintentionally deflected to *fine-leg* off the inside edge of the bat and passing between the batsman's body and the wicket, narrowly missing the stumps. It is also known as the Surrey or Chinese cut.

front-foot defensive stroke. A stroke whose main intention is to prevent a good-length ball from hitting the wicket or being lofted for a catch. The batsman steps forward from the *batting crease* alongside the line of the ball, stopping it with a vertical and *dead bat* by the side of his front pad and pushing it to ground by angling the blade of the bat downwards. The front side and leg lean towards the ball, and the head and eyes are over the point of contact with it.

front-foot drive. An attacking shot that strikes an *overpitched* but straight ball for runs. It is a *straight-bat stroke* played alongside the front pad, thus combining defence of the stumps with attack. The batsman steps forward from his crease, placing his front foot alongside either the bounce or the line of the ball, leaning into it with his front side by bending the front knee, and positioning his head and eyes directly behind the line of flight. At the point of contact, he hits hard, throwing first his top and then his bottom hand at the ball. This angles the bat blade downwards at the point of contact and keeps the ball on the carpet. Front-foot drives are classified according to the direction in which the ball is struck: e.g. *cover-drive, on-drive, square-drive, straight-drive*.

front-on. See *side-on; square up*.

full-length ball. An *overpitched* ball which bounces closer to the batsman than a *good-length* ball, and can be hit on the *half-volley* or *full-toss* by stepping forward. It is a bad ball and can be hit for runs. The definition also embraces the *yorker*, a dangerous ball which pitches on the batting crease, causing the batsman to hit over it, or bowling him.

full-toss. A delivery that does not bounce before reaching the batsman. The full-pitch (as it is also known) is a poor ball which raises no doubt in the batsman's mind about whether to play forward or back; it is therefore — at least in theory — easy to hit. (See also *intimidatory bowling*)

furniture. The batsman's *wicket*. When the batsman is bowled, it can be said that 'the furniture removers have been' — or that his furniture has been rearranged by the bowler.

g

gain pace off the pitch. A commonly used phrase describing a physical impossibility: a fast delivery which bounces on the pitch and is quicker after impact than before. The laws of physics dictate that hitting the ground must slow down a ball. There are bowlers, however, who, because of their body-action or a low skidding trajectory, appear to lose less pace than others. Because there is less contrast between the speed of the ball before and after it bounces and because the batsman's reflexes are more attuned to a greater retardation, such a delivery gives the impression of gaining pace off the pitch. Bowlers who have this capacity to hurry the ball on to the batsman are said to have pace off the pitch.

garden gate. See *gate*.

gardening. When the ball bounces on a damp pitch, it raises a divot and takes a piece out of the turf. Between deliveries and overs, the batsmen make good the damage by patting down the affected spots with the toes or backs of their bats. They are 'doing some gardening', to keep the wicket in as good a state as possible while they bat. Gardening may extend to repairing the havoc wrought by the bowler's feet on the pitch.

gate. To be bowled through the gate is to be bowled by a ball that passes through the gap between bat and pad which the careless batsman sometimes leaves or exposes when playing a straight-bat drive or a defensive shot. The delivery is often one that cuts back into the batsman who has 'left the garden gate open'. (See also *find the gap*)

get behind the ball. In batting, to position the head and eyes behind the *line of the ball*. This movement, in playing both forward and back, ensures that the batsman is in the best position to observe the behaviour of the ball both through the air and off the pitch: its *swing, curve, cut,* and *spin*. This in turn increases his chances of hitting it. The opposite of getting behind the ball is *backing away* to the leg-side and thus being unsure of the ball's movement.

In fielding, to gather the ball in such a way that the body is behind the line of its approach. This means adopting a defensive fielding posture such as the *long-barrier* or *ideal fielding position*. Thus, even if the ball bounces unpredictably or deviates enough to elude the hands of the fieldsman trying to gather it, it will strike his body, preventing the ball's further progress and possibly saving runs.

get over the ball. To place one's weight, head and the top of the bat over the ball at the point of contact, thus ensuring that it is hit immediately into the ground, avoiding any possibility of a catch. The placement of the player's weight over the point of contact automatically keeps the ball on the ground. If the fulcrum of balance lies behind the point of contact, the ball is lofted.

get the ball up (off a length). The make the ball lift abruptly and unexpectedly from a *good length*. Tall fast-bowlers, such as West Indians Joel Garner and Curtly Ambrose, have this ability to 'get the ball up', since, when they bowl, the angle of the ball's descent into the pitch produces a steep lift-off towards the batsman's body.

get to the pitch of the ball. To move out of the *batting crease*, down the wicket towards the bowler, and hit the ball on the *half-volley*. The head and eyes are directly over the *pitch (bounce)* of the ball, and behind its line. (See also *move into line with the ball*)

give out. The umpire, in signalling to a batsman that he has been dismissed, gives him out; the batsman is given out, or 'given' for short. The umpire signals the dismissal by raising the index finger of one hand above his head.

give stick. To hand out punishment. An expression used when a batsman shows a partiality for a certain bowler or bowlers, hits them to all parts of the ground and scores quickly.

give the ball air. To flight the ball or bowl it at a height and in an arc which creates indecision in the batsman's mind about moving down the wicket to meet the ball or playing back and waiting for it to reach him. A slow-bowler's skill.

glance. In batting, a deflected stroke: a term commonly employed to denote the *leg-glance*.

globe. Another expression for a duck — since a globe describes the shape of the figure 0.

gloves (batting). Used by batsmen to protect their hands against the ball, batting gloves are of a supple leather or other material for flexibility and a more comfortable grip on the bat. They are stoutly padded with kapok, rubber or synthetic material on the outside of the hand to prevent the ball injuring the batsman's fingers and thumbs. Sometimes they have an open palm for a firmer grip on the bat. They are secured around the wrist by an elasticized band or a velcro fastener. Manufacturers try to make the padding non-resilient, since a batsman can be caught off the hand. In hot climates, some batsmen wear cotton gloves under their batting gloves to absorb sweat during long innings.

Early batsmen played without gloves, and one of the delights and skills of the opposing bowlers was 'to grind the fingers against the bat'. The invention of early tubular batting gloves is often attributed to that innovative schoolmaster Nicholas Wanostrocht, whose *nom de plume* was Felix. He was also credited with the invention of a bowling machine called the 'Catapulta'.

gloves (wicketkeeping). Gloves are worn by *wicketkeepers* to protect their hands in gathering the ball bowled by the bowler or thrown by a fieldsman. Substantial, with backs of leather, their palms are padded and faced with pimpled rubber for a surer grip on the ball, and there is a flared and padded gauntlet-type protection for the wrist. The pimpled rubber is often treated with a substance such as neat's-foot oil to give it an adhesive quality. The rubber palms are stitched in a circular manner, so that when the keeper closes his fist in taking the ball, the palm forms a cup that closes around it (see *good cup*). The ends of the thumbs and fingers are protected by finger-stalls and the gloves can be tightened on the hand by a buckled strap on its back. Sometimes keepers remove the stalls to gain a more supple use of the fingers. Webbing between the thumb and forefinger ensures that the ball will not force its way through the gap between the two digits. Keepers usually wear inner gloves of chamois leather under their outer gloves; they tape the joints of the inners to prevent breakages and dislocations. The inners prevent bruising of the hands when taking very fast balls. England wicketkeeper George Duckworth used to insert thin slices of steak in his gloves for the same purpose when taking the thunderbolts of fast-bowler Harold Larwood. This had the desired effect of preventing bruising, though on a hot day in Australia it was not unusual to see George enveloped in a cloud of flies!

In the early days, wicketkeepers such as Tom Sueter of Hambledon kept wicket in the way that American baseball fans would know as 'meat hand'. Byes always contributed heftily to a team's score and it was considered essential for a keeper to be backed by a *long-stop*, an important fieldsman who was usually one of the fleetest on the ground. Without gloves or pads, keepers were frequently injured and sported crooked and broken fingers. The gloves of John Blackham, the Australian 'Prince of Wicketkeepers' in the inaugural Test of 1877, are on display in the Baer Museum at the Melbourne Cricket Ground. They clearly demonstrate that early keeping gloves were nothing more than riding gauntlets which merely took the sting out of the contact between ball and palm.

go for ten runs an over. To be struck for 10 (or any high number) of runs in one over. Describes the punishment of a bowler by a batsman — especially in a limited-over match, in which the success of a bowler is gauged by his ability to restrict the batsman to the fewest possible runs per over.

go with the arm. A spin-bowler's delivery which does not turn, but maintains the original direction imparted to it by the swing of the bowler's arm, is said to go with the arm. (See also *arm ball*)

golden duck. The worst of all possible *ducks*. A batsman out for a golden duck is dismissed off the first ball he receives. (See also *king pair*)

good cup. Like an excellent brassiere, a functional wicketkeeping *glove* needs a good cup. The cup of the glove is formed by the exact, concentric and close circular stitching of its palm. When the keeper closes his hand to grip and catch the ball, the dimpled, rubber-coated palm of his glove should assume a smooth, unwrinkled, rounded shape, like the inside of a shallow teacup. A cricket ball lodges perfectly in this cup.

good length. The part of the pitch which lies just outside the reach of the batsman, as he steps forward from the *batting crease*. The delivery bouncing on this section of the wicket is a good ball, particularly if it lands immediately in front of the stumps and is likely to hit them. Such a ball raises doubts in the mind of the batsman whether to step forward or back to hit it. This hesitation occupies decision-making time and leaves less time for the batsman to move. (See also *line and length*; *short of a length*)

good loop. To have a good loop is to possess good *flight*. The term is used to describe slow-bowlers who deliver the ball high in the air and make it drop suddenly just before it reaches the batsman. Generally this is achieved by imparting topspin and it has the effect of causing the batsman to drive at a ball that bounces on a length shorter than he anticipated. Consequently, since he fails to hit it on the half-volley, there is an excellent chance that he might hit it into the air as a catch. This possibility is increased by the fact that well-flighted balls tend to bounce more and are difficult to hit along the ground if they are not struck on the *half-volley* or *full-toss*.

googly. Another term used for the *bosie* or *wrong'un*; an expression believed to be of New Zealand origin.

gozunder. Familiar name for a *shooter* or creeper: a ball that 'goes under' the bat and emerges on the other side.

green wicket. Also known as a seaming wicket. A pitch that is firm, hard, covered with a light growth of succulent green grass, and in favour of the fast or medium-pace bowler. When a quick delivery bounces on such a surface it crushes the grass, making the ball skid on the resultant moisture, like a person treading on a banana-skin. This gives the impression that the ball gains pace off the wicket; the truth is that it merely loses less speed after bouncing. The crushed grass frequently lodges in the stitching of the ball's *seam*, causing it to swell and lift. When the ball bounces on this elevated seam it deviates unexpectedly to the left or right. This unpredictable lateral bounce is known as movement off the seam.

Moist or humid conditions before a match produce a green wicket — particularly after a dry spell. A pitch can 'green up' temporarily during a game if its grass covering is affected by a light drizzle. Mists, high tides and sea-frets can have a similar effect on wickets that are close to the coast.

grip. The manner in which a batsman holds the bat, or a bowler holds the ball. More efficient production of batting strokes occurs when the striker holds the bat with his two hands close together, behind and in the middle of the handle. This facilitates the swing of the bat along the line of the approaching ball and generates greater power. The lower a batsman holds the bat, the greater his control over it, but the lesser the power in his strokes; the higher the grip, the longer the swing of the bat, the greater the force imparted to the ball, but the lesser the control. Widely spaced hands on the handle cannot work well together: the stronger bottom hand then has control of the bat, and this usually results

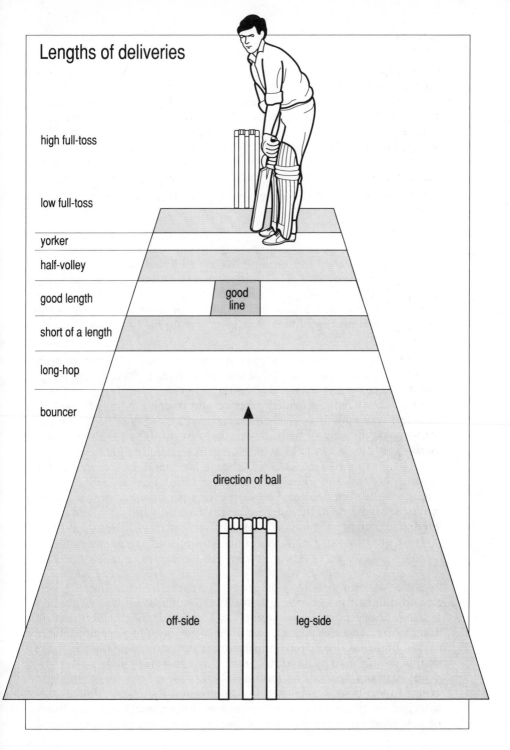

Lengths of deliveries

high full-toss

low full-toss

yorker

half-volley

good length   good line

short of a length

long-hop

bouncer

direction of ball

off-side   leg-side

in hitting *across the line* of the ball. (See also *bottom-handed* and *top-handed player*)

Bowlers hold the ball in different ways to *swing*, *cut* and *spin* it. Generally speaking, swingers grip the ball with the index and second fingers running alongside its vertical *seam*; spinners and cutters hold the ball with all of their fingers gripping it around the seam.

ground. Area on which a cricket game is played. (See also *ends of a ground*; *grounds, famous*; *maintenance of playing area*; *oval*; *playing area*; *playing surface*)

ground one's bat. In running to complete one or more runs, a batsman should always finish by grounding his bat: sliding it along the turf as it crosses the *batting crease*. This action enables him to ensure that some part of his person or bat is safely in contact with his ground as soon as it comes within reach. It avoids the stupidity of being *run out* when he has the crease within reach but neglects to ground his bat.

grounds, famous. Lord's cricket ground is acknowledged as both 'Cathedral' and 'Headquarters' of the Marylebone Cricket Club (MCC) and world cricket. It is named after Thomas Lord, a professional Yorkshire cricketer, who provided practice and match facilities for aristocratic patrons as early as 1789 on his land in Dorset Square. Subsequent moves brought him — with his original turf — to St John's Wood in north-west London in 1814, where his ground has remained ever since. Famous for its pavilion, its Old Father Time Stand, its Tavern and its Nursery ground (the second or practice ground), Lord's is traditionally the setting for the Second Test of the English season.

The Oval, home of the Surrey County Cricket Club since 1844, was the scene of the original *Ashes* Test of 1882 and usually hosts the Fifth Test of the summer (see *oval*). The Nottingham innkeeper William Clarke established the Trent Bridge ground just outside his hotel in 1837 and played many matches on it for his All-England team; the historic Midland ground is no longer a 'regular' on the English Test circuit. Edgbaston in Birmingham is both a suburb and Warwickshire's ground, and the occasional venue for Tests since 1902. Old Trafford, Lancashire, and the Manchester Test have been synonymous since 1884. For many winters and summers Yorkshire supporters have watched both international cricket and rugby at Headingley, Leeds.

In Australia, the vast Melbourne Cricket Ground is the largest and oldest in the land. Established on the original Richmond Police Paddock, 15 years after the club which gave it its name, the MCG holds several attendance records (see *spectators*). The Sydney Cricket Ground

(SCG) is now a wonderland of modern stands and 60-metre-high *light towers*. Once it was better known for its 'Hill', the home of Australia's most famous *barracker*, 'Yabba'. The Adelaide Oval nestles in the shadow of the Mount Lofty Ranges and St Peter's Cathedral and qualifies as one of the most beautiful grounds in the world. The Western Australian Test ground has the jarring acronym WACA and reputedly one of the fastest pitches in Australia. Tests have been played in Brisbane since 1928/29 — but at the present venue, the 'Gabba, only since 1931/32. The ground was infamous for its cloudbursts and 'sticky dogs' in the days of uncovered wickets. Its nickname is short for Woolloongabba: 'Place of the Flowering Gums' in the Aboriginal language.

Until its expulsion from the ICC, South Africa played its home Tests on four grounds: the Wanderers' Stadium in the Johannesburg suburb of Kent Park; picturesque Newlands, cheek by jowl with Table Mountain; seaside Kingsmead in Durban; and St George's Park in Port Elizabeth.

Tests are staged at five main centres in the West Indies: Port-of-Spain in Trinidad, Bridgetown in Barbados, Kingston in Jamaica, Georgetown in Guyana and St John's in Antigua. The Kensington Oval in Bridgetown and Sabina Park in Kingston are pocket-handkerchief grounds with boundaries much to the liking of the brilliant West Indian batsmen, but with crowd capacities that do little for the finances of the home side. The Bourda ground in Georgetown lies below the level of the Atlantic, which is held in check by dykes. Antigua is the home of the famed West Indian batsman Viv Richards. The St John's ground is situated outside the walls of the local prison, where Richards's father was once an officer; the ground and wicket were once maintained by the prison inmates. By far the largest Test ground in the Caribbean is the Queen's Park Oval, Trinidad, close to the Savannah parkland in the centre of the city, where every weekend in summer scores of games take place.

India has its Test centres in Bombay, Calcutta, Madras, Delhi, Kanpur and Bangalore. Major cricket in Bombay was once played against the Raj background of the Brabourne Stadium but has now been transferred to the Wankhede Stadium. Like the Calcutta Cricket Club, the Eden Gardens ground is one of the oldest in the sporting world. Feroz Shah Kotla is the name of the Delhi Test ground; while the Madras arena, now called the Chidambaram Stadium, was once known as the Chepauk ground and belonged to the East India Company. Green Park, Kanpur, was accorded Test status in 1951/52; Bangalore's first international game took place in 1974/75. Like its neighbour Pakistan, India has followed the policy of decentralizing its Test venues and in the past 20 years has played matches in Hyderabad, Nagpur, Jullundur, Ahmedabad, Cuttack and Jaipur.

Sri Lanka is a newcomer to Test cricket and played its first official international against England on the P. Saravanamuttu Oval in Colombo in 1982. A year later it played a Test in the Asgiriya Stadium in Kandy and has since staged games in Colombo at the Singhalese Sports Club and the Colombo Cricket Club.

Pakistan plays most of its home Tests in Lahore, Karachi, Hyderabad, Bahawalpur, Peshawar and Rawalpindi. Lahore switched Test venues from the Gymkhana ground to the Gaddafi Stadium in 1959. Hyderabad's ground stands on the edge of the Sind desert and is as arid as Bahawalpur is green and treelined. Peshawar is close to the Khyber Pass; while Rawalpindi is next door to Islamabad and the Western embassies. In 1978 the board of control took Test cricket to Faisalabad. Since that time Pakistan has also played games on the provincial grounds of the Ibn-e-Qasim Bagh Stadium, Multan, and Jinnah Park, Sialkot.

No national side plays Test matches closer to the South Pole than New Zealand. Carisbrook in Dunedin can turn on Antarctic weather for a Test. Wellington's Basin Reserve is less cold but infinitely more windy. It was the scene of New Zealand's first win over England in 1978 after 50 years of effort. The Kiwis' initial defeat of Australia took place in 1974 at Lancaster Park in Christchurch, a city bisected by a trout stream. Auckland's Eden Park is the archetypal New Zealand cricket ground: half church of cricket, half rugby citadel. It was the setting for New Zealand's first Test win against the West Indies in 1956; it also produced the lowest ever Test score — New Zealand's 26-run debacle against England in 1955.

groundsman. See *curator*.

grubber. See *shooter or creeper*.

guard. See *take guard*.

gully. Fielding position to the off-side of the batsman and behind him, beyond the widest slip and at an angle of about 45° to the ball's flight. Gully's distance from the bat varies from 2 to 10 metres according to the speed of the bowling. His function is to catch or stop a ball which is *cut* or *edged* thickly behind the wicket on the off-side.

h

half-century. A score of between 50 and 99 runs in a single innings: the first major scoring milestone passed by a successful batsman.

half-cock. A stroke played from a position which is neither forward nor back. Such a stroke disadvantages the batsman. He loses the front-foot advantage of hitting the ball on the *half-volley* or soon after it bounces and negating its spin and cut; moreover, he does not gain the extra time to hit the ball afforded by playing back.

half-pitcher or long-hop. A very bad ball which bounces halfway down the pitch, approximately 10 metres (half a pitch) in front of the batsman. The batsman enjoys a lot of time in which to make up his mind where to hit the ball as it hops tantalizingly towards him. The synonymous term 'long-hop' is sometimes misunderstood, as was demonstrated to me by a fast-bowler in Freddie Brown's Northamptonshire team in the 1950s. When his captain commented that one of the quickies in the opposing team was sending down a lot of long-hops, the innocent one replied: 'Aye, and they're bowling a lot of short ones too!'

half-volley. A poor delivery which bounces well within reach of the batsman stepping forward from the *batting crease*, and is struck as it bounces or immediately after. Usually it is hit for runs.

handle (of bat). See *bat*.

handled ball. One of the ten ways in which a batsman may be dismissed under the laws of cricket. The striking or non-striking batsman may be given *out*, on the appeal of the fielding side, if he touches or handles the ball, while it is in play, with a hand that is not gripping the bat — unless he first obtains the consent of the opposing side. The law is intended to prevent the batsman from grabbing or punching away a ball which would otherwise hit his wicket. Unfortunately it is open to abuse. In the Perth Test of 1978, Australian opening batsman Andrew Hilditch picked up a ball which had been struck gently down the wicket by his batting partner and politely handed it to the opposing Pakistan bowler. There was no thought of defending his wicket or preventing a fieldsman from gathering the ball. One of the fielding side, however, still smarting from what he considered to be an injustice perpetrated on him in the previous Test, appealed and Hilditch was given out! There have been more than 30 instances of batsmen being given out handled ball in first-class cricket since 1857.

hang the bat out to dry.   To play a hesitant and indeterminate stroke, a long way from the body, outside the off-stump. This shot gives the impression that the batsman is hanging out his bat, like wet washing, too far from his line of vision; it increases his chances of edging the ball to the wicketkeeper or slips.

hat-trick.   The capture of three wickets with three consecutive legal deliveries. Any bowler who performed this feat in the 18th century was rewarded with the gift of a hat; hence the name. The wickets must be credited to the bowler concerned: run-outs and others dismissals not caused directly by his efforts do not count. Modern records have credited bowlers with hat-tricks in which dismissals have been separated by intervals between innings, sessions, days, and sometimes matches.

heartwood.   Brown, brittle wood sometimes found on the outside edge of a *bat* blade. Heartwood is the young growth at the centre of a willow tree's trunk and manufacturers try to avoid incorporating it in the blade. (See also *knots*)

helmet.   Protective headgear worn by batsmen, wicketkeepers and close fieldsmen to prevent injury caused by the ball striking the head. English batsman and 'character' Patsy Hendren first used a padded headguard against the *Bodyline* tactics of Harold Larwood in county cricket in 1934; but it was not until World Series Cricket in the late 1970s that the wearing of helmets was widely adopted. In 1977 English batsmen Tony Greig and Dennis Amiss donned motorcycle crash-helmets to face the West Indian speedsters Andy Roberts, Michael Holding and Joel Garner. Equipment manufacturers were quick to seize on the idea and soon produced special helmets combining lightness, adequate protection and ventilation. Now helmets are made in club colours with adjustable protection for the temples and interchangeable face-visors with perspex or metal grilles. Helmeted fieldsmen can stand perilously close to the batsmen, confident that they are protected against serious head injury. (This has produced problems for cricket's legislators, who have introduced a law stating that a batsman cannot be caught off a fieldsman's helmet.) Umpires will not carry fieldsmen's helmets, which, when not in use, are generally placed on the ground behind the wicketkeeper or in the underground *water points* around the square. If a ball strikes a fieldsman's helmet lying on the ground, 5 runs are awarded to the batting side.

It is laudable that helmets have been made mandatory in Australian school cricket, where skill levels are lower and the possibility of serious injury is greater: there have been instances of young players being killed by balls that struck them on vulnerable parts of the skull. It may well be that the better option for junior cricket is the use of a softer ball which will not cause serious harm if it strikes the head.

Hercules. Nickname of the number 11 batsman. Being at the bottom of the batting pile, he is said to support the rest of the batsmen on his Herculean shoulders.

high action. Release of the ball from the highest point the bowler's frame can reach. Ideally all *bowling actions* should be high, deriving maximum bounce from the pitch. A high point of delivery is attained by bowling over a straight front leg. This means that the distance between the bowler's front foot and his hand at the point of delivery is maximized and provides the longest possible lever to project the ball. A long lever lengthens the arc of the bowling arm in its delivery swing. If a bowler moves the long lever of his bowling arm through its arc quickly, he will generate maximum speed.

hip-pocket short-leg. A *backward short-leg* fieldsman, standing so close to the batsman that he could almost pick his hip-pocket.

history of cricket. See pages xiii–xvi for a concise outline of the game's origins and history.

hit into the 'V'. To hit the ball into the area between wide *mid-off* and wide *mid-on*. The batsman's strokes are thus played straight at the line of the approaching ball. This enhances his chances of hitting the ball, particularly if the delivery is full-length.
   The policy of hitting into the 'V' is a golden rule of *limited-over* cricket, in which the bowler tries to project the ball straight at the stumps and well up to the bat. If the batsman tries to open the angles and hit outside the 'V' on both sides of the wicket, he hits *across the line* of the ball and stands a very good chance of missing it completely. But laudable as it is in the one-day game, hitting into the 'V' makes the job of the fielding captain all the easier: he can mass his fielders in that zone and make the task of scoring runs more difficult.

hit over the ball. In batting, to turn a delivery into a *yorker*. Sometimes a batsman misjudges the length of an *overpitched* ball and, in moving forward to strike it, steps too close to its bounce and is unable to bring his bat down in time to make contact. He hits over the ball's bounce and cannot *dig out* the yorker.

hit the ball on the up. To *drive* the ball as it rises towards the batsman after bouncing. West Indian batsmen, reared on bouncy wickets, seem especially adept at this skill, which enables them to punish a comparatively *full-length ball* without reaching it on the *half-volley* and without hitting it in the air. The secret of success in this shot is to push the top of the bat blade well ahead of the bottom and to delay the uncocking of the wrists and therefore the point of contact in the stroke.

hit the pitch hard. To bowl the ball with a *high action*, fast and short so that it digs into the pitch rather than skidding off it. On fast firm surfaces, hitting the pitch hard results in fast, lifting deliveries, sometimes from only just short of a *good length*; on such wickets this type of bowling, when very *short of a length*, produces bouncers. On slow, spongy wickets, however, hitting the pitch hard can be counterproductive, since the harder one digs the ball into shock-absorbent surfaces, the slower its bounce.

hit wicket. A batsman is *out* 'hit wicket' if, while the ball is in play, he breaks his wicket with any part of his person or equipment while preparing to receive the ball, playing a stroke, taking evasive action or setting off for a run immediately after playing or playing at the ball. Early laws permitted the batsman to be given out only if he struck his wicket while playing a stroke. But because of difficulties in determining when a stroke began and ended, the law was extended to embrace the instant when a batsman sets off for a run. Thus a batsman can now play a stroke, slip in setting off for a run, dislodge the bails and be given out hit wicket.

hitting the ball twice. A batsman may lawfully hit a ball a second time with his bat or any part of his person — except the hand not holding the bat — if he is defending his wicket. But if, after the ball is struck by the bat or stopped by any part of his person, he wilfully strikes it again with his bat or person, while not defending his wicket, he can be given *out* 'hit the ball twice'. The interesting facet of this law is that hitting the ball with one's person is regarded as striking the ball. Thus if a batsman is struck a painful blow on the body by a bouncer and, in a fit of pique, subsequently kicks the ball away while not defending his wicket, he can be given out! (See also *obstructing the field*)

hoick. An *agricultural stroke* or slog, usually in the air in the direction of deep mid-wicket. A portmanteau word which describes a hoisted hook, it also applies to the act of slogging or 'hoicking' the ball to leg.

hold up an end. To maintain resistance against the bowlers, usually in support of a more adept batting partner at the other end. Normally used to describe the last-ditch defiance of a *tail-end* batsman.

hook. An attacking horizontal-bat stroke, played against a *bouncer* rising to chest- or head-height in line with, or to the leg-side of, the batsman's middle- or leg-stump. The batsman moves his body and head *back and across* the wicket towards the off, until he is to the off-side or inside the line of the rising ball. Simultaneously he lifts his bat back, pulling it high behind his head with his bottom hand until it is in a horizontal posture. As the rising ball draws level with his body, he pivots on his rear foot and leg, hitting down on the ball and steering it to ground in the area beteween *square-leg* and *fine-leg*.

This stroke yields many runs to the batsman who plays it well; but it is considered risky, since many players attempt it against balls that are too high or too wide of the off-stump and hold the potential of a catch. The shot often has the unwary batsman caught at deep fine-leg. (See also *sucker hook*)

hoop. A *swing*-bowler who hoops the ball moves it evenly a long way in the air.

howzat? See *owzat?*

i

ICC. See *administration*.

ideal fielding position. A baseball term sometimes applied in cricket, describing the posture of a fieldsman moving in to gather the ball, shuffling forward, feet together, body and arms behind the ball and leaning forward. In this position, if the ball misses the fielder's hands it hits his body and drops in front of him, where it is easily retrieved and thrown. (See also *long-barrier position*)

incricket. Action or play of the fielding side which occurs in the *in-field*, on the square and close to the pitch.

indoor cricket. The indoor version of cricket is played between two teams of eight players on a carpeted area, slightly larger than a tennis court — approximately 28–30 metres long, 10–12 metres wide and 4.5 metres high — and completely enclosed by tensioned netting. The players hit an indoor ball using a wooden bat, and score runs as in outdoor cricket. The ball is a tennis ball encased in the yellow leather shell of a cricket ball. It is much lighter than the normal cricket ball and this reduces the risk of physical injury to the batsmen, and to the wicket-keeper and fieldsmen (who are often perilously close to the bat). As a result, batsmen and keepers dispense with pads entirely, and their gloves have less padding than standard gloves. On the other hand, players often wear knee and elbow guards to protect those joints against friction injuries caused by contact with the synthetic grass on which the indoor game is played.

The teams toss for *innings* and the eight players on the batting side are then divided into four pairs, each pair batting in turn for 32 deliveries. The batting side faces 128 balls before allowing its opponents the opportunity of outscoring it. Each batting pair tries to score runs by hitting the ball into different areas of the surrounding netting, for which they are rewarded with boundaries of varying proportions. They also score runs by running between two creases 11 metres apart, just over half the length of a standard 20-metre pitch. Each member of the bowling side must bowl two overs of 8 balls, either overarm or underarm. The fielding team seeks to restrict the batting side's scoring by the strategic placement of fieldsmen guarding the vital boundary.

Unlike in outdoor cricket, the batsman's *dismissal* does not lead to his leaving the crease — he must remain there until the expiry of his pair's 32 balls — but to the deduction of 5 runs from his and the team's score. There are seven main ways of dismissing a batsman, all of them found in the outdoor version of cricket. Distinctions are to be seen, however, in the fact that the ball is never *dead* and batsmen may be *run out* at any time — and in the fact that batsmen may be *caught* out off rebounds from the nets. There is one umpire for the game, usually positioned on an elevated platform above the batsman's head, from where he can give decisions for both ends of the wicket.

In Australia, the speed of the game, its fixed time-frame and its immunity to bad weather have brought indoor cricket tremendous popularity. Commercial indoor centres cater for as many as 300 teams — male, female, mixed, social, factory-centred or office-based — graded into leagues comprising sides of comparable ability. Elite teams compete in 'Super Leagues', and each year an Australia-wide interstate carnival takes place in a major city. Indoor Test matches are played between New Zealand and Australian teams.

inducker. A late *inswinger*. The word denotes a ball which 'ducks' or moves suddenly and late into the batsman from the off-side.

infield That part of a cricket field which is found on or close to the *square* of carefully cultivated turf from which the pitches of a ground are prepared.

infielder. A player who fields in the *infield*: on the *square* or less than 30 metres from the bat. His main function is the attacking one of taking close-to-the-wicket catches or running out batsmen from the infield.

inner ring of fieldsmen. In a conventional game of cricket, the inner ring of fieldsmen is made up of men strategically positioned 20 to 30 metres from the bat to take catches or stop the batsmen from taking singles. In the *limited-over game*, the inner ring carries out the same functions, but it consists of those fieldsmen who, by regulation, must remain within the *circle*, either for the duration or for the first 15 overs of the game. (See also *field restrictions*)

innings. The extent, duration and yield of a player's or team's batting effort. A game can consist of one or of two innings. A team's innings lasts for the amount of time its eleven members occupy the batting crease; its yield is the total amount of *runs* accumulated by its batsmen. An individual's innings also occupies a certain period of time and produces a given number of runs. Qualitatively, an innings may be good, bad, brilliant or lucky.

The highest recorded innings in first-class cricket is Victoria's massive 1107 against New South Wales in 1926/27. The highest individual score at the same level is Hanif Mohammad's 499 for Karachi against Bahawalpur in 1958/59. The highest Test total is England's 7/903 declared against Australia at the Oval in 1938. The highest individual Test score is Garfield Sobers's 365 not out for the West Indies against Pakistan in Jamaica in 1957/58. The lowest first-class innings was achieved by Oxford University and Northamptonshire, each of which managed to accumulate 12 runs in 1877 and 1907 against the MCC and Gloucestershire respectively. The lowest ever Test total, 26, was recorded by New Zealand against England in Auckland in 1954/55. I was privileged to play in that game and was removed from the attack with an 'expensive' analysis of 2/10! (See also *points*; *result*; *win by an innings*)

inside edge. The vertical edge of the bat, the one closer to the batsman's body and to the leg-side when he takes up his *stance. Inswing* and *off-spin* bowlers sometimes swing or spin the ball sufficiently into the batsman's body for it to cramp the striker in his stroke and clip the inside edge. Dismissals occasionally result from this mis-hit: batsmen *play on,* or play the ball on to the pads to lob it up as a catch to the *bat-pad fieldsmen.* Occasionally, skilful wicketkeepers standing back from the stumps take exceptionally difficult catches off fast deliveries, deflected off the inside edge. The problem in taking such catches is that they *wrong-foot the keeper* who habitually moves towards the off-side in anticipation of a catch off the outside edge; consequently he has to reverse his initial movement in the split-second after the ball hits the inside edge — and then catch the ball!

inside the line of the ball. To the off-side of the *line of the ball*; not to be confused with 'alongside the line of the ball', which means slightly to the leg-side of the delivery's line. (See *back and across; move inside the line of the ball; move into line with the ball*)

inswinger. A delivery which, governed by the aerodynamic principles of *swing*, curves in the air from the batsman's off-side towards his *leg-side* (i.e. in towards the stumps) before bouncing. It frequently causes the downfall of batsmen who neglect to play close to the front pad in a *front-foot defensive stroke*; they are usually bowled 'through the garden gate'. The inswinger may also defeat batsmen who are strong bottom-handed players — by inducing them to give a catch to fieldsmen placed close to the bat on the leg-side. This ball is not regarded with the same respect as that reserved for the *outswinger* — the theory being that the batsman can always defend his stumps at the last minute against the ball moving in towards them.

To bowl an inswinger, the bowler holds the ball between the first two fingers and the thumb of the bowling hand. The index and second finger rest on top of the ball on each side of the vertical *seam*. The flat of the thumb supports the seam underneath the ball. As the bowler releases the inswinger, he angles the perpendicular seam towards fine-leg, pushing the delivery in, from outside the batsman's off-stump, towards his wicket with an open action.

International Cricketer of the Year. A prize peculiar to Australian cricket and awarded at the end of a season to a visiting or home player who, in the opinion of various impartial panels of judges, has been the outstanding performer in Test and international limited-over cricket. The prize is usually a prestige car. Past winners have included Viv Richards (1979/80, 1983/84 and 1984/85), Dennis Lillee (1980/81), and Richard Hadlee (1985/86).

intervals. Pauses in play. The laws of cricket permit only 10 minutes between each innings, 7 of these being taken up by the rolling of the wicket. The time and duration of the other intervals, i.e. those for lunch and tea, are agreed by the ground authorities or the *captains* and *umpires* before the game. If an innings ends or there is an interruption because of weather or light conditions within the 10 minutes before the *lunch* interval, that adjournment is extended and occurs immediately. If such an interruption occurs within 30 minutes before the *tea* interval, tea is taken at once without any extension of the time involved, unless the interval is prolonged by bad weather. If the ninth wicket of the batting side falls within the 10 minutes before an interval, play continues for a further half an hour, so that, if possible, the innings may be terminated and the interval between innings incorporated into the meal or tea break. Captains may agree to forgo the tea interval.

In *limited-over* matches, because of television commitments, innings are scheduled to begin at specified viewing times. The interval between innings therefore varies according to the amount of time existing between the end of the innings of the side batting first and the scheduled telecast of the beginning of the other side's innings. If, for instance, the side batting first is dismissed shortly before the end of its allotted time or number of overs, the between-innings interval is extended. If, on the other hand, *rain* interrupts play, the umpires may curtail the interval to regain some or all of this time lost.

intimidatory bowling. A method of bowling fast which threatens physical harm to the batsman, often forcing him to choose dismissal rather than injury. Law 42 of cricket states that the bowling of fast *short-pitched balls* or head-high *full-tosses* is unfair if, in the opinion of the umpire at the bowler's end, they are intended or likely to inflict physical injury on the batsman, bearing in mind his relative skill. If a bowler violates this law, the umpire calls *no-ball*, cautions him and informs the other umpire, the fielding captain and the batsmen of his action. A repetition of the offence occasions a final warning. Should the bowler again try to intimidate the batsman, the umpire calls no-ball and instructs the fielding skipper to remove the offending bowler from the attack. He may not bowl again in that innings and the incident is reported to the batting captain, the match authorities and the administrators of the fielding team.

Intimidatory bowling tarnishes the image of cricket. It threatens the batsman's safety, and reduces the game to an unspectacular survival exercise. In spite of this, umpires and the ICC have failed to resolve the thorny problem. Umpires have been denied support when they have imposed the penalties of law 42 and consequently are reluctant to enforce the regulation. Test nations with an abundance of fast-bowlers have steadfastly opposed any attempt to hobble their match-winners. The lawmakers have argued that the limitation of the number of permissible bouncers per over or per series of overs makes the trend of a game too predictable. The problem appears insoluble, yet the issue of intimidatory bowling has plagued cricket for decades, particularly in the *Bodyline* years of 1932–34 and during the Australian domination of postwar fast-bowling in 1948. More recently it has been highlighted by the West Indies' fast-bowling dominance in Test cricket.

Irish swing. The lateral movement or *swing* of a delivery in the air in the direction opposite to that expected. Most fast and medium-pace bowlers *work on the ball* to retain the *shine*, raise the *seam* and swing the ball longer. Working on the ball involves cleaning the seam, and dampening one half of the ball with sweat and saliva before polishing that side vigorously on the shirt or trousers.

A weary Queensland quickie was slogging his way through a late spell one torrid Brisbane day with an old and tattered ball. In a desperate attempt to retain the shine, swing the ball and take a wicket, he saturated one half of the ball with saliva, bowled, and released it with its wet side facing right or the batsman's leg-side. With the shiny side facing in that direction, and the seam pointing towards the slips, the ball should have swung away towards the slips. Instead it moved in, and bowled the batsman! The only explanation so far offered for this unusual phenomenon is that the bowler's saliva and sweat make one side of the ball so heavy that it acts like the bias of a lawn bowl and drags the ball in the direction of its moistened half.

j k

jag back. See *break-back*.

jockstrap. Athletic support worn around the waist and between the legs for the genitals. It prevents groin strains and is used to hold up the slip-in *box*.

juice. The *moisture* squeezed out of the grass on a *green wicket* by the impact of the ball. The moisture causes the delivery to skid quickly on to the batsman and swells the *seam*, occasioning movement off the pitch.

just over the top. Short for, 'The ball passed just over the top of the wicket, almost bowling the batsman'. A bowler's appeal for *lbw* is turned down by the umpire if, in his judgment, the ball would have gone just over the top. (See also *too high*)

keep the strike. To retain the opportunity of facing the bowling. A batsman who takes a *single* off the last ball of an over, in order to face the next delivery at the other end from another bowler, retains the strike. This is a tactic consciously pursued by an expert batsman seeking to shield a *tail-ender* from the bowling.

keeper. Abbreviation for *wicketkeeper*.

king pair. A pair of *golden ducks*, or dismissal off the first ball faced in each innings of a two-innings match. (See also *bag a pair*)

knee-roll. That part of the *pad* at the height of the knee, where the longitudinal ribbing is replaced by three horizontal folds. These enable the player to bend his knee. Any delivery hitting the batsman on or above the knee-fold strikes the upper *flap* and is generally deemed to be too high to warrant the upholding of an *lbw* appeal.

knock. The innings of an individual batsman who hits ('knocks') the ball several or many times.

knots. Blemishes in a *bat* blade, caused by the growth of branches from the trunk of the willow tree. Such marks are now barely noticeable, thanks to the modern technique of bleaching the wood from which the blades are turned.

know where the off-stump is. A batsman who knows where his off-stump is plays an off-side defensive stroke only when failure to do so would result in his being bowled. Often players fend unnecessarily at good-length deliveries that swing away outside the off-stump. The man who is aware of the line of his off-stump may begin to play at such a delivery; but once he knows that it no longer poses a threat to his wicket, he withdraws his bat to avoid being caught behind. (See also *take guard*)

late-cut. A stroke which deflects the ball on the off-side behind the wicket, through the slips and towards *third man*. It is a horizontal-bat stroke played off the back foot to a delivery wide of the off-stump and holding no danger of bowling the batsman. In the backlift the bat is raised behind the batsman's head as he steps *back and across* his wicket towards the off-side and into a position that brings him to an arm's length from the line of the ball. He then hits down on the ball, making contact when it has passed him, guiding it to ground and steering it away for runs. Contact with the ball is very late — so much so, that it is said that one Lancashire League batsman who revelled in the stroke regularly rapped wicketkeepers across the top of the gloves as they tried, prematurely, to take the ball. His repeated admonition was: 'Leave it alone until I've finished with it!' (See also *square-cut*)

late swing. The movement in the air of a fast or fast-medium delivery which maintains a straight path for most of its flight, but then, just before reaching the batsman, curves either from off to leg or from leg to off. The explanation of this behaviour is that when the ball travels at more than 110 km/h, it is moving too quickly for the optimum degree of *swing*. When it slows down to the ideal pace for swing, however, movement takes place, demanding a quick and late response from the batsman. The skill of moving the ball late cannot be acquired; the bowler must possess an innate ability to deliver a ball at the requisite speed.

laws, codification of. There are 42 written rules governing cricket: its participants, the playing area, the equipment used, the conduct of the game, the players and the umpires, and ethics. The first written code of the laws of cricket dates back to 1744, when the rules of the game as settled and used by 'The Cricket Club' of London were set down. They were first printed in the *New Universal Magazine* in 1752 and revised in 1774, when the home side was given the choice of both pitch and innings. The Marylebone Cricket Club (MCC) was one of the authorities responsible for the 1774 and 1788 revisions of the laws. It later became the established legal authority on the game and was the author of the 1835, 1947 and 1980 recodifications. Nowadays the revamping of the laws does not rest solely in the hands of the MCC; revision suggestions emanate from the International Cricket Council, and amendments usually undergo a trial period as *experimental laws* before they are adopted or rejected by the ICC and the MCC. (See also *administration*)

lay off (come off) the stroke. The batsman who leans back prematurely in a stroke and fails to transfer his weight wholly forward and in the direction of the shot 'lays off the stroke'. The fault robs the shot of power and can result in the ball being lofted for a catch.

lbw. See *leg before wicket*.

leg before wicket (lbw). One of the ten ways in which a batsman may be dismissed under the laws of cricket. A batsman may be given *out* lbw if any part of his body or equipment, except the hands holding the bat and the gloves on those hands, is struck by the ball, thereby preventing it from hitting the wicket. (If the ball hits the hands or gloves holding the bat, a batsman may be *caught* off the resultant deflection.)

The *umpire* at the bowler's end is alone empowered to give an lbw decision, and only if he is satisfied that the following three questions can be answered in the affirmative:

(1) The ball pitched in line with the stumps (i.e. within the imaginary rectangle extending from wicket to wicket), or pitched outside the line of the off-stump.
(2) The ball hit the batsman's body or equipment (excluding the hands holding the bat) within the area bounded by the stumps.
(3) The ball would have gone on to strike the batsman's wicket.

If the umpire decides that the delivery meets all of these criteria (or, in the case of a full-toss, the last two), he should give the batsman out lbw. (He should not, however, give him out if the ball is deflected off the bat on to the body or equipment.) The batsman may also be given out lbw if the ball hits his body or equipment to the off-side of the line of his off-stump, and would have struck the wicket but for the fact that the batsman, making no attempt to hit the ball, used his body or equipment to defend his stumps (see *not offering a shot*). This law was introduced to prevent the striker from using his *pads* unfairly as a first line of defence.

One of the inconsistencies of the lbw law, long opposed by such eminent cricket jurists as Sir Donald Bradman, is that a batsman may not be adjudged lbw to a delivery that bounces outside the line of the batsman's leg-stump, even though the ball makes contact with his body or equipment in line with the wicket and would have hit it.

The interpretation of lbw depends solely on the opinion of the umpire at the bowler's end; the law is usually invoked only when he is certain that the batsman is out. The benefit of any doubt is generally

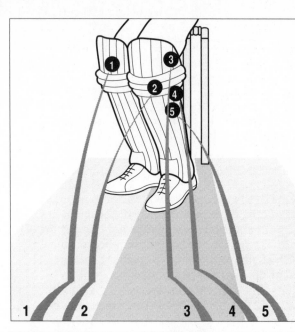

Leg before wicket

1 Not out. The ball has struck the pad well outside the line of the stumps (and the batsman offered a shot).

2 Probably out. The umpire may rule not out if he thinks the ball was turning sharply enough to miss the stumps.

3 Possibly out. The umpire may rule not out if he thinks the ball was rising sharply enough to clear the stumps.

4 Out. The ball pitched in line with the stumps and would have gone on to hit them.

5 Not out. The ball pitched outside leg-stump.

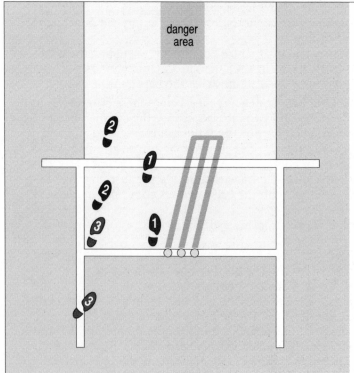

danger area

No-ball

Position 1 is a fair delivery.

Position 2 is a no-ball because no part of the front foot is behind the popping crease.

Position 3 is a no-ball because the rear foot is touching the return crease.

given to the batsman. If, for instance, a delivery fulfils the first two requirements of the law, but hits the batsman's pad as he stretches forward a metre or so in front of the batting crease, the umpire will usually give him not out: he is reluctant to guess what might have happened to the ball in the 2 metres between its point of contact with the pad and the batsman's wicket. A batsman is also frequently given the benefit when, in the opinion of the umpire, the ball strikes the batsman too high on the body and might have passed over the top of the wicket, or moves so much that it might have gone down the leg-side past the stumps. The subjectivity of the law's interpretation makes it one of the most contentious decisions in the game.

The lbw law did not appear in the 1744 code: it was introduced in 1774 after one of the best hitters in the game 'was so shabby as to put his leg in the way and take advantage of the bowler'.

leg theory. A tactic of the fielding side in which the bowler directs his line of attack at the leg-stump or at the batsman's body by slanting, swinging, cutting or spinning the ball from the off, and takes wickets or restricts scoring by *packing* the on-side field. This ploy denies the batsman room to swing his bat freely and play his strokes, restricts his scoring opportunities and frequently frustrates him into a mistake that leads to his dismissal.

The English bowlers F.R. Foster and S.F. Barnes perfected leg theory as an offensive weapon, bowling for the MCC and England in Australia in 1911/12. Frank Foster, a medium-fast left-hander with a short run and easy action, slanted the ball into the Australian right-handers, who had to fend it off their thighs and avoid giving catches to the six fieldsmen strategically positioned on the leg-side. The legendary Sydney Barnes was the perfect complement to Foster, taking 34 wickets in the series and beginning the First Melbourne Test with a spell of 4 wickets for 1 run in 5 overs. Significantly, both Barnes and Foster had the ability to move the ball into the batsman and then *seam* it away off the wicket to the slips.

In English county cricket, Worcestershire's Fred Root refined leg theory to the extent that it yielded him 219 wickets at 17.21 runs each in 1925.

Douglas Jardine, England's captain in Australia in 1932/33, added a frightening facet to leg theory when he instructed his express bowlers, Harold Larwood and Bill Voce, to direct their 150 km/h deliveries at the batsmen's bodies, to a crowded leg-side field. This blueprint for disaster represented a physical threat to Woodfull's Australian batsmen and sparked off the *Bodyline* controversy.

leg-break. See *leg-spinner*.

leg-byes. Runs scored off a ball which is not struck by the batsman but is deflected off his person or equipment, except the hand holding the bat, and allows the batsmen time to change ends and score one or more runs. If such a deflection reaches the boundary, 4 leg-byes are awarded, signalled by the *umpire* and recorded as *extras* in the appropriate box on the scoresheet.

leg-cutter. A delivery of medium or medium-fast pace which, because the hand cuts down the left side of the ball, turns quickly from leg to off after it bounces. The ball is held around the *seam* with a similar grip to that for the *off-cutter*, except that the first and second fingers are more widely spaced. It is delivered with the open action suited to the *inswinger*, and at the moment of release the wrist of the bowling hand snaps the first three fingers smartly down the left side of the ball in the direction of gully or third slip. The ball *curves*, before it bounces, from off to leg. Because of its speed, it does not always deviate after bouncing.

The incurving leg-cutter is an extremely dangerous delivery. If the bowler does not know when it will grip the turf, the batsman is also ignorant about whether or not the ball will cut towards the slips. Because the ball curves in towards the wicket, the batsman must always play at it for fear of being bowled. If the ball then cuts away, it does so at the very last moment and may bowl the striker or take the edge of the bat for a catch. (See also *leg-spinner*)

leg-glance. A defensive stroke played to a ball directed at or outside the leg-stump. The face of the bat is angled towards *fine-leg*, and the ball is glanced or *deflected* in that direction. The leg-glance is played off the front foot to a *full-length* delivery, or off the back foot if the ball is *short of a length*.

leg-gully. See *backward short-leg*.

leg-side. That side of the *playing area* which lies to the right-handed batsman's left (and the left-handed batsman's right), on the same side of the wicket as his legs, as he faces the bowler. It is also known as the on-side.

leg-side field. Fielding arrangement in which a preponderance of the fieldsmen are positioned by their captain on the leg-side; a negative, defensive tactic designed to stop the scoring of runs, particularly when the bowler directs his attack at leg-stump and close to the batsman's body to cramp his stroke-production. To counteract this stultifying manoeuvre, certain countries have introduced regulations preventing the deliberate overpopulation of the leg-side. (See also *defensive field*; *field restrictions*)

leg-slips. Leg-side fieldsmen positioned behind the batsman and alongside the wicketkeeper. They are the leg-side equivalent of the *slip* fieldsmen and are placed to take the finely deflected catch. The laws allow only two leg-slips, restricting the number of players permitted behind *square-leg*. The distance between the leg-slips and the batsman is determined by the speed of the bowler.

leg-spinner. A slow ball which, because of the spin or twist imparted by the bowler at the moment of release, turns from the batsman's leg-side to his off-side after it bounces. The leg-spin bowler (or 'leg-spinner') is usually a left-handed *finger-spinner* or a right-handed *wrist-spinner*. The former is accurate and faster through the air, but turns the ball less; the latter spins the ball a long way and makes it bounce but is less accurate. In both cases the ball *drifts* from off to leg before it bounces. Consequently both like to bowl with the breeze coming from mid-off, or the batsman's right, to increase the curve and loop of the delivery. A headwind produces the same effect. (See also *leg-cutter*)

leg-stump. One of the two outside *stumps* making up the *wicket* defended by the batsman. It is situated to that side of the *middle-stump* which lies to the batsman's leg-side as he faces the bowler; from the bowler's point of view, it is the right-handed batsman's far-right stump, or the left-hander's far-left one. (See also *off-stump*; *take guard*)

leg-trap. A planned field setting which, allied to a bowler's attack on the batsman's leg-stump, is designed to dismiss him by compelling him to offer a catch to the deliberately positioned fieldsmen. (See also *leg theory*)

length. See *full-length ball*; *good length*; *line and length*; *short of a length*.

let the ball go. A batsman lets the ball go when he does not attempt a shot but allows a delivery to pass through to the wicketkeeper. Players often permit a good-length outswinger outside the off-stump to go *through to the keeper* to avoid the risk of being caught behind.

life. When a fielding side fails to take advantage of a chance to dismiss a batsman, that batsman 'has had a life' — he lives on to continue batting. A pitch that 'has life in it' gives assistance to the bowlers.

lift the head. To throw back the head in attempting to hit the ball. The batsman who lifts his head in executing a stroke takes his eye off the ball and usually fails to make contact. Even when bat does meet ball the shot is often lofted, since the batsman's head and weight are moving back and away from the point of contact.

light (accustom the eyes to). Cricket is played in varying conditions of light, ranging from bright sunny mornings to dark overcast evenings. Moreover, batsmen about to go in often wait in pavilions or dressing-rooms where the light conditions are vastly different from those in which they will have to bat. This can make it extremely difficult to pick up the flight of the ball when facing the first few deliveries. To remove such an obvious handicap it is wise for the next-in batsman to wait, or even to have a short practice, outdoors; this accustoms his eyes to the light. Batsmen walking to the wicket are often seen staring fixedly into the skies — as Ian Chappell used to do — in a last-minute attempt to gain a true appreciation of the light out in the middle. (See also *bad light*)

light towers. Tapered hollow towers, approximately 10 metres in diameter at the base and some 60 metres high, erected around major cricket grounds in the southern hemisphere. Enormous banks of many powerful floodlights surmount the towers and illuminate the ground at night, for the playing of *day/night limited-over* matches in visibility which is thus the same for both teams. Spiral staircases within the towers provide access to the floodlights, so that they can be repaired or serviced. In Australia, towers have been erected around arenas such as the WACA ground in Perth, the SCG and the MCG. Similar arrangements are found on some Indian, Pakistan and South African grounds. But there is no need for them in England, where summer evenings are light enough to permit cricket at least until 9 o'clock.

limited-over competitions. In addition to periodic participation in the Olympiad of the *World Cup*, Test nations seek to maximize the crowd-drawing (and hence money-making) capacity of visiting sides by incorporating a series of *limited-over games* before or during their annual programs of home Test matches. These games usually bear the name of the home team's sponsor and may observe varying formats. The number of matches in each competition and the number of overs per game vary from nation to nation. Generally, however, limited-over internationals are restricted to 50 or 60 overs, with some tournaments catering for bad weather by providing a reserve day in which to complete a game. Each Test series in England is preceded by several 60-over matches. In Australia a competition comprising a series of 50-over elimination games and several finals is played over the summer between international teams and is known as the World Series Cup. The West Indies play a number of one-day games against visiting tourists, a pattern also followed by New Zealand and Pakistan. In March each year, an international one-day triangular tournament is played at Sharjah in the United Arab Emirates for prizemoney which in 1989 earned $150 000 for the victors. Such rewards are typical of most international limited-over competitions. On the domestic scene, England, Australia, New Zealand, Pakistan, the West Indies and South Africa all stage varying numbers of limited-over games at first-class level. In England, county sides compete in almost 250 games in four one-day competitions. Most of these tournaments receive corporate sponsorship and vary in format between 40 and 60 overs. England even has national one-day competitions for club, village, school and old-boys' teams. Limited-over games of differing structures are also used as the basis of amateur league and club competitions all over the world. (See also *day/night match*; *one-day match*)

limited-over game. A single-innings match in which each team is restricted to a predetermined number of *overs* and the side scoring more runs, irrespective of the number of wickets lost, wins. To distribute bowling responsibilities amongst the less able performers in the fielding team and to increase run-scoring opportunities, bowlers are usually confined to bowling no more than one-fifth of the total number of balls sent down (see *bowling restrictions*). Ultra-defensive field placements on the boundary are outlawed by regulations that insist that at all times six men must be within an area known as the *circle*; in some competitions, only two fieldsmen are permitted outside the circle for the first 15 overs of an innings (see also *field restrictions*).

The main theme of this type of game in international and first-class cricket is the entertainment of the public. For this reason a result is guaranteed, even when bad weather interferes in a game; mathematical formulae have been evolved to produce a winning team in all but the most abbreviated matches, on the basis of runs scored per over. Limited-over games are frequently staged as *day/night matches* under lights, providing entertainment at times that are convenient to the spectators. The scoring of runs and *bowling containment* are the keynotes of limited-over cricket: a sad scenario for the bowler who likes to bowl to dismiss batsmen! (See also *limited-over competitions*; *one-day match*)

line and length. The shortened term for good line and good length. It is used to describe accuracy in bowling, indicating that a bowler is landing the ball on a *good length* in line with the stumps. Such a tactic, particularly in limited-over cricket, stops batsmen from scoring, frustrates them, and often leads to their dismissal. (See also *bowling containment*; *line of the ball*)

line of the ball.   The direction in which the ball is projected by the bowler and approaches the batsman. A bowler whose line is *outside the off-stump* directs his attack slightly to the off-side of the wicket. A batsman who hits *across the line* aims to hit the ball at an angle across the direction in which it is approaching. (See also *move inside the line of the ball*)

lob-bowling.   See *underarm bowling*.

loft.   To hit the ball into the air.

lofted drive.   A front-foot or back-foot *drive* struck into the air. Sometimes the ball is lofted unintentionally, and can lead to the batsman being caught. Often, however, the shot is deliberately played, with the intention of hitting the ball over the head of a fieldsman specifically placed to block a scoring avenue. (See also *chip*; *over the top*)

logo.   Emblem of a *sponsor*, team or country displayed on a player's clothing.

long-barrier position.   Defensive fielding posture assumed by a player to stop a hard-hit stroke. The *fieldsman* faces a point at right-angles to the path of the ball, before kneeling on the ground on the leg closer to that path. The other leg is bent and the foot positioned alongside the knee touching the ground. The body is directly behind the line of the hit, the head and eyes behind its approach. The hands, with fingers pointing downwards, are contingent, directly in line with the ball's path, in contact with the ground and immediately in front of the fieldsman's grounded knee and foot. This position ensures that if the ball bounces unexpectedly and eludes the fieldsman's grasp, it will be stopped by the second line of defence: his body. (See also *ideal fielding position*)

long-hop.   See *half-pitcher*.

long-leg.   Another term for *deep fine-leg*.

long-off.   Off-side fieldsman behind and to the left of the bowler, in the outfield or on the boundary, behind *mid-off*. Long-off is both an attacking and a defensive fieldsman whose role is to cut off potential boundary strokes, and to take lofted catches hit past or over the head of the bowler and mid-off.

long-on. Leg-side fieldsman, positioned to the right of the bowler and behind *mid-on*, in the outfield or on the boundary. His role is to cut off potential boundaries, and to take lofted catches hit past or over the head of mid-on.

long-stop (back-stop). In the days when wicketkeepers wore a minimum of protective gear and were less proficient, long-stop was a very important run-saving position on the field. He stood on the boundary immediately behind the wicketkeeper and swiftly retrieved the deliveries missed by him, thus reducing to a minimum the many *byes* that occurred. Long-stop needed to be a fast runner, a sure stop and a good thrower of the ball. With the improvement in the quality of keeping, he has been replaced by *deep fine-leg*, who fields strokes deflected or hooked behind *square-leg* and doubles as occasional long-stop.

look around the field. When a batsman first goes to the wicket, he *takes guard* before looking around him to pinpoint and memorize where the opposing captain has placed the fieldsmen. Subsequently he reassesses field placements whenever the opposing captain changes them. He thus knows where to hit the ball for runs, and where not to hit it in the air.

Lord's. See *grounds, famous.*

lost ball. A ball which remains in play but has been lost and cannot be found, or is unable to be recovered, by a member of the fielding side. For example, the ball may be struck by the batsman and picked up by a ferocious dog which cavorts around the outfield with it in its mouth. The fieldsmen would naturally be reluctant to retrieve it from the dog; but since the ball is still in play, the batsmen are at liberty to continue running between the wickets and take as many runs as they wish. By calling 'lost ball', however, the fieldsmen can restrict the batsmen's scoring to 6 runs — unless they have already taken more. (See also *runs*)

lost run-up. The predicament of a bowler who, in his *run-up* to the wicket before bowling, loses his step or rhythm in the middle of his approach. Thinking that he may overstep the batting crease and bowl a *no-ball*, he shortens or lengthens his stride, or changes step by hopping. He loses his run-up, and the rhythm and balance of his approach evaporate, reducing his speed and making an effective delivery of the ball impossible. Under such circumstances, a bowler should stop, go back to his bowling *marker*, and restart his run-up. (See also *bowling action*)

lunch. Pause in play to allow players, officials and spectators to eat lunch. The luncheon *interval* occurs between the first and the second *session* of play in games lasting a whole day or more. Scheduled duration is usually 40 minutes, but the interval's start and extent can be varied according to the match and weather conditions, and by the mutual agreement of the captains.

m

maiden over. An *over* from which no runs are scored. *Byes, leg-byes, wides* and *no-balls* do not violate a maiden over. Maidens are entered in a bowler's analysis to indicate his economy and the difficulty experienced by the batsmen in scoring off him.

maintenance of playing area. See *curator; drying the ground; moisture; mower; pitch; rollers; shaving the wicket; super-sopper; watering the wicket.*

major boundary. A hit by the batsman which clears the agreed *boundary* without bouncing and earns the striker six runs.

make one's ground. See *fail to make one's ground; ground one's bat; out of his ground.*

make room for a stroke. When the ball is being delivered on a line close to the batsman's body, he is denied space in which to swing the bat vigorously; he is too cramped to make a stroke. The counterploy to full-length inswingers that pitch virtually on his toes is for the batsman to make room to play a shot. He disregards the position of the wicket and discards his primary duty of defending it: when the ball pitches in line with the stumps, he retreats to the leg-side and attacks it as though it were outside his off-stump. This move permits him the room in which to swing his bat — and, because the bat swings through a wide arc, to hit the ball hard. The tactic is often used by batsmen in quick-fire *limited-over* games — or in longer matches when they are *well set* and want to get on with the game.

maker's name. The name and insignia of the manufacturer of a *bat,* printed on an adhesive label stuck on the face of the *blade*. Batsmen who 'show the bowler the maker's name' play very correctly and straight in defence.

Man of the Match.   A prize awarded to the player from either team who contributes most, as a batsman, bowler, keeper and/or fieldsman, to the efforts of his side in a game. Such prizes are given as a matter of course in Test and representative or international limited-over games. The principle has also been extended to club and minor matches. The award is not necessarily given to a member of the winning side, and is decided by one or several impartial judges. It may consist of a trophy, a cash award, or a combination of both.

manager.   Administrative officer and general factotum charged with the on-the-spot business affairs of a team or touring party. The manager is usually the appointed agent of a national board, a provincial or county committee, an association or a club; he supervises travel and accommodation arrangements, payment of expenses and emoluments, the provision of medical services, equipment, laundry and participation in official social functions. He is also the liaison officer with the home authorities and the media. In professional circles he has a financial role, his additional duties including the verification of gate takings to ensure that his team receives its appropriate share and that the players are paid.

Often a former player, the manager frequently shares in the on-field direction of the side, arranging practice sessions and facilities, participating in selection and having his say about tactics. Managers of international touring teams are so busy that they invariably need the support of an assistant manager. Whatever their backgrounds and skills, managers always attract the nickname 'Ger'.

Different countries adopt different policies towards the appointment of managers of Test and touring teams. England, Pakistan and the West Indies favour players-turned-administrators (such as Jackie Hendriks, Intikhab Alam and Alec Bedser), who add much to the cricketing nous of a touring team. Australia inclines towards members of the ACB (administrators such as Col Egar), who ensure that the tour progresses smoothly but may never have played a game of first-class cricket. (See also *administration*)

mankadding.   The action of a bowler who pretends to bowl but does not release the ball. Instead, without warning, he runs out the batsman at the bowler's end, who has already left his batting crease. There is nothing in the laws of cricket to prevent this occurring, since the batsman who *backs up* too far is himself contravening the rules by cribbing a few metres. It is, however, regarded as unsporting for the bowler not to warn the batsman that he will run him out if he continues to back up too far. In 1947 at the Sydney Cricket Ground, Indian spin-bowler Vinoo Mankad ran out Australian opener Bill Brown in this way without warning. The cricket-watching public did not forget: they bestowed Mankad's name on an act that they regarded as highly unsportsmanlike.

marker (bowler's). Small strip or circle of painted white metal, wood or plastic, which the bowler places on the ground well behind the bowling wicket to indicate where he should begin his *run-up*. Some bowlers employ more than one marker. England speedster Brian Statham used a second marker one-third of the way along his run to show him where to accelerate in his approach. Other bowlers set down a marker up to a metre behind the *bowling crease*; this indicates where the bowler should place his rear foot in his delivery stride. If he oversteps this disc he knows that the following stride will carry his front foot over the *batting crease* and he will bowl a *no-ball*.

MCC. The Marylebone Cricket Club, the premier club in the cricketing world. It was founded in 1787 by members of the White Conduit Club and in 1788 was responsible for the first revision of the *laws* of cricket. Since that time it has been the watchdog of the laws and the body responsible for their revision. Its president nominates the chairman of the ICC and it is represented on the Cricket Council and on the TCCB (see *administration*). Its ground at Lord's is regarded as the Headquarters of Cricket.

'MCC' also happens to stand for Melbourne Cricket Club, the oldest cricket club in Australia, founded in 1838. Its ground, the MCG, was the scene of the inaugural Test played between England and Australia in 1877.

meat of the bat. The centre and thickest part of the *blade*, some 14 cm from the toe of the *bat*. Since there is more wood in this part of the bat, balls hit with the meat of the blade are struck the hardest.

medium-pace bowler. A bowler who delivers the ball at speeds of 100–130 km/h, attempting to dismiss batsmen by using *variation in pace*, *swing* and *cut*. Medium-pacers either open the bowling for the fielding side or are brought into the attack as the first- or second-change bowlers. Like the *fast-bowlers*, they gain the advantages of swing, seam, bounce and pace from the *new ball*. Since the ball swings most at about 110 km/h, medium-pace bowlers move it in the air more than the genuine pacemen. The heavy and humid conditions often found in England may help them to swing the ball a prodigious amount. Australian medium-pacer Bob Massie demonstrated a facility to move the ball enormously in overcast conditions when he captured 16/137 on his Test debut against England at Lord's in 1972. Not surprisingly, England has produced three of the game's greatest medium-pacers in Sydney Barnes, Maurice Tate and Alec Bedser. Since they are usually more accurate, concede fewer runs and hit the seam more often, medium-pace bowlers are frequently more effective than fast-bowlers on helpful *green wickets*.

members' enclosure. That part of a cricket ground, usually enclosed and separated from the public spectator area by a fence, which is exclusively the domain of the members of the club or association whose ground it is. The players' and club members' *pavilion* is usually found in the members' enclosure.

Mexican wave. A mass crowd phenomenon which seems to have originated on Mexican soccer grounds during the World Cup competition. To demonstrate their enthusiasm for the game and their side, before and during a match, individual spectators rose to their feet, waved their hands or scarves and resumed their seats, giving way to their neighbours, who did the same. The up-and-down movement of humanity around the football stadium gave the impression of a sea-breaker surging around the ground. This spontaneous demonstration of emotion is now often emulated by cricket crowds.

mid-off. Fielding position on the off-side, about 10 metres to the left of the bowler as he runs in to bowl, and level with a point a few metres behind the bowler's wicket. Mid-off stops the drives and defensive strokes placed just to the left of the bowler, and takes any catches offered him.

mid-on. Leg-side fieldsman, positioned about 10 metres to the right of the bowler as he runs in and a few metres behind the bowling wicket. Mid-on stops drives and defensive strokes placed just to the right of the bowler, and takes any catches offered to that position.

mid-wicket. Leg-side fieldsman, stationed level with the midpoint of the pitch, some 20 to 30 metres from the bat. Mainly a defensive position, designed to prevent the intended single pushed in front of square on the on-side, mid-wicket sometimes catches the indiscreet lofted on-drive.

middle. Synonym for the *square*. Thus, 'in the middle' refers to the centre of the playing area, as opposed to the *outfield*.

middle of the edge. That part of the bat midway between the centre of the *blade* and either vertical edge. To hit the ball 'with the middle of the edge' means that, whilst the batsman has not made true contact with the ball in the middle of the bat, he has hit it fairly solidly. Such contact imparts force to the stroke, but seldom results in the ball going in the direction for which it was intended. This mis-hit can result in a catch. Many modern bats have edges only slightly thinner than the *meat* of the blade, so that when the ball is struck with the middle of the edge it is still hit very solidly, minimizing the chance of giving a catch.

middle-order batsmen. Batsmen in the middle of the *batting order*. They are usually numbers 4, 5, 6 and 7 on the skipper's list. Whilst they possess good technique and might have to bat with restraint when their side is in trouble, their outlook is generally aggressive. Their role is to consolidate, with attacking cricket, the sound start that the early batsmen have (presumably) given the team.

middle-stump. The centre *stump* of the three that make up the *wicket* defended by the batsman. (See also *leg-stump*; *off-stump*; *take guard*)

midfield. That part of the playing area which lies halfway between the *square* and the *boundary*. A midfielder catches, gathers and returns balls hit or travelling into the midfield.

miscue the ball. To mis-hit the ball, sending it in an unintended direction.

misfield. To attempt to stop a ball ineptly or incorrectly, fumbling or missing it completely. A favourite dictum of older cricketers imparted to learner batsmen is 'Never run on a misfield'. The reason is that, when a player misfields, the batsman often loses sight of the ball and is unsure whether the fieldsman can recover it quickly enough to effect a *run-out*. (See also *fox the ball*)

missed. A batsman who escapes dismissal when a fieldsman muffs an opportunity to catch him has been missed. (See also *dropped*)

mix-up. A confused situation created by misunderstanding between batsmen running between the wickets. Mix-ups generally result from bad *calling* for runs, and end in a *run-out* with both batsmen at one end or in the middle of the wicket.

moisture. Dampness in the pitch as a result of *watering the wicket* during its preparation, or because of rain falling on the playing surface during the game. Watering before a match binds the pitch, ensuring that it lasts the duration of an extended game and does not become a *crumbling, dusty wicket* which favours the spin-bowler in the early phases. Too much watering, however, applied too close to the beginning of a game makes for a lively *green wicket* favouring the seam-bowlers in the early passages of play. Similarly, rain during the game can make the playing surface spiteful and hazardous for batting.

move inside the line of the ball. Tactic used by the batsman against the fast-bowler's *bouncer*. The striker moves *back and across* towards the off-side of the wicket, taking his body and head to the off and *inside the line of the ball* to avoid being struck. He is then in an ideal position to play the *hook* stroke — or he may decide to allow the short-pitched delivery to go through unmolested to the keeper.

move into line with the ball. In batting, to move into a position just alongside (i.e. slightly to the leg-side of) the line of the approaching ball, with the head and eyes directly behind its flight. This tactic entails moving *back and across* in the back-foot strokes, and playing front-foot strokes with the leading foot as close as possible to the *pitch (bounce)* and line of the approaching delivery. It enables the batsman to detect the behaviour of the ball through the air and off the wicket and be in a position to play the appropriate stroke. Failure to move into line with the ball can have disastrous consequences. Outside the off-stump it usually leads to a batsman *hanging out his bat to dry* and an edged catch behind the wicket. If the batsman fails to move into line with a straight ball and *backs away* to the leg-side, he is unable to observe its behaviour from behind its line and risks being hit by the short-pitched delivery that follows him.

move the ball both ways. The bowler's ability to *swing* or move different deliveries either way in the air — i.e. his ability to bowl both *inswingers* and *outswingers*.

move the ball in the air. See *swing*.

move the ball off the seam. To deliver the ball in such a way that its *seam* or stitching is vertical and pointing directly down the pitch — so that, when it bounces and lands on the seam (protruding from its surface), the ball 'slips' off the seam and changes direction slightly. Bowlers usually move the ball off the seam when the wicket is 'green' (i.e. covered with moist green grass). Some (such as England's medium-pacer Maurice Tate) have been expert at moving the ball off the seam; but none can really forecast which way the ball will deviate on pitching.

move the ball up/down the hill. Sometimes cricket pitches are situated on grounds that slope slightly across the playing surface, from leg to off or from off to leg. This used to be the case at the Lord's ground in London, where the pitch had a slight incline from the Father Time Stand side of the playing area to the Tavern side. Quicker bowlers operating from the pavilion end had little difficulty making the ball cut back after bouncing, 'down the hill', from off to leg, or from Father Time to Tavern. Occasionally, however, the ball would land on the seam and, quite unexpectedly, move 'up the hill', against the incline, from leg to off. (See also *bowl up/down the hill*)

mower. A machine for cutting grass on the wicket area and surrounds; it may be worked by hand, or by a petrol or electrical engine. On the *square*, the *curator* must be able to lower the mower's blades so that it crops the grass very short. The finish to a first-class or Test wicket is usually provided by a final *shaving*. The pitch and outfield should be mown before the beginning of the game, and before each day's play in matches of more than one day's duration.

A 'gang mower' is a large, wide mower usually pulled behind a tractor. Its ability to cut wide swathes means that it can mow large areas quickly, and it is therefore used exclusively for cutting the *outfield*.

n

Nelson. The point in an individual batsman's or a team's innings when the score stands at 111: according to English cricketing tradition, an unlucky total at which disaster is likely to strike. The term stems from the misconception that the famous English admiral Horatio Nelson lost one eye, one arm and one leg in battle. In fact Nelson remained a biped until his death in the battle of Trafalgar in 1805 — another case of a superstitious myth based on a fallacy (see *devil's number*).

I always thought of 111 as a lucky score. It was the total for which the England side of which I was a member twice dismissed Australia to win the 1954/55 Ashes series 3–1 in Australia.

nets. An area of cultivated turf alongside or on a ground, specially prepared for effective practice. A number of adjacent single-ended pitches are cut, watered and rolled, to a standard comparable to the surface of a centre *pitch*. The batsmen practising on these pitches are separated and protected by nets, approximately 2 metres high and 20 metres long, which stop hits and expedite the return of the ball to the bowler. A back net substitutes for the wicketkeeper and stops the balls the batsman edges, misses or allows to pass. The nets are supported by poles and guy-ropes or by a metal frame. Bowlers operate in rotation from the bowling crease at the open end of the net. Rubber mats are sometimes placed on the ground over the bowling creases to prevent excessive wear and tear. A further refinement is the placement of a net behind the bowlers to prevent the ball travelling too far into the outfield. Batsmen and bowlers are allocated a set amount of time to bat and bowl — to 'have a net', in the vernacular. The net system is ideal for the club situation because it provides the maximum practice for the greatest number of players in the shortest period of time.

new ball. The bowling side is given the advantage of a hard, new ball at the beginning of each innings of the batting side. The new ball *swings* pronouncedly, bounces higher, and goes through to the keeper more quickly. Naturally as the batsmen strike the ball, and as it bounces on the pitch or hits the boundary, it becomes worn and loses its *shine*, hardness, and consequently movement through the air and bounce (see also *seam*). Until the early 20th century, only one ball was permitted per innings: this severely handicapped the bowlers who had to bowl with a soft old ball. The laws have since remedied that fault and permit the periodic replacement of a worn ball with a new one. The intervals between the taking of the new ball have varied considerably. Just after World War II, fast swing-bowlers were encouraged by the provision of a new ball after only 65 overs. But the law was revised to stipulate that the bowling side could take a new ball only after every 200 runs scored by the batting side. Nowadays a new ball is taken in first-class games after every 85 overs (the laws stipulate a minimum of 75 overs). The bowling side may, for tactical reasons, delay the introduction of the new ball when it becomes due, and take it when it deems fit. When a batting side occupies the crease for many overs, it is not unusual for more than one extra new ball to be taken. The first replacement is called the second new ball, the next replacement the third new ball, and so on. (See also *old ball*)

new-ball bowler. The faster type of bowler, who is given the advantage of bowling with the ball when it is new at the beginning of the opposing side's innings. The pace-bowler is afforded this bonus because of his ability to make the hard *new ball* swing and bounce more, as well as to make it go through to the wicketkeeper more quickly. The bowling team relies on its new-ball bowlers to make the most of their advantage by dismissing the opposition's early batsmen.

nick. Another word for an *edge* — as in 'he nicked the ball'.

nicknames. Alternative, familiar names have been given to prominent players since the inception of the game. Edward Stevens of Surrey was known in the 18th century as 'Lumpy' because of his preference for bowling over a rise in the pitch; William Beldham, the last survivor of the Hambledon club, was called 'Silver Billy'. Such was the status of the 19th-century cricket colossus, Dr W.G. Grace, that he was accorded the title 'The Champion'; while his brother E.M. Grace, because of his profession, was called 'The Coroner'. The demon fast-bowler of the 1932/33 Bodyline series, Harold Larwood, was called 'Lol'. The enormous size of the Australian captain in 1920/21, Warwick Armstrong, earned him the sobriquet 'The Big Ship'. One of his successors, Bill Lawry, caught reading a Phantom comic, became 'Phanto'. So great a player was Bradman that he became affectionately known to all of his fellow Australians as 'The Don'.

My own *nom de guerre*, 'Typhoon' Tyson, emanated from a comparison of my bowling speed with that of the tropical stormwind. My contemporaries included 'Ferocious' and 'Fiery' Fred Trueman, named after his temperament; 'Scrubs' Peter Loader, after his crewcut hair; 'Bo' Lock, because of the effect achieved by combining the two names; 'Kipper' Cowdrey, after his job in the bedding department of his father-in-law's London store; and Denis 'Compo' Compton and Godfrey 'Godders' Evans.

More recent Australian nicknames have included Dennis 'Fot' Lillee, so called because his Western Australian skipper, 'Bo' Lock, said he had bowled like a 'Flippin' Old Tart'; Rodney 'Bacchus' Marsh, not named after the God of Wine but after the Victorian town Bacchus Marsh, where the train bearing him and a Western Australian side to Melbourne once stopped; 'Chappelli', the epithet by which Ian Chappell was known, because 'Chappell I' was the way his name appeared on scoreboards to distinguish him from his brother 'Chappell G'; Max 'Tangles' Walker, who earned his title from his wrong-footed bowling action; and Ashley 'Rowdy' Mallett from his quiet demeanour.

Modern cricketers differ from their predecessors. Players used to be unofficially christened according to a characteristic or attribute; nowadays they prefer to play on words and sometimes to use literary allusions to name their teammates. Geoff Lawson has become 'Henry', after the writer; David Boon changed into 'Daniel', after the Texan patriot; Geoff Marsh was accorded the damp monicker 'Swampy'; and Terry Alderman was dubbed 'Clem', after Brisbane's Alderman Clem Jones, the cricket administrator who in 1974/75 gained notoriety by sacking the 'Gabba curator on the eve of a Test match and preparing an atrocious pitch himself.

Brian Statham was sometimes called 'The Whippet' by his fellow England players, but he preferred 'George'. Why? He had the best reason of all for a nickname. He liked it!

nightwatchman. A *tail-end* batsman who, with only a short time remaining in a day's play and with light and pitch conditions far from ideal, goes in to bat in place of the *recognized batsman* who would normally be next in the *batting order*. A valuable batsman is at risk in these circumstances and may lose his wicket, whereas the loss of a less accomplished player's wicket is of lesser significance. The term refers to the role the substitute batsman is expected to play: to watch over the innings until the following morning.

There have been instances of players being sent in as nightwatchmen and succeeding as batsmen. Australian leg-spinner Tony Mann scored 105 in a Test against Bishen Bedi's Indians in Perth in 1977/78. The most famous employment of more than one nightwatchman occurred in the second Australian innings of the 1937 Melbourne Test against England. Caught on a wet spiteful wicket, Australian captain Don Bradman opened his side's innings with the lowliest of the low batsmen: his twin non-batting spin-bowlers, 'Chuck' Fleetwood-Smith and 'Tiger' Bill O'Reilly. His hope was that these players, who had batted at number 9 and 11 in the first innings, could, together with leg-spinner Frank Ward (promoted from number 10 to number 3), hold out against the England bowlers until the pitch improved. They did, and the tactic paid dividends: Bradman himself batted at number 7 and scored 270. His opening batsman, Jack Fingleton, went in at number 6 and notched 136 on an improved wicket. As a result, Australia won the game by 365 runs.

nip-backer. See *break-back*.

no man's land. Vacant areas of the outfield in which there are no fieldsmen. In the early phases of a *limited-over game*, batsmen will deliberately hit *over the top* into no man's land, because rules forbid the positioning of more than a few fieldsmen in the outfield and there is little danger of being caught.

no-ball. An illegal delivery. The umpire calls and signals no-ball to the scorers by extending one arm horizontally from the shoulder. A ball is deemed a no-ball if:
- the bowler's rear foot touches the *return crease* or its forward extension;
- part of the bowler's front foot, whether grounded or not, is not behind the *batting crease*;

- the ball is *thrown* not bowled;
- there are more than two fieldsmen behind *square-leg*;
- the wicketkeeper moves in front of the stumps to take the ball before it touches or passes the batsman's body;
- the bowler failed to notify the *umpire* of his method of delivery;
- the bowler violates law 42 governing *intimidatory bowling*;
- (in some limited-over games) the bowler bowls a *bouncer* rising above shoulder-height.

A no-ball does not count as a ball in the over and an extra ball has to be bowled. A batsman may strike and score off a no-ball without any danger of dismissal — except by *hitting the ball twice, handling* it, or being *run out*. Runs scored by a batsman off a no-ball are credited to him; *byes* and *leg-byes* scored off a no-ball are designated *extras*.

non-striker. Batsman who is at the wicket, but is not the batsman receiving or about to receive a delivery from the bowler. As the ball is delivered, the non-striker waits at the bowler's or *non-striker's end*, ready to run between the wickets when the striker hits the ball or runs are possible from *byes* or *leg-byes*.

non-striker's end. Also known as the bowler's end, this is the end of the pitch at which the *non-striker* stands as the bowler delivers the ball. The non-striker stands by the bowler's wicket and behind the batting crease at that end of the pitch, and *backs up* as the bowler bowls. When the batsmen run between the wickets, a fieldsman, usually mid-off or mid-on, must get to the wicket at the non-striker's end ready to take a possible return from another fieldsman and effect a *run-out*.

not cricket. Unsportsmanlike, unethical. An epithet which has passed into the English language from cricket and its connotations of fair play.

not offering a shot. A batsman may be adjudged *out* lbw even when struck on the pad or person outside the line of the off-stump, if, in the opinion of the umpire, the ball would have gone on to hit the stumps and the batsman has made no attempt to play it with his bat. (See *leg before wicket*)

not out. The status of a batsman who has not been *dismissed* by the opposite team in any of the ten ways described in the laws of cricket (see *out*). Batsmen are recorded in the scorebook as not out when they remain undefeated at the end of an innings, a match or a day's play. The more frequently a batsman remains not out at the end of an innings, the higher his *batting average*. (See also *carry one's bat*; *red ink*)

notch. To score (runs). The term comes from the original method of recording the number of runs scored in a match. (See *scoring*)

O

obstructing the field. The batsman at either crease may be given *out* 'obstructing the field' if, by word or action, he deliberately prevents a fieldsman from taking a catch or gathering the ball — even if the obstruction takes place while the batsman is lawfully defending his wicket with his bat or person.

Wisden lists only one instance of such a dismissal in a Test match. At the Oval in 1951, England opener Len Hutton was hit on the glove by South African off-spinner Athol Rowan. The ball ballooned into the air and, just as wicketkeeper Russell Endean was about to take the catch, Hutton, thinking the ball was going to drop on his wicket, hit it a second time — thereby, however, unwittingly preventing Endean from taking the ball. (See also *hitting the ball twice*)

off the mark. The batsman who is off the mark has scored the first run of his innings. To fail to get off the mark is to score a *duck*. In friendly or charity games — matches in which it is *not cricket* to score a duck — batsmen are always 'given one off the mark'. The bowler sends down a delivery which it is easy to hit for an initial run.

off-break. See *off-spinner*.

off-cutter. A medium-pace or medium-fast delivery which, because the delivery hand cuts down the right side of the ball, turns quickly from off to leg after it bounces. To bowl such a delivery, the bowler holds the ball around the *seam* with the first two fingers on top of the ball and the thumb and third finger supporting it from beneath; he employs a closed action and cuts the first two fingers hard down the right side of the ball at the moment of release. Because of the off-cut imparted, the delivery *curves* out towards the slips before it bounces. (See also *leg-cutter; off-spinner*)

off-drive. A front-foot or back-foot *drive* struck towards the *off-side* between the bowler and *cover*.

off-side. That side of the *playing area* which lies off to the right-handed batsman's right, and the left-handed batsman's left, when he faces the bowler.

off-spinner. A slow or slow-medium ball which, because of the *finger-spin* imparted by the bowler, turns, after it bounces, from the batsman's off-side to his leg-side. The spin imparted to the ball usually makes the delivery *drift* from leg to off before bouncing; because of this, the off-spin bowler (or 'off-spinner') prefers to bowl with a breeze from the leg-side accentuating the drift. A headwind also has this effect, as well as making the ball drop in the air. (See also *off-cutter*)

off-stump. One of the two outside *stumps* making up the *wicket* defended by the batsman. It is situated to that side of the *middle-stump* which lies to the batsman's off-side as he faces the bowler; from the bowler's point of view, it is the right-handed batsman's far-left stump, or the left-hander's far-right one. (See also *leg-stump*; *take guard*)

oil hole. A misnomer and misconception concerning the small, round puncture found in the base of the toe of the *bat*. It was once thought that a bat, stood upright in a shallow receptacle containing raw linseed oil, would soak up oil through this hole. In fact, the hole is left by the lathe on which the bat is turned and shaped.

old ball. The state of the ball, generally after 20 or 30 overs of use, when it has lost its *shine* and hardness. In this condition the ball's leather is scuffed and the *seam* is flat: the ball will not swing, nor will it bounce very high. The spinner may find the old ball easier to grip and spin, but generally it will favour the batsman. (See also *new ball*)

on the full. Without bouncing. A delivery struck by a batsman on the full is a *full-toss*. A hit that reaches a fieldsman on the full is a *catch*.

on-drive. A front-foot or back-foot *drive* struck towards the *on-side* between the bowler and *mid-wicket*.

on-side. An alternative term for *leg-side*.

one short. The call and signal of the umpire when a batsman runs a *short run*.

one-day match. A game played to a conclusion in a single day. One version of the one-day format, played mostly between English clubs, permits the team batting first to determine how long it bats before

Batting strokes

square-cut

front-foot
leg-glance

front-foot
off-drive

back-foot
defensive

sweep

front-foot
defensive

hook

pull

back-foot
drive

declaring, and thus how long it allows its opponents to score the runs needed to win. Under these conditions, four results are possible: win, tie, loss or draw. The side batting second may still force a draw, even though it fails to reach its run-target, because its adversary has to bowl it out to gain victory, as in the standard game.

The more common types of one-day game are those that restrict the innings of both sides — on the basis either of time or of the number of overs faced — and award the victory to the team scoring more runs. A less common version of this kind of match amalgamates the time and over restrictions by allowing the team that bats first to occupy the crease for a set period or number of overs — whichever comes first — and then allocating the same number of overs to the side batting second.

Spectators are attracted to the *limited-over* or limited-time game, because a result is guaranteed — even though it produces defensive bowling and fielding approaches.

one-day stroke. A stroke that a batsman would not normally play in an extended match, but is characteristic of the *limited-over game* — i.e. a shot that is designed to combat defensive bowling and fielding tactics and involves improvisation and some risk. An example of such imaginative strokeplay is when the batsman moves to the leg-side and risks driving, through the off-side field, a ball that is pitched on the leg-stump and could bowl him. (See also *make room for a stroke*)

one-day wicket. A pitch that provides a good playing surface for the *limited-over game.* Ideally dry, it does not change during the 120-odd overs of the match, is suited to strokeplay, and is equitably fair to the batsmen of both teams. It has no covering of green grass and so does not contain the 'juice' that facilitates movement off the *seam.* It is firm and fast with an even bounce, and the ball comes on to the bat. Bowlers receive no satisfaction from such surfaces, which allow them only a containment role and very much favour the batsmen.

open the angles for the batsman. To allow the batsman to play strokes at any angle of a 360° circle around his stumps: a fault stemming from a bowler's inability to maintain good line and length or to *bowl to his field.* Such a bowler in limited-over cricket creates an impossible situation for his captain, who is expected to save runs yet does not have enough fieldsmen to stop strokes played to all points of the compass. By contrast, the bowler who pitches the ball straight and on a good length compels the batsman to temper aggression with discretion for fear of being bowled. He cannot attempt a cross-bat stroke *across the line*; he must play a straight-bat stroke directly at the line of the ball and try to hit it into the 'V' between mid-off and mid-on.

The bowler who overpitches one ball and then sends down a short delivery permits the batsman firstly to drive him straight, and then to cut, pull, hook or glance the ball to any of the boundaries square of or behind his wicket. The bowler has opened up the angles outside the 'V' for the batsman.

open the batsman up. To bowl a ball which is in line with the batsman's body before it moves or spins away towards the slips. Such a ball provokes the initial response of playing at its original line towards mid-on, with the chest facing down the pitch in an 'open' posture towards the bowler. The ball's subsequent away-movement towards the off is in precisely the opposite direction to the bat's swing. Consequently the bowler's chances of evincing an edged stroke are greatly increased.

open the face of the bat. To pronate or turn the wrists outwards (away from the body) in the *backlift* so that the blade of the bat opens to face the off-side. Consequently, when the bat descends and makes contact, the ball is angled in that direction and slices the shot away towards the off. Opening the face of the bat assists in the placement of the *off-drives* and in running the ball through the slips. It also involves the risk of hitting slightly *across the line* towards the off-side.

open the shoulders. In batting, to become aggressive, attack the bowling and hit the ball hard.

opener. An *opening batsman*.

opening batsman. One of the two *batsmen* who go to the wicket first to open the innings; also known as the openers. They head the *batting order*.

opening bowler. One of the two bowlers used by a team to begin the bowling in an innings; usually a fast-bowler who is able to swing the *new ball* effectively.

opening up. The failure of a batsman or bowler to maintain a *side-on* position. When a bowler opens up in his delivery stride, his head, leading arm, shoulder, side and leg turn or *fall away* to the left or the batsman's off-side. Thus, as the bowler's momentum shifts towards the slip fieldsmen, rather than the batsman's wicket, he presents his chest and not his front shoulder towards the batsman, and is said to bowl with an open action, or to be chest-on. This denies him the full use of his weight in the delivery stride and reduces his pace; the ball often passes wide of the leg-stump. The bowler's one advantage from such an action is that it is easier to bowl an inswinger and a leg-cutter.

When a batsman opens up while executing a straight-bat stroke, his head, leading shoulder, arm, side and leg move to his left or leg-side, away from the line of the approaching delivery. Since his weight is moving in that direction, so will his bat. Usually, with the stronger bottom hand controlling its movements, the bat's backlift is towards the slips. Consequently its downswing is towards mid-on or mid-wicket. In following such a path, the bat swings *across the line* of the ball, and its chances of making contact are reduced. (See also *square up*)

orthodox. Term applied to the usual and most effective way of performing a cricket skill. An orthodox batting *stance* is classically *side-on*, with the batsman's toes aligned with the middle-stump of his wicket and his front shoulder and side pointing down the pitch towards the bowler. This position facilitates the straight swing of the bat and increases the batsman's chances of hitting the ball. An orthodox *bowling action* is also side-on, with the bowler releasing the ball as his weight passes over the front foot.

out. When a batsman is out, he has been *dismissed* and is out of the game for the remainder of his side's innings (unless called upon to be a *runner*). A batsman may be out in ten ways: (1) *bowled*, (2) *caught*, (3) *hit wicket*, (4) *run out*, (5) *leg before wicket*, (6) *stumped*, (7) *obstructing the field*, (8) *handled ball*, (9) *hitting the ball twice*, (10) *timed out*. (See also *give out*)

out of his ground/crease. Vulnerable position of a batsman who, while the ball is in play, moves out of his *batting crease* to hit a delivery or take a run, leaving himself open to being *stumped* or *run out*. (See also *ground one's bat*)

outcricket. Action that takes place in the *outfield*, away from the pitch, the batsmen and the bowlers — i.e. the fielding skills of catching, stopping, chasing, throwing, backing-up, relaying throws, preventing singles, closing gaps in the field and keeping the weaker batsman on strike. Thus, bad fielding and bad fielding tactics are described as 'poor outcricket'.

outer. A large section of the spectator area of a ground allocated to members of the public who have paid the basic entrance fee. Soccer supporters would call the area 'the terraces', and baseball fans 'the bleachers'. Spectators in the outer, unlike those in the stands or the *members' enclosure*, have no reserved seats; sometimes they have no seats at all and stand or sit on the ground, in the open air.

outfield. That part of a cricket field which lies outside the area of the carefully cultivated *square* of turf from which all the pitches of a ground are prepared. It is generally the part of the playing area close to the *boundary*.

outfield throw. A fieldsman's *return* from the outfield to the keeper, to a fieldsman at the bowler's wicket, or to a cut-off relay fieldsman. After stopping and retrieving the ball, the thrower aims at the target with the front arm, stepping towards it with the front leg. He swings the throwing arm in a wide circle, moving it down in front and to the side of the body, bringing it back behind him and then upwards and forward to release the ball at just above shoulder-level, with the throwing arm in an 'L' configuration. Some fielders can make such returns from more than 100 metres.

Baseball coaches help their players to master the outfield throw by asking them to imagine that there is a dwarf standing in front of them and a giant behind. When they throw for distance they are instructed to swing the arm in a wide arc so that they hit the dwarf on the head in the forward downswing, and the giant under the chin in the upward backswing, before releasing the ball.

outfielder. A player who fields in the *outfield*, more than 30 metres from the batsman: a defensive fielder whose main roles are to save runs, take lofted outfield catches and run batsmen out. (See also *boundary rider*)

outright win. A victory in a two-innings match, in which the winning side scores more runs in its two completed innings than its opponents in their two completed innings. (See also *result*)

outside edge. The vertical edge of the bat, the one further from the batsman's body and on his off-side when he takes up his *stance*. One of the *outswing* and *leg-spin* bowler's tactics is to swing or spin the ball sufficiently to the off-side to 'find the outside edge' — to clip it with the ball and, from the resultant mis-hit, produce a catch to the wicketkeeper or a slip fieldsman.

outside the off-stump. Area lying to the *off-side* of the batsman's *off-stump* as he faces the bowler. The term is generally used to describe a delivery directed to that part of the wicket, or a batsman's stroke played from that region: e.g. 'a leg-spinner, spinning away outside the off-stump', or 'a ball pulled from outside the off-stump'. (See also *hang the bat out to dry*)

111

outswinger.   A delivery, usually bowled at fast or medium pace, which curves in the air from the batsman's leg-side to his *off-side* before bouncing. Outswing is caused by the *seam* and *shine* of the ball creating a weaker air-pressure on its left side as it moves towards the batsman. The stronger air-pressure on the right side of the ball forces it in a curve towards the slips and the batsman's off-side. Outswing may occur as soon as the bowler releases the ball, or it may take place late in its flight.

To bowl an outswinger, the bowler grips the ball with the index and forefinger on top and on each side of its seam; he supports the bottom of the seam with his thumb. It is imperative that the seam be vertical at release and pointing towards first slip. The delivery should be served up on a *full length* to gain maximum flight-time and allow it to swing more. It is also more effective when bowled *over the wicket* from close to the stumps: the ball is released over the top of middle-stump, and, if aimed at the batsman's leg-stump, has only to swing half the width of the vertical bat (i.e. 5.4 cm) to pass it and hit the wicket. When *bowled from wide on the crease* the ball has to curve more to pass the bat — since it is first angled in towards the batsman's wicket before swinging away.

The outswinger aims to bowl the batsman or have him caught off the *outside edge*, behind the wicket or in the slips. To bowl the batsman, the bowler aims the outswinger at the batsman's pads to tempt him into a leg-side shot; the subsequent movement of the ball towards the off causes the stroke to be aimed towards the leg-side and directly *across the line* of the delivery, increasing the batsman's chances of being bowled. The outswinger that begins its flight in line with the stumps and then moves away to the off is designed to tempt the batsman into following it, flirting with it and edging a catch to fieldsmen behind the wicket.

By common batting consent, the outswinger is deemed to be one of the most dangerous balls in cricket. A delivery moving in towards the batsman's wicket can always be fended off at the last moment. The ball moving away, on the other hand, has no single final target; it may hit the stumps, but its real danger usually lies in the temptation it provides outside the off-stump. (See also *swing*)

oval.   A cricket ground on which a game is played. 'Oval' is an Australian term, deriving its name from the shape of the ground: contours which cater for the winter game of Australian football often played over the same area. An oval consists of the *wicket*, the *square*, the *outfield* and often a *net* area.

The most famous cricket ground called an oval is the Kennington Oval on the south bank of the Thames in London. The home of the Surrey County Cricket Club, it is the perennial setting for the Fifth Test of the English season — and the scene of Australia's first-ever triumph over England in 1882 and the birthplace of the *Ashes* legend.

over. A sequence of 6 legal balls delivered by one bowler from one bowling crease; after which the game is continued by the delivery of a further 6 balls from another bowler at the opposite bowling crease. *No-balls* and *wides* do not count in an over: an additional ball must be sent down for each illegal delivery.

The segmentation of the game into overs was designed to permit a greater participation in the sport by different types of bowlers and batsmen. Originally an over consisted of 4 balls delivered consecutively by a different player in a team of four. When the number of players in a side increased to five with the addition of a captain, an over became 5 balls. In Australia at one stage, overs were made up of 8 balls; but this has been reduced to 6 in the name of uniformity, and because it is said that a slightly greater number of balls can be bowled per hour. At the end of an over, the umpire at the bowler's end calls 'over' to indicate that the bowling should move to the opposite bowling crease. (See also *field restrictions*; *limited-over game*)

over the top. To hit the ball over the top is to defy the schemes of both bowler and opposing captain by striking the ball intentionally over the heads of fieldsmen placed specifically in strategic positions, often on the boundary. The term is sometimes applied to strokes that loft the ball over the ropes for six. (See also *chip/loft the ball over the infield*; *field restrictions*)

over the wicket. The area immediately above the stumps. In bowling over the wicket, the bowling arm is on the side of the body nearest to the bowler's wicket, and (if he bowls from close to the wicket) virtually above the stumps at delivery. Thus the right-arm bowler going over the wicket delivers from left of the stumps. The zone over the wicket is the ideal target for fieldsmen returning the ball to the bowler or wicket-keeper for run-outs. (See also *around the wicket*; *bowl from over the top of middle-stump*)

over the wrist. The bowler described as bowling over the wrist bowls *wrist-spin*.

over-rate penalties. Fines imposed on fielding teams in some international and representative *limited-over* matches for failing to bowl the specified number of overs within the time allotted to an innings. The greater the delinquency of the bowling team, the higher the fine. The purpose of the punishment is to maintain a fast and entertaining over-rate for the benefit of the spectators. Its efficacy is unquestioned, since the cost to the offending side can erode the whole of the prizemoney usually allocated to such matches.

113

overarm bowling. The bowler's most effective way of projecting the ball at the batsman's wicket. The ball is delivered with a straight arm raised above shoulder-level. This style permits the maximum use of the shoulders and body, and endows the bowler with greater speed. When the arm is raised vertically alongside the head, the bowler gains more bounce from the pitch and has greater control of direction, length, swing, curve, spin and cut. Overarm bowling was popularized by bowlers such as Kent's Edgar Willsher and received official blessing in 1864. It is now the universally accepted way of bowling. (See also *bowling action*; *roundarm bowling*; *underarm bowling*)

overpitch. To bowl a bad ball which does not bounce, or bounces closer to the batsman than a *good length*, allowing him to step forward and punish it. An overpitched ball is usually a *half-volley* or *full-toss*.

overthrow. A poor *return* from a fieldsman to the wicketkeeper or bowler, or at the stumps. The throw is not gathered, misses the wicket or is deflected off it with the batsman safely in his ground; it passes over or beyond the stumps, sometimes giving the batsmen time to take an extra run or runs. The passage of the ball beyond the wicket is described as an overthrow; the extra runs scored are designated 'overthrows', but are recorded in the scorebook in the normal way. (See also *back-up*)

owzat? Appeal to the umpire uttered by bowlers and fieldsmen to ask if the batsman has been dismissed: literally, 'How's that?'. This appeal is sufficient to cover any method of dismissal. (See also *appeal*; *out*)

p q

packed off-side/leg-side field. The positioning of fieldsmen in such a way that the majority are packed on either the off-side or the leg-side of the pitch. Captains attempt to restrict the scoring rate by instructing their bowlers to *bowl to one side of the wicket* and packing that side with most of their fieldsmen.

pad the ball away. To defend the wicket with the pads, against deliveries that cannot trap the batsman *lbw* but present difficulties because they swing or spin inordinately or bounce in the *rough*. In padding the ball away, the batsman deliberately deflects or kicks the ball away with one of his pads so that there is no threat of it striking his stumps.

Batsmen *pad up* against big *outswingers* that pitch on off-stump and are moving further to the off. They take this precaution against the possibility of the ball hitting the seam and cutting back towards the wicket rather than continuing towards the slips. They also defend their wickets against leg-spin and off-spin bouncing in the rough outside the line of the stumps. Such deliveries have a tendency to stop, turn and jump; to play a stroke runs the risk of being bowled, hitting too soon or edging a catch either directly or off the pad.

pad up.   To put on the *pads* before going in to bat. Also, to present the pads, in the act of *shouldering arms*, so as to prevent the ball hitting the stumps if it cuts back. (See also *pad the ball away*)

pads.   Protective casing for batsman's and wicketkeeper's legs, made of buckskin or canvas stuffed with kapok or plastic, or of thick synthetic material. Pads are ribbed lengthwise down the leg, have a *knee-roll* to facilitate the bending of the knee, a round upper *flap* to protect the front of the thigh, and a flap on each side of the leg to defend the calf muscles. The base of the pad is shaped to rest on the top of the instep. Pads are secured to the leg by three straps, two below the knee and one above. These are fastened by buckles or velcro on the inside of the leg, so that there is no danger that the sound of the ball flicking a buckle will be mistaken for a deflection off the bat. The strap above the knee is loosely buckled to allow the batsman to bend his leg.

Pads were introduced into cricket only with the advent of *roundarm* and *overarm bowling*, which was sufficiently fast to injure the legs of batsmen. Early cricketers did not consider it sporting to defend their wickets with their legs, so there was no need for pads — nor indeed for an lbw law. Faster bowling subsequently produced horrific injuries. The 19th-century Kent batsman Alfred Mynn, a mountain of a man, was once so dangerously bruised around the legs that he had to be transported home from a game in Nottingham on the roof of a stagecoach; at one point his physicians despaired for his life. The first pads were of wood. Then, in 1836, H. Daubeney invented the forerunners of modern pads and batsmen's wellbeing against fast-bowling was more assured.

Protected by pads, batsmen began to misuse them. Against difficult deliveries, they deliberately defended their wickets with their legs rather than their bats, necessitating the introduction of more stringent lbw laws. Arthur Shrewsbury, perhaps the finest professional batsman of his time, was a master of back-foot play and the use of the pads as a second line of defence. (See also *leg before wicket*)

pair. See *bag a pair; king pair.*

partnership. The association of two batsmen at the crease over a period of time. A partnership is valued by the number of runs it realizes or the number of minutes it occupies, and is often described in terms of when in the *batting order* it occurs (thus, an 8th-wicket partnership is reckoned from the fall of the seventh wicket, and so on). Records are kept of club, league, first-class and Test partnerships. They are measured in terms of the most prolific, the longest, and sometimes the slowest or fastest in run/time ratios. The bowler who dismisses one member of a partnership is said to break that partnership. (See also *stand*)

pavilion. Structure erected on a cricket ground, housing seats for spectators, and the dressing-rooms in which both teams change before the game and where the members of the batting side await their turn to go in. Large windows in the wall overlooking the playing area enable spectators in the pavilion to watch proceedings on the field. Some pavilions have provision for the serving of lunches and teas, and a bar.

Fences on either side of the pavilion, extending from the periphery of the ground to the boundary of the playing area, mark the members' enclosure. As the name implies, this area, usually provided with comfortable seating and extra facilities, is reserved for members of the home club or association and their guests: a privilege for which members pay an annual subscription. Some members' pavilions, such as that at Lord's, are large, imposing and historic buildings. The Lord's pavilion has several storeys, and is so high that, since its completion in 1890, no batsman has ever straight-driven a ball cleanly over its crest. It contains seating for many members, administrative offices, committee rooms, changing-rooms and bathrooms for members and players, players' dining rooms, bars and the famous Long Room, from which the privileged members obtain the best view of the game. The members' enclosure is large, incorporating the Warner, Allen and Tavern stands and some private boxes. It is not surprising that membership of the Marylebone Cricket Club, the private body that owns Lord's, is much sought after and exclusive.

The members' pavilions at the Melbourne and Sydney Cricket Grounds are as large as that at Lord's and cater in the same way for the players and the watching public. They also contain delegates' viewing rooms, but more emphasis is placed on the provision of seats for members.

penalties. Bonus runs and advantages awarded to the batting team for infringements of the laws by the bowling team. If the bowler sends down a *no-ball*, the batting side is accorded an *extra* run and the batsman a hit at the ball without the possibility of being dismissed bowled. A ball delivered so *wide* of the wicket that the batsman, standing in his normal position, is unable to reach it, also earns a penalty run. If a member of the fielding side stops the ball with any item of equipment or clothing, such as a cap, the batting team is awarded 5 runs in addition to those already run by the batsmen. A *lost ball* incurs a penalty of 6 runs. But the severest penalty of all affects the batsman who may be adjudged *timed out* if he wilfully takes more than 2 minutes to step on to the field of play after the fall of a wicket.

There are also penalty fines in some *limited-over* competitions for teams that fail to bowl their allocated number of overs in the stipulated time. (See *over-rate penalities*)

photo-finish. A very close *run-out* decision which can be clarified only with the assistance of a photo-finish camera of the type used at racecourses; an expression attributed to English umpire extraordinaire Alec Skelding (see *umpires, famous and amusing*). Instant *action replays* on electronic scoreboards and on television can now clarify such decisions for spectators and viewers, but do not help the umpires — which has led to the suggestion that a third umpire should be stationed in front of a TV in the pavilion to inform his colleagues in the middle about the correct decision.

physiotherapist. Qualified paramedical person seconded to a team to prepare it physically for competition and attend to injuries in the course of tours or matches. In the lead-up to games, the 'physio' treats the injuries sustained in previous encounters, conducts *warm-ups* and fitness-training sessions, and advises on diet; he also massages.

In the English first-class circles of the 1950s, physiotherapists were cynically viewed as 'slap-and-tickle merchants'. They themselves regarded many of the injuries brought to their attention as pure 'gold-bricking' to get a rest from the rigours of the county circuit. One Northamptonshire physio became so blasé about 'pulled muscles' that he would tell the so-called sufferers to 'take two aspirins and run it off'. Nowadays physiotherapists are held in high esteem by players. The physios nurse them like their own children to keep them on the field. More, they become integral members of the tight-knit community which is a touring side.

pick-up and balance. The comparative ease with which a *bat* is picked up in the backlift, and the manner in which its weight is distributed about a fulcrum. If a bat is well-balanced, it has a good pick-up and can be wielded quickly and effectively.

117

ping spot. The very centre of the *meat* of the bat: the most effective part of the bat with which to hit the ball. Balls struck in the ping spot really 'ping' their way to the boundary.

pitch (bounce). By common usage, 'pitch of the ball' has come to mean the actual spot where the ball bounces. An accurate bowler is described as able to 'pitch the ball on a sixpence'. A bowler who bowls a good *line and length* pitches the ball on a good length in line with the stumps. If he *overpitches*, he bowls a *half-volley, yorker* or full-pitch (i.e. *full-toss*). If he pitches short, he bowls *short of a length*.

A batsman who moves out of the batting crease down the wicket towards the bowler and uses his feet to hit the ball on the half-volley is described as 'getting to the pitch of the ball'. Batsmen frequently adopt this aggressive tactic against spin-bowlers, whose slow flight through the air affords the batsman enough time to meet the ball as it lands on the wicket. Getting to the pitch of the ball increases the chances of hitting it and minimizes the possibility of dismissal, since the batsman can stifle all spin and cut as the delivery bounces.

pitch or wicket. That part of the *playing area* which lies between the two *bowling creases*, and 1.52 metres to each side of the middle-stump at both ends. The cut-turf pitch is therefore 20.12 metres long by 3.04 metres wide. The length of the pitch was set by tradition at 4 Saxon 'gads' each of 16½ feet, or the exact width of a strip-farmer's acre holding under the medieval open-field system of agriculture. The width of the pitch exceeds the distance between the two *return creases*, which is 2.64 metres. No fieldsman is allowed to stand or have any part of his body on or over the pitch before the ball hits or passes the bat or strikes the batsman. Until the captains toss for choice of innings the authority governing the ground is responsible for the selection, mowing, rolling and watering of the pitch. After the toss, *maintenance* of the pitch is entirely in the hands of the *curator* under the direction of the umpires. No watering of the surface is allowed once the game has started.

The pitch is rolled before the game; thereafter the captain of the batting side may request that it be rolled for 7 minutes in the half-hour before each day's play and before his side begins its innings. The sweeping of the pitch to remove loose soil must not affect the rolling time. The playing surface is mown before the game at the discretion of the ground executive, and, in matches of two or more days' duration, on each morning before play resumes. If the weather intervenes, the pitch may be mown just before the game resumes. The *outfield* is mown before play each day. The curator is permitted to dry and mend any holes made by the bowlers' and batsmen's feet.

The word *wicket* is often used as an interchangeable term for the pitch on which the game is played. (Cross-references to types and conditions of wicket are listed under that entry.)

placards. See *banners*.

play and miss. To attempt a stroke at the ball — usually outside the off-stump — and not make contact, narrowly escaping edging the ball as a catch to the fieldsmen behind the wicket. The baseball exclamation 'a swing and a miss' has gained some currency among television commentators in recent years.

play back. The action of a batsman who steps back behind the *batting crease* to wait for the ball and hit it. In moving back, he transfers his weight onto the back foot, giving himself extra time to see the ball and hit it; but this weight-transfer makes it difficult to impart power to strokes played into the area in front of the wicket. Playing back produces *back-foot drives*, the *back-foot defensive stroke*, *cuts*, *pulls*, *hooks*, and the back-foot *leg-glance*.

play close to the pad. To play *straight-bat strokes* with the bat alongside the pads, covering the wicket with both the width of the bat and the pads. The striker may edge the ball on to the pads, preventing it from hitting the wicket; but because he has hit the ball, he escapes the *lbw* fate. Playing close to the pad, off either the front or the back foot, prevents the batsman being bowled through the *gate* by the ball that swings, spins or cuts back into him. The danger lies in the possibility of offering a *bat-pad* catch.

play forward. The action of a batsman who steps forward from his *batting crease* to meet the ball, placing his front foot alongside the *line of the ball* before hitting it. In moving forward, the batsman transfers his weight onto his front foot, which enables him to impart power to the resultant stroke. Playing forward produces *front-foot drives*, the *front-foot defensive stroke* and the front-foot *leg-glance*.

play on. To hit the ball with the bat and unintentionally deflect it on to the stumps. A batsman dismissed in this manner is deemed *out* 'bowled'.

play on the run. To execute a stroke and embark immediately on a run, giving the impression that the batsman was already running when he hit the ball.

play oneself in. The defensive process of beginning an individual innings by gradually and cautiously becoming accustomed to the state of the wicket, the light, and the character of the opposing bowlers. Once a batsman has played himself in, he should be *well set* and ready to play strokes.

play straight. The correct method of playing a *full-length ball* directed at the stumps, in which the downward swing of the vertical bat is directed straight towards the line of the approaching delivery. Playing straight greatly increases the striker's chance of hitting the ball. It is the antithesis of the *agricultural* swing of the bat *across the line* of the ball towards the leg-side.

play with the spin. To hit the spinning ball to the side of the pitch to which it is being taken by the direction of its turn. Thus, the common theory is that *off-spin* can be struck more safely and efficiently with the turn, towards the leg-side; and conversely, that it is less risky to hit *leg-spin* towards the off-side. But science does not bear out this hypothesis: the batsman can in fact hit a ball harder by striking diametrically back along the path of the approaching delivery. Thus off-spin should be hit towards the off-side and leg-spin towards the on-side. It is, however, undoubtedly true that by playing with the spin and allowing for the angle of its deviation, a batsman can place the ball more accurately between the fieldsmen.

Player of the Series. A prize awarded to the player from any team who contributes most as a batsman, bowler, keeper and/or fieldsman to the efforts and success of his side in a series of Test or international limited-over games. The award is decided by one or a panel of several impartial judges. It is not necessarily given to a member of the victorious side, and may take the form of a trophy or a cash award, or a combination of the two.

playing area. That part of the cricket ground lying within the *boundaries* settled by agreement between the captains before the beginning of the cricket match and on which the match is played. It comprises the *wicket*, the *square*, the *outfield*, and often an area set aside for *nets*. (See also *maintenance of playing area*)

playing surface. In the wider sense: the area of ground within the agreed boundaries on which a cricket match is played. In the particular connotation: the *wicket* or *pitch*.

plumb. Clearly, directly and without any doubt: a term often used to describe the unquestionable dismissal of a batsman who is out 'plumb' *lbw*. Plumb can also mean 'true', and is employed to describe a pitch that gives no assistance to the bowler.

point. Fielding position to the off-side of the batsman and level with him in line with the *batting crease*. Point is at right-angles to the ball's flight and may be an attacking and catching fieldsman, just a few metres from the bat, or a defensive and run-saving man, 30 or more metres away from it. Deep point is a *sweeper* cutting off the boundary. The position is so called because the end or point of the bat is inclined in that direction in the execution of the *cut* stroke. (See also *cover-point*; *silly point*)

points. Rewards given to teams for the results they gain in competitions based on the league principle. The number of points awarded to a team for a game varies according to whether it gains an *outright* victory, a *first-innings win*, a *tie* or a *draw*; it diminishes to nothing for a loss. As the season progresses teams accumulate points, and at the end of the summer the side with the most points wins the competition or the right to appear in the final round of matches. Below is an example of the variety of results possible in a two-innings game, showing the number of points that the various results might attract:

• Outright win – winning team leads on first innings: 20.
• Outright win – first innings a tie: 16.
• Outright win – winning team behind on first innings: 12.
• Outright tie: 10.
• First-innings win: 12.
• First-innings lead – points retained if beaten outright: 8.
• Tie on first innings: 6.
• Outright loss – tie on first innings: 4.
• Drawn game: 4.
• Abandoned game: 6.

One-innings competitions award proportional points for a win, a tie, a draw, an abandoned match, and sometimes (in school games, as a small compensation) a loss.

polish the ball. See *shine*; *work on the ball*.

popping crease. The *batting crease*. In the early days of cricket a 'popping hole' was scooped in the turf, at a *cloth-yard*'s distance in front of the stumps. In order to run out a batsman, a fieldsman had to 'pop' the ball into the hole before the batsman had made his ground. A line drawn through the popping hole became the popping or batting crease.

pouched. A colloquial term for *caught*; it refers, of course, to the ball not the batsman.

prod. Derogatory term applied to a tentative and ineffectual *front-foot defensive stroke*. The English cricket writer E.W. Swanton, coining the phrase 'the post-war prod', ascribed its origins to the uncertain post-1945 period.

promote up the order. To change a batsman's position in the *batting order*, asking him to bat earlier than originally planned. This tactic is usually stimulated by a need for solid defence or quick runs: the captain throws in a hitter (in baseball parlance a 'pinch-hitter') or a *stonewaller* to meet the crisis.

pudding. A very wet *wicket*, usually found in England; one which is as soft as a boiled pudding. The surface is so saturated and yielding that it offers no assistance to the bowler. The ball comes off the pitch very slowly, sitting up, without movement off the seam, cut, spin or bounce, and asks to be hit. A pitch very much in favour of the batsman, especially if he plays off the back foot.

pull. An aggressive horizontal-bat stroke addressed at a *long-hop* or *full-toss* which, since the ball reaches the batsman at above waist-height, holds no threat of bowling him. The pull is the most natural stroke in cricket: a scything shot which pulls the ball to the leg-side. The backlift takes the bat high behind the batsman's head as he steps *back and across* his wicket, adopting a feet-astride position towards the bowler or mid-off. He then swings his bat down on the ball with arms extended as though chopping at a tree, smashing the ball down in a direction that can vary between *square-leg* and *mid-on*. The pull may be played at a ball on any line: outside the off-stump if it is not too wide, straight, or outside the leg-stump. But the delivery must be of the right height, and the shot must be executed with the point of contact at the requisite distance from the batsman's body.

pull the ball on. To *play on*, usually in the execution of a *pull* shot.

pull the parachute. To abandon one's teammates when the side is in difficulties and struggling. The analogy is that of jumping from a crashing plane with the last parachute, leaving the rest of the crew to take their chances. A batsman pulls the parachute when he 'chickens out' or surrenders his wicket because he is frightened of being hit by a really fast bowler. The recognized batsman 'looking for the *red ink*' — a not-out and the consequent improvement in his average — pulls the parachute when he makes no attempt to *farm the bowling* to shield his tail-end partners from the attack. (See also *pull up the ladder*)

pull up the ladder. To *pull the parachute*. This time the analogy is that of climbing up a ladder from a place of danger to safety, then raising the ladder and abandoning those below.

push the ball through. When a spin-bowler pushes the ball through, he bowls at a quicker pace than normal, refusing to flight the ball. He adopts the tactic either to avoid being hit or to exploit a *turning wicket*. It is a policy normally used by slow-bowlers in limited-over games, since the quicker the flight of the delivery, the less time the batsman has to use his feet, reach the pitch of the ball and drive it for runs. On good wickets, pushing the ball through reduces a spin-bowler's ability to turn the ball past the bat: the ball is in contact with the ground so briefly that it does not have time to grip and deviate. On soft or turning pitches and 'sticky dogs', however, the slightest amount of spin changes the ball's line: under these conditions the spin-bowler pushes the ball through to deny the batsman time to reach the pitch of the ball and hit it, and he can still turn it sufficiently to beat the bat. (See also *bowling flat*)

push to cover's left hand. The act of playing an off-side stroke just in front of *point* and to the left of *cover*. To return such a ball, most fieldsmen — being right-handed, and having stopped the ball with the left hand — must transfer it to the right hand before throwing it to the keeper or bowler. This operation takes enough time to allow the batsmen to cross for an easy single; consequently a push to cover's left hand is synonymous with a comfortable run. To prevent a plethora of such singles, fielding captains station a left-handed fieldsman at cover: a move that often leads to the undoing of the complacent batsman strolling through for his statutory single from the push to cover's left hand!

put down. A fieldsman who puts down a batsman *drops* a catch off one of his hits. If, on the other hand, a fieldsman or the keeper puts down a batsman's wicket in a run-out or stumping, he *dismisses* him: the wicket is down.

pyjama game. Disparaging term used by critics of *limited-over* cricket in reference to the distinctive coloured uniforms ('pyjama suits') worn by players in *one-day* and *day/night* matches. Traditional cricket is

Batting
the hitting arcs

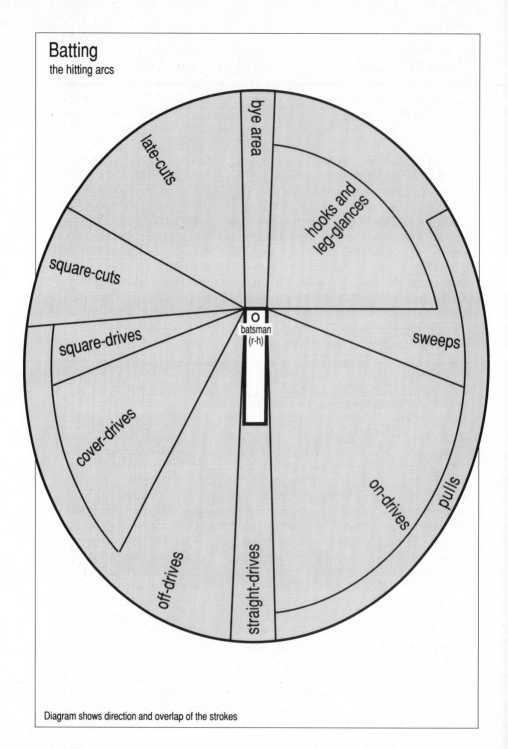

bye area

late-cuts

hooks and leg-glances

square-cuts

square-drives

O
batsman
(r-h)

sweeps

cover-drives

on-drives

pulls

off-drives

straight-drives

Diagram shows direction and overlap of the strokes

played by competitors clothed all in white. Particoloured shirts and trousers are worn by limited-over players to distinguish teams and add colour to matches not uncommonly played under floodlights; even the *umpires* wear coloured (usually yellow) jackets. The night-time setting of some of these contests and the dreamlike quality of the results led to the coining of the 'pyjama' sobriquets.

quick on the draw. Describes an impetuous *umpire* who gives batsmen out without enough consideration of the factors governing his decision. Like a gunman in a Western, he is quick to draw his 'weapon' — the raised finger. A batsman who falls victim to a quick-draw umpire is described as having been 'gunned out'.

quick single. A *short single*, or one quick run.

quickie. A fast-bowler.

quota of overs. The number of overs which any one bowler is permitted to send down in a *limited-over* game: usually one-fifth of the total bowled.

r

rabbit. A poor *tail-end* batsman: one who tends to capitulate to the bowling as timidly as a rabbit. A batsman who is repeatedly dismissed by one bowler is designated as that bowler's bunny.

rain. Rain is the natural enemy of cricket, flooding grounds, rendering playing surfaces treacherous at best, and at worst soggy and unplayable, making the outfield so slippery that fieldsmen cannot stand up and bowlers cannot run up to the wicket, preventing the batsmen from seeing a delivery clearly, and reducing a leather ball to the untenable condition of a wet bar of soap. The *umpires* are the sole judges of the fitness of the ground, weather and light for play; they may suspend or delay play if conditions are unsatisfactory. Before rain stops or holds up play, however, the umpires must establish that neither the two batsmen nor the fielders wish to continue or begin. For instance, if the batting team, in an effort to win the game, wishes to stay on the field while light rain is falling, the umpires will accede to its wishes — provided conditions are not unreasonable, and provided the other team does not object. No match may begin or restart while rain is falling. After any rain interruption, the umpires must inspect the ground as soon as conditions improve, and must resume play as soon as possible. If heavy rain precludes any possibility of play for a foreseeable period, they may cancel or postpone play for that amount of time, adjusting the hours of previously agreed *intervals* (see also *target*). A suspension owing to rain is noted in the socrebook and the media as RSP (rain stopped play).

raise the finger. To give a batsman *out*. (See *umpires' signals*)

raise the seam. To run the thumbnail or some sharp object along the stitching of the ball to make the *seam* stand out more from its surface. The increased prominence of the seam augments the movement of the ball before and after it pitches on the stitching. Interfering with the ball in this way is totally against the laws and spirit of the game. (See also *work on the ball*)

rattle the stumps. To bowl a batsman out.

recognized batsman. A player who is acknowledged and chosen in the side as a competent batsman, going in to bat early in the *batting order*.

records. See *statistician*; *Wisden*.

red ink. To be 'looking for the red ink' (or be 'after the red ink') is to seek to remain *not out* at the end of an innings. When a batsman achieves this feat, it is usually recorded by the scorer in his book in red ink. The ambition is often regarded as selfish, particularly if it involves the sacrifice of other batsmen's wickets.

red rambler. A 19th-century colloquialism for the cricket ball.

referee. An impartial official appointed by the governing authorities of a *limited-over* competition and stationed off the field to adjudicate on match regulations. The referee may be called upon to confirm the target needed by a side batting second when its innings is curtailed by weather. He may also be required to decide the winner of a tied game, if the outcome hinges upon which side lost the fewer wickets. In rain-affected one-day games he determines the number of overs each side will bowl and bat. His role in no way impinges upon that of the *umpires*, who rule on all on-field situations.

relay return. See *cut-off relay return.*

result. The outcome of a match. In a two-innings game such as a Test, the side that scores more runs in its two completed innings than its opponents in that team's two completed innings wins the game *outright.* A team which bats only once yet totals more runs in its one innings than its opposition in its two completed innings *wins by an innings.* Usually this situation arises when a side notches a large total in its first innings, *declares* its innings closed without all of its players having batted, dismisses the opposing team for a score which is between 75 and 200 runs short of its own (depending on the duration of the match), and asks it to *follow on.* Sometimes a side may have a substantial but, under the laws, not large enough lead on the first innings to enforce the follow-on; in those circumstances, it may attempt to force a win by *forfeiting* its second innings and requiring its adversary to bat twice in succession.

A team which outscores its opponents in the first innings of a two-innings contest, yet fails to dismiss them a second time to win outright, *draws* the match, but is deemed to have gained a *first-innings win.* A game which concludes with the aggregate scores of both sides equal, with each having completed its two innings, either by having declared or been dismissed, is a *tie.* In certain competitions based on a league system, proportional *points* are awarded according to the result. A side may win if its opponents refuse to play or concede the match.

In one-innings matches, results are based on the comparison of a single completed innings. One-innings games may be won, tied, drawn or lost according to the regulations governing the various competitions.

Limited-over contests, based on the premise that the side scoring more runs or scoring faster over a preordained number of overs is the winner, always produce a result. In this one virtue lies much of the appeal of one-day cricket. In my assessment the virtue is overestimated, for there is often considerable excitement and merit in a drawn game.

retire hurt. To withdraw or retire from the batting crease because of injury or sickness. The batsman who retires hurt must notify the umpire at the bowler's end of his intentions, and may resume his innings at the fall of a wicket or the retirement of another batsman. A batsman who retires through injury or illness, or some other unavoidable cause, and is unable to resume his innings is recorded in the scorebook as 'Retired not out'; if he retires by choice, he becomes 'Retired out'. Having retired for a reason other than incapacitation (e.g. to attend a wedding!), a batsman may resume his innings only with the permission of the opposing captain.

retreat. To *back away*.

return. Fieldsman's throw which returns the ball to the wicketkeeper, the bowler, or the man ready to put down the wicket at the bowler's end. (The various types of throw and return are listed under *throw*.)

The word is also an alternative expression for a *bowling analysis*. Thus, a bowler's return may read: 24 overs, 4 maidens, 50 runs, 7 wickets, 4 no-balls, 0 wides.

return catch. A catch which is hit back to the bowler off his own delivery, dismissing the batsman *caught and bowled*.

return crease. The crease marked at each end of the *bowling crease* and at right-angles to it. Its function is to prevent a bowler from delivering from an angle which is too wide of the stumps at the bowler's end. The inside edges of the return creases mark the length of the bowling crease (2.64 metres); and although the return crease is considered to be unlimited in length, it must be marked for a minimum of 1.22 metres behind the wicket, and as far as the batting crease in front of the wicket. If a bowler touches the inside edge of the return crease with any part of his rear foot while bowling, the umpire calls and signals a *no-ball*.

reverse sweep. A *sweep* hit to the off-side, by changing the grip on the bat and hitting the stroke as if it were a double-handed tennis backhand. An extremely risky, unorthodox shot, it is attributed to Pakistan batsman Javed Miandad, who first played it in the 1970s to overcome the slow-bowlers' defensive tactic of bowling wide of the leg-stump to a *packed on-side field*. The stroke has caused the downfall of such English batsmen as Ian Botham and Mike Gatting and called down accusations of irresponsibility on their heads; it has been compared to taking a soccer penalty kick with the head.

rollers. Weighted cylinders revolving on axles and used for pressing and levelling the wicket and outfield. Most grounds possess a light and a heavy roller. The light roller, similar to a garden roller, is a single solid cylinder of not more than 200 kg, pulled by hand. The heavy roller is a mechanically or electrically propelled vehicle, usually but not always with a front and rear cylinder, driven by an operator who sits on it or steers it from the front; it may weigh a few tonnes. In the pre-season preparation of a ground, the *outfield* is smoothed with a heavy roller. The wicket area or *square* is also heavily rolled both laterally and longitudinally. This process is known as cross-rolling, and ensures that the levels of the pitches will be correct.

Before a game the *curator* prepares the wicket to be used by *watering*, *mowing* and rolling it. It is he who decides what type of roller should be used. If the wicket is damp on the morning of the match, he generally opts for a lighter roller, since the heavy one would bring moisture to the surface and place in jeopardy a prompt start to the game. If the wicket is extremely dry and cracked he will also choose a light roller, since the pressure of the heavy roller might make its surface crumble and deliver the match into the hands of the spin-bowlers. In ordinary conditions, however, the groundsman will opt for the heavy roller to compact the pitch into a firm, hard playing surface. Before the game begins, the *captain* of the side batting first may have the wicket rolled for no more than 7 minutes in the half-hour before the start. He also chooses the type of roller he prefers, based on the same judgments as those used by the groundsman.

In one-day games, the pitch is rolled for no more than 7 minutes during the interval between innings. The skipper of the side about to bat chooses the size of the roller; he may opt not to have the wicket rolled at all. In matches lasting two or more days, the pitch is rolled before play, under the same conditions as on the first day. It is also rolled between innings. (See also *super-sopper*)

rope.   On many grounds the *boundary* (or part of it) is marked by a white rope laid along the turf. Thus, 'over the rope' is synonymous with 'over the boundary'.

rough.   That part of a turf *pitch* which is scuffed and roughened by the feet of the bowlers and batsmen during play. These rough patches usually occur in front of and outside the line of the stumps. However, no player may roughen the area in front of the batsman, known as the *danger area*. (See also *running on the pitch*)

roundarm bowling.   Projecting the ball at the batsman's wicket with a straight arm, just below or just above shoulder-height. Roundarm bowling evolved from *underarm*. In the early 19th century, Christina Willes helped her brother John to practise in a barn near their Canterbury home. Finding that she could not bowl underarm because of her fashionable voluminous skirt, she started throwing the ball 'high handed'. Her brother recognized the possibilities of this new technique and imitated it. But his methods were regarded as unfair. He was no-balled for throwing in Kent's game against the MCC at Lord's in 1822; whereupon he threw down the ball, mounted his horse and rode out of the ground and the game. William Lillywhite popularized roundarm bowling, which was made legal in 1835; it was not until 1864, however, that bowlers were permitted to bowl from above shoulder-level.

rubber. The rubber grip on a bat *handle*. Also, an alternative name for a series of Tests.

run. See *runs.*

run the ball. In batting, and especially in limited-over cricket, to steer or *deflect* the ball through the vacant slips area towards *third man.*

run-chase. The pursuit by a team and its batsmen of the total number of runs needed to surpass their opponents' score and win the game.

run-out. One of the ten ways of dismissing a batsman according to the laws of cricket. Either batsman is run out if, in running between the wickets, or at any time while the ball in in play, he is out of the *batting crease* nearer to him when the wicket at that end is put down by a member of the fielding side. If the batsmen have *crossed* in running, the player running for the wicket which is put down is out; if they have not crossed, the player who has left the wicket which is put down is out. A batsman may be run out off a *wide* or a *no-ball.* A batsman who is assisted by a substitute *runner* is run out if either he or his runner is out of his ground when the wicket closer to him is put down. The run on which a batsman is run out is not scored, although the runs preceding that run are. Thus, a batsman run out on a third run is credited with 2. The non-striker may be run out by a ball hit back by the striker along the wicket and into the stumps at the non-striker's end, but only if the ball first touches the person of one of the fielding side. A run-out dismissal is not credited to the bowler.

Two batsmen may not be run out off the same ball, as they can in the double-play of baseball. There have been some instances, however, when two contemporaneous run-outs were theoretically possible. In one famous fictional account, a batsman hit a steepling catch to deep mid-off and set off for a run with his eyes firmly fixed on the ball. Unfortunately, at the other end of the wicket his partner also had his head in the air and his gaze on the ball. They collided in the middle of the pitch with a clang worthy of two medieval knights clashing at a joust. Both fell unconscious to the turf as the catch was missed — though the fielding side was still left with the option of running out either batsman! (See also *out*)

run-rate. The average number of runs scored per over in an innings that has been completed, is being played, or is about to be played. A run-rate measures the achievement of a team that has already batted; it records the progress of one that is batting; and it sets a target or *asking rate* of a certain number of runs per over (i.e. run-rate required) to reach a total within a specified number of overs. The run-rate is also used to assess the achievements and progress of, and the challenge facing, individual batsmen.

The run-rate and asking rate vary in the course of an innings. A side needing 200 for victory in 50 overs requires a run-rate (scoring rate) of 4 per over. If, after 20 overs, it has scored only 50 runs, its run-rate then stands at 2.5 runs per over and the task it faces has grown to 150 runs in the remaining 30 overs — an asking rate of 5 per over. If the side subsequently fails and is dismissed for 180, it has scored at a run-rate of 3.6 per over.

run-saving. Bowling tactics, or the positioning of fieldsmen, designed primarily to prevent the batsmen from scoring runs rather than to get them out.

run-up. The bowler's prefatory forward motion or run to the bowling wicket before he moves into his *bowling action* and delivers the ball. The run-up adds forward momentum and additional pace to that obtained from the strength of the action, contributing approximately 20 percent of the fast-bowler's speed. It brings him to the bowling crease in a balanced, rhythmical fashion, increasing the effectiveness of his delivery: its speed, flight, length, swing, curve, cut and spin.

The bowler begins his run-up slowly, accelerates until he reaches his maximum speed in the penultimate step, then slows up slightly in order to turn into a *side-on* position for the delivery stride. (Australian fast-bowler Dennis Lillee, for instance, hit a top speed in his run-up of 32 km/h but slowed to 27 km/h to deliver the ball.) The length of a bowler's run-up depends upon his speed and his power of acceleration. A slow-bowler's approach is usually short and slow, but energetic, rhythmical and poised. A fast-bowler's run-up is longer and more rapid; but it is not impossible for a speedster (such as the Australian Keith Miller) to explode into a brief approach and deliver the ball at lightning velocity. In contrast, some medium-pacers (such as the England left-hander John Lever) employ an exorbitantly long approach, pleading the necessity of cadence and equilibrium before they can bowl.

The bowler's run-up compels him to *follow through* after releasing the ball, thus absorbing the energy of the bowling action and preventing injury. (See also *lost run-up*; *marker*)

runner. Under the laws of cricket, a batsman who is incapacitated by injury or illness during a match is allowed to have a substitute from his team to run for him between the wickets. The runner must wear the same external protective equipment as the batsman, and if possible shall already have batted in the innings concerned. While the injured batsman is facing the bowling, the runner stands where he will not interfere with the play — normally at *square-leg*. He may be dismissed by being run out, obstructing the field or handling the ball.

The presence of runners on the field often seems to lead to confusion in the calling for runs and the scampering between the wickets — particularly when players such as the former England master of indecisiveness, Denis Compton, are involved. A call for a run from Compton was never regarded as more than a basis for negotiation. In one game, Compton was batting when both batsmen had runners. The confusion was indescribable. Finally Compton called a mid-wicket conference of all members of the discussion group and told them that he was CIC between the wickets. A subsequent Compton call of 'Yes! no! wait! bugger it!' resulted in all four runners meeting in the middle of the wicket, while the bails were removed at both ends!

running between the wickets. The batsmen's action of running to change ends and score runs after the ball has been hit. 'Running between the wickets' has virtually become a stock-phrase and is used constantly by commentators when discussing batsmen's speed and assurance in taking runs. (See also *call for a run*; *ground one's bat*; *turn blind*)

running on the pitch. The bowling sin of running straight down the wicket after releasing the ball, roughing up the playing surface immediately in front of the *batting crease* and so increasing the difficulties the batsman at that end will encounter in defending his stumps or striking the ball for runs. Technically the ideal *follow-through* takes the bowler straight down the wicket after he releases the ball; this underwrites his accuracy. But the bowler must also ensure that he does not trespass on that part of the playing surface which lies up to 1.22 metres in front of the batting crease and 30.48 cm either side of middle-stump. This zone is designated the *danger area*.

The roughing-up of the danger area constitutes a real threat to the batsman, since it presents an opportunity for the bowler from the opposite end to pitch the ball on the damaged turf (see *bowl into the rough*), which makes it easier to turn or cut the ball. Law 42 forbids the bowler running on the pitch. Moreover, it sets down a procedure, similar to that outlined against *intimidatory bowling*, to be followed should the bowler persistently damage this part of the wicket by scuffing it with the studs or spikes in his boots. The bowler is cautioned twice, and the other umpire and both teams are informed of the warning. Should the cautions go unheeded the bowler is removed from the attack for the rest of the innings.

Although bowlers are the most common offenders, batsmen also do their share of damage while running between the wickets; they may be advised by the umpire to run by the side of the wicket. Batsmen have been known to run on the wicket deliberately, when their team has been about to bowl in the last innings of a game, to scuff it up and make it more helpful to their spin-bowlers!

runs. The units by which a team's and a batsman's score, a partnership between batsmen, a bowler's economy and a wicketkeeper's effectiveness are measured in cricket. A side scoring more runs than its opponents in one or two *innings* wins the game (see *result*). Batsmen who notch 50, 100, 200, 300 runs or more are adjudged eminently successful. Bowlers who concede few runs in dismissing the opposing batsmen win matches (see *bowling analysis*). Wicketkeepers who prevent runs being scored by byes restrict the opposition's score.

A run is scored when, with the ball in play, the batsmen *cross* and make good their ground from end to end and *batting crease* to batting crease. Runs are also scored from *boundaries*. All runs scored off the bat are credited to the batsman making the hit. Penalty runs are awarded or taken for *wides*, *no-balls*, *byes*, *leg-byes* and *lost balls*, and are recorded as sundries or *extras*. Five *penalty* runs are given to a batsman when a fieldsman stops a hit with anything other than his person. No runs are scored by a hit off which a batsman is *caught*. If a batsman is *run out*, only the runs completed before the run off which he is dismissed are counted.

runs on the board. Runs that have already been scored. A batting side with runs on the board is in a relatively sound position: it has successfully completed its batting task, and the opposing team still has to rival its score.

S

safe/good pair of hands. Attribute of a *wicketkeeper* who catches well. He may be exceptionally mobile, or adept at preventing *byes*; but his match-winning function is to *catch*, *stump* or *run out* batsmen. A good pair of hands ensures that the ball goes into the keeper's gloves and stays there: there are few fumbled stumping or run-out chances and missed catches are a rarity.

The signs of a safe pair of hands are unmistakable. The keeper stays down in his stance until the ball pitches, and only then does he rise with its bounce. He never snatches at the ball, but waits for it, cushioning its entry into his gloves by allowing his hands to give as though he were catching a precious piece of porcelain. A good pair of hands is thus also described as 'soft hands'. The phrase is the opposite of 'Iron Gloves', the nickname given by his English opponents to Australian keeper Rod Marsh, in his early hard-handed snatching days.

sandshoe crusher. A *yorker* pitched on the batsman's legs, and consequently too close to the body to allow the free swing of the bat and the successful production of a stroke. As a result the delivery hits the batsman on the foot — painfully 'crushing his toes' should he be unwise enough to wear soft-toed sandshoes!

save the single. To stop the batsman from scoring one run. The fieldsman positioned to save the single is stationed close enough to the batsman to prevent his tapping the ball and scampering between the wickets for a sharp, surprise run.

scone ball. Another term for the *bouncer* or the *beamer* — the connotation being that the ball has been aimed at the batsman's 'scone' or head.

scoop bat. A specially designed and contoured bat, the *blade* of which is hollowed or 'scooped out' at the back. The weight is distributed more towards the edges of the blade, which are therefore thicker, and enable the batsman to hit the ball hard even when he does not hit it in the middle of the blade.

scoreboard. A structure erected on the cricket ground outside the boundary to inform the players and spectators of the history and current state of the game in progress. The simplest club scoreboards are upright wooden screens with three horizontal lines of hooks or nails. Squares of sheet metal, each painted with a number, are suspended from these hooks. The top line gives the present score, the second line the number of wickets down, and the last line the number of runs scored by the last batsman to be dismissed.

In higher grades of competition, the scoreboards are more elaborate. Though still operated by hand, they may give the names of the batsmen and bowlers both current and past, runs scored, the order in which the batsmen were dismissed and the bowlers bowled, extras, the scores at which the wickets fell, the bowling analyses and the scoring rate. On some Test and first-class grounds such as Melbourne and Sydney, score-boards have entered the high-tech age. Electronically controlled, and costing millions of dollars, they show every detail of every event in the immediate or distant past, including slowmotion *action replays* of exciting and contentious incidents.

scorebooks and scoresheets. See *scoring.*

scorecard. See*card.*

scoreline, short. The short scoreline is an abbreviated report on a match, given in the electronic and print media, stating the side's score, the number of wickets lost, the not-out batsmen, the latest batsmen dismissed and their scores, the extras, the short bowling figures and the opposing team's score. For example: 'In reply to India's first-innings total of 445, Pakistan are 3/179, with Miandad 17 not out, Imran 12 not out, extras 10. The last batsmen out: Shoaib 25, Salim 89. Kapil has 2/56 and Hirani 1/4.'

In the above analysis, the 3/179 is shorthand for '3 wickets down for 179 runs'; and the 2/56 is short for '2 wickets taken at a cost of 56 runs'. (It is important to note that in countries other than Australia, the score would be stated as 179/3 rather than 3/179!)

scorers. A scorer is appointed by each side to record the statistical details of a match: all runs, dismissals, bowlers used and their analyses, the fall of wickets, individual and collective totals, and so on. The scorers accept and immediately acknowledge all signals and instructions given to them by the *umpires.* They should frequently check to ensure that their sheets agree. (See also *scoring*)

scoring. The recording of the collective and individual performances in a cricket match: number of runs scored, wickets taken, runs conceded, catches accepted, extras yielded, time needed, and so on. The first cricket competitions were recorded by two *scorers,* one from each team — so that they could keep an eye on one another! They sat inside the field of play, cutting a notch on a stick for every run scored and gouging out a deeper notch for every tenth run. Individual performances of batsmen and bowlers were ignored. In the 18th century, when the press began reporting matches, detailed written scoresheets were introduced — the first being that of the famous Kent vs All England match of 1744. By the turn of that century more details appeared on scoresheets, but it was not until well into the 1800s that the names of the bowlers, catchers and wicketkeepers appeared alongside the dismissals in which they shared.

Today, standard scoresheets, bound into books, are used as the official record of every game. At the head of each sheet, space is provided for the name of the competition, the number of the round, the sides playing, the team batting, the date and venue of the game and the winner of the toss. Each sheet is devoted to one innings of a team and the bowlers who opposed it. From the left of the page, columns are devoted to the times of the start and end of each batsman's innings, his name, his runs as they were scored, how he was out, the bowler who dismissed him, and his score. The lower half of the page provides a grid recording the team's progressive score, spaces for byes, leg-byes, wides and no-balls, times for the team's progressive half-centuries, the scores at the fall of each wicket, the total score, and the progressive and summated bowling analyses.

A batsman's runs are written, as they are scored, on horizontal lines opposite his name. The value of a stroke is indicated by a digit from 1 to 6; boundaries are set down in red. In a long innings a batsman's score is periodically tallied and recorded in brackets. Two parallel chevrons drawn vertically across the lines of a batsman's RUNS AS SCORED column denote his dismissal. How he was out — 'stumped Jones', 'bowled', 'caught Smith', 'lbw', 'run out', 'c & b', etc. — is entered in the HOW OUT column and the bowler responsible or involved is noted in the BOWLER slot. The batsman's final total, and the number of balls faced, are entered in a box opposite his name on the right of the page. Batsmen undefeated at the end of an innings are entered as 'not out' in the HOW OUT column — in *red ink*. Byes, leg-byes, wides and no-balls are entered on lines separately devoted to each category of sundries and found beneath the record of the batsmen's scores. The team's progressive total is registered on a grid further down the page, followed by the score at the fall of each wicket; the name of the batsman dismissed and of the not-out batsman occur lower down the page.

Bowlers' analyses are noted at the bottom of the sheet. Their names appear near the left of the page. To their right is a series of small printed boxes, each recording one over. A scoreless delivery is indicated by a dot. Runs taken off the bowler are indicated by figures from 1 to 6; boundaries are written in red. No-balls are logged as NB, byes as B, leg-byes as LB, and wides as W. Wickets are marked in the over square by a red X. The number of runs taken off a bowler's over is minuted in the bottom right-hand half of the over box; an over that yields no runs merits an M, for maiden over. At the far right of the bowling analysis, separate boxes tally the number of overs delivered, maidens bowled, runs conceded, wides, no-balls, wickets taken, and average number of runs per wicket.

Leading scorers also compile schematic line-diagrams that depict a batsman's scoring shots from both ends, their direction, and the number of runs scored off each. Because the lines drawn to represent the strokes radiate, like the spokes of a wheel, from the centre point of the pitch towards a circular boundary, the diagrams are known as 'wagonwheels'. They are often used on television to illustrate an innings. (See also *card*; *scoreline, short*; *scoring, line-by-line system*)

scoring, line-by-line system. A multi-column spreadsheet method of *scoring* invented by the former Australian and international scorer W. Ferguson ('Fergie') in the early 1900s. This system enables the scorer to trace the progress of the whole match with absolute precision, detailing every ball of every over bowled by every bowler from each end; it records which batsman faced which balls in every over, how many runs he scored off each ball, how many boundaries he hit, how many runs came from the over and what the scores of the team and the respective batsmen were at the beginning and end of the over.

The system works like an accountant's ledger. Each over is scored along one line across vertical columns drawn across the page. The first column records the number of the over within that innings. Subsequent columns detail the name of the bowler, the number of the over he is bowling, the end from which he bowls, the names of the batsmen and details of each ball they face and the runs they score, the number of balls received by each batsman in the over, the score at the end of the over, the time at the end of the over, the batsmen's scores after the over, the boundaries they hit, and the number of minutes they have been batting. The final column is wider and devoted to notes on the over: catches missed, off which ball, by whom, off which batsman, time lost to rain or bad light, and unusual occurrences.

This method has been used widely in first-class and Test cricket since 1905, by such renowned scorers as Roy Webber, Jack Price, Irving Rosenwater and Bill Frindall. It is usually employed in conjunction with the conventional scorebook method. (See also *scoreline, short*; *scorers*)

seam. Six parallel rows of coarse, protruding and waxed stitching which encircle and hold together the two halves of the leather casing of the *ball*. First-class balls are quartered. The two quarters of one half of the ball are sewn together by non-protruding seams which could be replicated throughout the stitching of the ball, making it completely smooth. But the seam joining the two halves is deliberately raised above the surface of the ball to help the bowler grip it, and to make it *swing, cut* or *spin*. The seam must consist of a stipulated number of *stitches* and its thread must be of a specified thickness. Thick thread and fewer stitches raise the seam abnormally above the ball's casing, allowing the bowler to spin, cut and swing the ball more. Sometimes in humid conditions the

Line-by-line scoring

Australia   v   New Zealand   at   Brisbane   on   Nov. 28, etc. 1980

Umpires R.C. Bailhache at Stanley St end; Umpire M.W. Johnson at Vulture St end

	BOWLERS						BATSMEN							INNINGS					
DAY	Stanley St.	E	Vulture St.	E	L of s/board			R of s/board			NOTES	Totals at End of Over					
TIME	NAME	O	NAME	O	NAME	b/r/c	4	NAME	b/r/c	4		O	Runs	W	L bat	R bat	Extras
					1st day — 28.11.1980												
11.00	Lillee	1			WRIGHT	7		EDGAR			nb	1	2	0	1	0	1
11.05			Pascoe	1		10			4		w	2	4	0	2	0	2
11.10	"	2				17					nb 4b	3	9	0	2	0	7
11.15			"	2					11		nb	4	10	0	2	0	8
11.20	"	3				23					M	5	10	0	-	-	-
11.23			"	3		27			13			6	13	0	4	1	-
11.28	"	4	"			29			17		1b	7	14	0	4	1	9
11.32			Lawson	1		33			19		M 1b	8	15	0	4	1	10
11.37	Pascoe	4							25		M 4b	9	19	0	4	1	14
11.41			"	2		39	1					10	23	0	8	1	-
11.44	"	5							31		M	11	23	0	-	-	-
11.48			"	3		46	2				w	12	30	0	14	1	15
11.55	Chappell	1							36		M w	13	31	0	14	1	16
11.59			Lillee	5		48			43		DRINKS at end of 13th over	14	35	0	14	3	18
12.06	"	2				52			45			15	38	0	15	5	-
12.09			"	6		54			49		M	16	39	0	15	5	19
12.12	"	3				60						17	44	0	20	5	-
12.15			"	7		66						18	46	0	22	5	-
12.18	"	4				63	3		53		50 at 12.20 (80m)	19	56	0	29	8	-
12.22			"	8		74					M	20	56	0	-	-	-
12.26	Pascoe	6				75			58	1		21	61	0	29	13	-
12.30			Lawson	4					65		w	22	64	0	29	15	20
12.35	"	7			McEWAN 1						M	23	64	1	0	15	-
12.41			"	5		2			70			24	67	1	0	18	-
12.45	"	8				5			75		nb	25	71	1	1	20	21
12.51			"	6				HOWARTH 4			M	26	71	2	1	0	-
12.58	Higgs	1				10	1		5			27	76	2	6	0	21
								Lunch: 1.00				120m		21m	6m	
1.41			Lillee	9	W	1					M	28	76	3	0	0	21
1.48	Pascoe	9				4			8		21b	29	79	3	0	1	23
1.52	"		"	10					14			30	82	3	0	4	-
1.57	"	10				10			15		nb	31	84	3	0	5	24
2.01			"	11					21		5-ball over.	32	88	3	0	9	-
2.06	"	11				16						33	90	3	2	9	-
2.10			"	12		19			25			34	94	3	2	12	25
2.15	Lawson	7							31	2	100 at 2.16 (155m)	35	102	3	2	20	-
2.19			Pascoe	12		24			32		Lillee back end of 36th.	36	105	3	5	20	-
2.23	"	8				28			35		nb	37	107	3	6	20	26
2.27			"	13		29			40			38	108	3	7	20	-
2.32	"	9				31			44		1b	39	113	3	11	20	27
2.36			"	14		37					DRINKS at end of 40th over	40	115	3	13	20	-
2.44	Higgs	2							50		M	41	115	3	-	-	-
2.46			Lillee	13		38			55	3		42	120	3	14	24	-
2.51	"	3				43	1		56			43	125	3	19	24	-

seam swells with moisture, enabling the swing-bowler to *move the ball* more. (See also *work on the ball*)

seam-up. Method of bowling in which the ball is released with the *seam* vertical, thus increasing the ball's chances of landing on the seam and deviating off the pitch.

seamer. A ball that *moves off the seam*.

seaming conditions. Weather and pitch conditions that assist the seam-bowler. A humid atmosphere helps the faster type of bowler to make the ball deviate off the seam after bounding; dampness in the air swells the stitching on the ball, making it protrude more and thus increasing the degree of the ball's movement off the uneven surface of the *seam*. A firm pitch with a covering of moist green grass also helps the seam-bowler, since it too increases the height of the seam, and the juiciness of the grass makes the ball skid unpredictably at various heights and in various directions. (See also *move the ball off the seam*)

seaming wicket. Alternative term for a *green wicket*: a pitch on which the ball deviates unpredictably off the seam.

send back. A batsman will sometimes *call for a run* which, in his partner's opinion, is impossible and will result in a *run-out*. In such instances, the dissenting batsman refuses the run and sends his partner back with a call of 'No' or 'Wait'.

series. Abbreviation for a series of *Test* matches, played between two national teams, one of which is the host or home side and the other the touring or visiting team. A series is played during the home team's season and consists of from one to six Tests. The team winning more matches is deemed the victor. If the two sides share an equal number of wins, the series is drawn. The series between England and Australia is known as the *Ashes*.

session. The period of play between two *intervals* — i.e. between the commencement of play and lunch, between lunch and tea, or between tea and stumps.

set a field. The action of a *captain*, in consultation with a bowler, in placing fieldsmen in the appropriate positions to catch out the batsmen and stop them scoring runs. The captain selects the apposite field placements according to the bowler's style of delivery and the strengths and weaknesses of the batsmen.

shake hands with the batsman at the other end. A batsman who advances a long way out of his crease in hitting the slow-bowler, or in *backing up* at the non-striker's end, is described as having ventured so far from safety that he seems intent on shaking hands with his partner at the other end. The description is usually applied to batsmen who have been *stumped* or *run out* by wide margins.

shake the head. An umpire shakes his head to convey or reinforce a negative response to an *appeal* for a batsman's dismissal.

shaving the wicket. The finishing trim applied to the playing surface. The grass is shaved very close to the soil, as if with a razor — the aim being to leave as little grass on the surface as possible. The wicket is usually shaved with a very sharp sickle, or with a *mower* whose blades are set as low as possible. (See also *curator*)

Sheffield Shield. The trophy awarded annually to the state team that wins the Australian domestic first-class competition. It is named after its donor, the Third Earl of Sheffield, who brought out the twelfth English team to tour Australia, captained by Dr W.G. Grace, in 1891/92. Upon his departure, Lord Sheffield gave the sum of £150 to the Australian Cricket Council for the advancement of the game in the colonies. The Council invested the money in a shield measuring 46 × 30 inches (117 × 76 cm) and bearing the Sheffield and the Australian coats of arms. The colonies of South Australia, New South Wales and Victoria competed for the Shield for the first time in 1892/93; they became states on federation in 1901, and in 1926/27, 1947/48 and 1977/78 were joined in the competition by Queensland, Western Australia and Tasmania respectively.

shine. The glossy finish to the *ball*, obtained by lacquering its leather casing. The better the sheen on a ball, the greater its capacity to *swing* through the air. For this reason, the bowler and fieldsmen polish the *new ball* at every available opportunity between deliveries to smooth the scuffing of the ball's leather surface caused by its coming into contact with the ground. Fieldsmen help retain the shine on the ball by throwing the ball on the full to the keeper or bowler, reducing the number of times it bounces. The outfield with a lush covering of grass also helps to retain the shine, for it is less abrasive to the surface of the ball. (See also *work on the ball*)

shirt. White garment covering the cricketer's chest, shoulders and arms. Formerly made of light *flannel*, it is now manufactured from lightweight, synthetic stretch material. Sleeves are generally short to obviate rolling them up — though only a generation ago short sleeves were frowned upon as not good form. In the 19th century, shirts were not completely white; different colours and designs were used to identify teams and individual players (much as in today's *limited-over* competitions). Thus H.H. Stephenson's eleven, which toured Australia in 1861, wore dove-grey shirts decorated with brown spots. Today's shirts are frequently adorned with logos of the team *sponsor* or the insignia of the relevant cricket association.

shock bowler. An extremely quick *fast-bowler* used by his captain in short spells to shock his opponents out with sheer speed.

shooter or creeper. A ball that keeps low after it bounces, shooting or creeping close to the turf. The early days of cricket saw bowlers who specialized in 'shooters'. When the winning of the toss meant that the fielding side could choose the match wicket, it was said of the *lob-bowler* 'Lumpy' Stevens (a great length-bowler with a passion for shooters who always sought to choose his ground, so that he might pitch on a downward slope): 'Honest Lumpy did allow, he ne'er could pitch but o'er a brow.' Shooters are also known as 'grubbers'.

short. A term applied to fielding positions and meaning closer than normal to the batsman. Thus, backward short-leg is the fielding position just behind square-leg and within a few metres of the striker. Short cover is a cover fieldsman who is nearer than usual to the bat. (See also *silly*)

short mid-wicket. Leg-side fieldsman, posted level with the midpoint of the pitch and about 5 metres from it; much closer to the bat than *mid-wicket*. Essentially a catching position, intended to accept chances popped up by the batsman in front of the wicket on the on-side, it is sometimes referred to as *forward short-leg*.

short of a length. That part of the pitch lying well outside the reach of the batsman stepping forward from the *batting crease*. The ball bouncing on this part of the wicket, approximately 3 metres in front of the batting crease, leaves no doubt in the batsman's mind about the necessity to step back to hit it. Playing back to strike the delivery gives the batsman more time to defend his stumps or hit the ball for runs. (See also *bowling containment*; *hit the pitch hard*)

short run. A run made by the batsmen but deemed incomplete (i.e. not run the full distance) because of failure to *ground the bat* behind the rear edge of the batting crease at one or both ends. When such an event takes place, either or both umpires shout and signal 'one short' and the run is not scored. If, however, one or both batsmen run one short on two different runs, 2 runs are deducted from the total coming from that shot.

In the 1930s Don Bradman, knowing that only one run was denied him if both batsmen ran one short on the same run, used this loophole to his advantage. When he batted towards the end of an innings with a tail-end batsman, he would try to hit the last ball of the over for three runs to retain the strike. Sometimes, however, the ground was too small or the field too well set to allow him three runs. He and his partner therefore deliberately ran their second run short: after passing each other in mid-wicket, they touched down their bats, well short of the batting crease, returned to the other end and then completed the third run! This tactic denied Bradman only one of his three runs and enabled him to keep the strike. It also forced the legislators to change the laws, denying any run to a batsman who deliberately made short runs for tactical advantage.

short single. One quickly taken run, usually the outcome of a batsman hitting a ball very slowly, short or wide of a fieldsman. Not to be confused with a *short run*.

short square-leg. Leg-side fieldsman placed a few metres from the bat on a line which is the extension of the *bowling crease*. This is a catching position designed to pick up opportunities popped up by the batsman playing defensively on the leg-side. Short square-leg is sometimes known as the *bat-pad fieldsman* because he catches the chance deflected from the inside edge of the bat on to the pad and into the air.

short-arm throw. See *sidearm throw*.

short-leg. A fieldsman stationed *close to the bat* on the leg-side, in front of, square of or behind the wicket. (See also *backward* and *forward short-leg*)

short-pitched delivery. A ball that bounces well outside the reach of a batsman stepping forward from the batting crease. *Short of a length*, it compels him to step back and play it off the back foot, employing shots that range from a *back-foot defensive stroke* to a *hook* or *cut*.

shoulder arms. Term that describes the action of a batsman in allowing a delivery to pass through to the keeper outside the off-stump by *padding up* and raising his bat high above his shoulders and head, in the manner of a soldier shouldering arms with his rifle. The raising of the bat ensures that there is no danger of a rising delivery jagging back into the batsman and striking the bat by accident for a catch behind.

shoulders. Top right and left corners of the rectangular face of the bat *blade*. The back of the blade tapers towards the shoulders, which are the thinnest parts of the bat. They are also the parts of the blade most easily broken. The ball that bounces unexpectedly and strikes one of the shoulders usually produces a catch to the fieldsmen close to the bat. Some manufacturers have produced blades with sloping rather than square shoulders to minimize the possibility of such catches. (See also *bat*)

shy at the stumps. To throw hard at the wicket in an attempt to effect a *run-out*. Sometimes fieldsmen gamble by shying at the stumps without there being a man at the wicket to take the return or a *back-up* fieldsman in position. This often occurs when the batsmen attempt to steal a *quick single* and a fieldsman swoops on the ball before his teammates have time to position themselves. If he hits the stumps, the result is a spectacular run-out; a miss can produce *overthrows*. On occasion, fieldsmen will impulsively shy at the stumps when there is clearly no chance of a run-out.

side-on. The position of the bowler's body in the ideal delivery stride. Also, the correct attitude adopted by a batsman in his stance and when playing straight-bat strokes. When the bowler is side-on in his *bowling action*, he appears to have jumped in his run-up and turned sideways by doing a feet-astride jump to face the stumps at the bowler's end. His leading shoulder, arm, side and leg point and move straight down the pitch towards the batsman's wicket. This maintains his forward momentum and greatly augments his ability to bowl a good line.

In an orthodox side-on batting *stance*, the toes of both feet are aligned with the middle-stump of the batsman's wicket or the guard he has taken. His chest faces *point*, and his left side, shoulder, arm, elbow and leg point towards the line of the approaching ball. From this position, when he moves forward to execute a vertical-bat shot he maintains the swing of his shoulder girdle, and therefore his arms and bat, on the same line as the approaching delivery. He therefore plays straight and not *across the line* of the ball and his chances of hitting it are greatly increased.

'Side-on' is a favourite catchphrase of coaches, largely because it eradicates one of the most common batting faults: playing across the line. Gerry Weigall, a player and coach with the Kent County Cricket Club, would stomp around Lord's in the last overs of his life, shouting entreaties to the batsmen at the crease to stay 'Sideways, sideways!': a technique he demonstrated with his neatly furled umbrella. When Gerry died in 1944, a kind obituarist penned his farewell: 'Rest in peace, Gerry Weigall. Sideways!'

sidearm throw. A fast roundarm throw used to *return* the ball to the keeper or bowler from fielding positions no more than 30 metres from the pitch. The fielder bends to retrieve the ball and, without standing up, draws back his arm level with his shoulder before flicking the ball in towards the stumps. Sometimes called a short-arm throw, it should never be used over long distances because it increases the chances of the fieldsman throwing out his arm. (See also *throw*)

sightscreen. A wooden, plastic or metal structure erected or placed on or outside the *boundary* behind the wicket at both ends to provide a colour contrast between the ball and its background and thus enable the batsman to see the ball more clearly. Sightscreens are essential on grounds ringed by 'bad' visual backgrounds such as trees or buildings, though some clubs with skyscapes as a setting for the bowler's arm do not need them. Where they are in evidence, they are recognized by the umpires and captains before the match. A ball passing underneath or striking the sightscreen after bouncing is deemed a four. If a boundary hit clears the sightscreen it is adjudged a six.

Club sightscreens are usually latticed wooden structures, approximately 5 or 6 metres square and 5 cm thick, raised and fixed on a wheeled chassis. They are painted white to provide a contrasting backdrop for the red ball. Their latticed construction makes them more wind-resistant and prevents them being blown over by a moderate breeze. The wheels facilitate movement along the boundary when different pitches are used. It is also necessary to move sightscreens in the course of a game, when right-handed and left-handed bowlers operate from the different positions of over and around the wicket, and in accordance with adjustments requested by the batsmen. The sightscreen attendant pushes the sightscreen a few metres to the right or left, so that the ball and the bowler's arm remain framed against it at the moment of delivery. To expedite such changes, the umpire often assists the batsman by holding up his arm so that the adjustment takes place while the bowler is walking back to his mark.

On some English first-class grounds, where cricket is a daily event in summer, authorities have created permanent sightscreens by painting walls and whole blocks of seating white and preventing spectators from sitting or moving in front of them. At Headingley in Leeds, spectators are permitted to sit behind the bowler's arm at the Kirkstall Lane end, but only their heads protrude above successive strata of whitewashed walls: it gives the impression of a shooting gallery — which is precisely the name given to that stand by the crowd on the terraces. Lord's at the pavilion end poses many problems of vision for the batsmen. The bricks of the members' pavilion are dark, the English weather is sometimes gloomy, the sightscreens are of pocket-handkerchief dimensions and the cramped accommodation makes it almost impossible for members to remain still for any length of time.

Modern technology has revolutionized sightscreens, constructing them of lightweight metal and plastic and making them easy to move. Changes in the game have also had their effect. With some *limited-over* games being played under lights, using a ball which is white or yellow for better visibility, sightscreens at some Australian grounds have turned black. These make the light-coloured ball stand out — though when it is in the hands of a black West Indian fast-bowler, its method of propulsion can be invisible!

signals. See *scorers*; *umpires' signals*.

silly. A term applied to fieldsmen stationed close to the batsman: *silly mid-off, silly mid-on, silly point, forward short-leg* and *bat-pad*. The term obviously originates in the fact that it is physically silly, sometimes suicidal, to field in such a position.

silly mid-off. A *close-to-the-bat* fielding position, slightly to the off-side and in front of the batsman, just a metre to the right of the pitch and only 3 metres from the bat. A *bat-pad* or *catching position* designed to pick up the opportunities popped up from tentative defensive strokes.

silly mid-on. A *close-to-the-bat* fielding position slightly to the leg-side and in front of the batsman. Silly mid-on is in line with the more distant *mid-on* and stands just off the cut wicket. His role is to pick up the short catches which the batsman fails to keep on the ground when driving or playing the defensive stroke towards mid-on. (See also *forward short-leg*)

silly point. A *point* fieldsman stationed 2 or 3 metres from the bat to take catches popped up off tentative defensive strokes, or deflected from the bat edge via the pad into the air.

single. One run.

sit on the bat handle. To fail to *back up*. The non-striking batsman who neglects to move up with the bowler and be prepared to embark on a run is said to be sitting on his bat handle.

sit on the splice. A batsman sits on the *splice* when he concentrates on defending his wicket for long periods of time, and does not attempt to play any strokes. Like a horseman sitting motionless on his mount, the defensive batsman seems to be sitting astride his bat, physically incapable of propelling it into any scoring motion.

sit up. Term applied to the movement of a delivery which rises sluggishly from a slow wicket, giving the batsman time to punish it.

sitter or dolly. An easy catch; a ball that just 'sits' in the air for the taking — or could virtually be taken sitting down! To miss a sitter or dolly is therefore particularly embarrassing for a fielder.

six. Short for six runs. By previous agreement between the captains of the two competing teams, 6 runs are normally awarded when the ball in play, usually from a batsman's hit, crosses, touches or is carried across the *boundary* without bouncing. A six is also known as a major boundary. In the event of a *lost ball*, 6 runs are awarded.

skipper. A familiar synonym for *captain*; derived from a Dutch word for a ship's captain.

slant the ball across the batsman. A bowler slants the ball across the batsman to vary the angle of his attack. He may bowl *over the wicket* from wide on the return crease, pushing the ball towards the leg-side and trying to hit the wicket or induce the batsman into giving a catch on the leg-side; or he may bowl *around the wicket*, angling for a catch on the off-side. Because the bowler slants the ball across the face of the wicket, and must pitch outside the line of the stumps to hit them, this method of attack rarely produces an lbw decision.

sledge. To attempt to distract an opposing player when he is batting, bowling or fielding, by engaging him in a diversionary, aggressive and usually abusive exchange of words. Sledging is theoretically illegal under the laws of cricket. Law 37 allows the umpire to give *out* any batsman who wilfully obstructs the opposite side by word or action; law 42 permits the intervention of the umpire if any member of the fielding side incommodes the striker by noise or action while he is receiving the ball. Nevertheless, the practice of sledging is widespread in all countries in all grades of cricket, and is regarded by some as part and parcel of the adult game. In the lexicon of sportsmanship, however, sledging downhill on the ill-mannered psychological discomfiture of an opponent must remain 'not cricket'.

The origin of the expression is uncertain, but it appears to have stemmed from a comment passed by former Australian captain Ian Chappell, on the subject of certain remarks made by one of his bowlers to an opposing batsman. The remarks were, according to Chappell, 'as subtle as a sledgehammer', and from that time comparable insults and behaviours have been subsumed under this graphic back-formation.

slip cordon. See *slips*.

slips. Fielding positions to the off-side of the batsman and behind his wicket. The distance of the slip fieldsmen behind the wicket may vary from 2 to 20 metres according to the speed of the bowler. The slips try to catch the batsman off balls deflected finely from the *outside edge* of the bat.

The fielding captain may station just one slip for his slow spin-bowlers. But sometimes he positions a slip cordon of as many as four for his faster bowlers when the ball is swinging or cutting away, or seaming off the wicket. The slip cordon forms an arc behind and to the right of the batsman. First slip stands a metre or two to the wicketkeeper's right — according to the amount of ground the keeper thinks he can cover — and slightly behind him. Second slip is two arm's lengths away from first and sometimes slightly closer to the batsman than first slip. Third and fourth slips are in similar positions in relation to second slip and each other. In order to ensure that an edged catch cannot pass between them, the slip fieldsmen stretch out their arms and touch hands to check that there is no penetrable space between them. When the ball is bowled they crouch with hands cupped in anticipation of a catch — the theory being that when a catch is edged in their direction, it is quicker and easier to stand up to take it than to stoop suddenly.

The slip fieldsmen are so called because they were originally positioned to prevent the batsman from playing the *cut* stroke to 'slip' the ball past the wicketkeeper. (See also *leg-slips*)

slogger. An uncultured batsman, lacking technique, who scores his runs by swinging wildly, or 'slogging', at the ball. Sometimes good batsmen have to slog when their side needs quick runs. (See also *agricultural stroke*)

sloggers' corner. The *deep mid-wicket* and *long-on* areas of a cricket field: the leg-side outfield to which a slogger naturally tends to hit the ball.

slow-bowler. A bowler who delivers the ball at slow speed, usually trying to dismiss a batsman with a combination of *spin* and *flight*. He is suited to *turning wickets* and the *old ball*, which he can grip securely, and gains advantages of flight by bowling into the breeze.

The Scottish writer Sir James Barrie, an enthusiastic cricketer, claimed to be the slowest bowler ever known. So slow, in fact, that if he did not like one of his deliveries after he had released it, he could go after it and bring it back!

soft hands. Hands that give or yield, in the act of catching or stopping the ball, cushioning its impact. Soft hands make for efficient catching and stopping, whereas hard, unyielding hands push the ball forward and out of the fieldsman's grasp. (See *catch*)

spectators. The largest crowd to attend one day of a cricket match was the 90 800 who crammed the Melbourne Cricket Ground on the second day of the Fifth Test between the West Indies and Australia in 1960/61. The World Series Cup game between the same two teams in 1983/84 was watched by 86 133 spectators. The greatest number to witness a Test was the 350 534 who attended the Third England vs Australia Test at the MCG in 1936/37; while the greatest number to see a Test series is calculated to be the 943 000 who went to the five games of that rubber. Unconfirmed figures estimate that more than 350 000 people saw England play India in the Fourth Test in Calcutta in 1981/82. It is also thought that more than 90 000 spectators saw the one-day international between India and Pakistan in Calcutta in 1986/87.

Crowds at cricket matches used to behave with decorum, acclaiming achievement with ripples of applause rather than mindless chants, and sipping tea rather than gulping beer. Nationalism and the mass hysteria of football partisanship have invaded cricket grounds in recent decades, bringing huge problems of hooliganism and crowd control. Riots and pitch invasions have occurred during Tests in places as far apart as Perth, Port-of-Spain, Calcutta and Karachi, provoked by alcohol, student unrest, racial tensions, politics or contested umpiring decisions. On grounds such as the MCG, police control is strict, coordinated by radio and rigidly and quickly applied before real trouble develops. Hot heads are often given time to cool off sitting on blocks of ice in the police paddy-wagon. In countries where enforcement is less rigid, it has not been unknown for umpires to receive death threats or be menaced with a revolver while waiting for the train home. (See also *barrack*; *Mexican wave*; *pavilion*; *stands*)

spell. A number of overs sent down by a bowler in one stint of bowling before he is rested. Paradoxically, to 'spell a bowler' means to rest him.

Spettigew dropper. Mythical delivery named after a fictional character. Spettigew was an imaginary club cricketer who perfected a ball that descended vertically on the bails. The phenomenal success of his bowling in club and county cricket gained him lightning promotion to the England side, and he won a Test match for his country. (See also *donkey drop*)

spikes. Pointed metal protrusions, screwed, hammered or set in the undersides of cricket *boots*. They enable players to move surely on damp, slippery or hard surfaces. Primitive spikes were merely nails, hammered into the leather soles and heels of boots. Modern spikes (also called 'sprigs') are secured under the sole of the boot in the manner of running spikes, or screwed into baseplates set in the sole. Spikes may be long or short, sharp or blunt, and can be changed according to conditions underfoot. Batsmen favour short sharp spikes for quick movement down the pitch to the slower bowlers; bowlers use longer spikes to gain purchase in the footholds worn in one spot on the bowling crease by the repeated pounding of bowlers' feet. Sometimes batsmen and fielders opt for shoes without spikes, relying on rippled rubber soles to provide an adequate grip on the turf.

spin. To make the ball revolve from right to left, left to right, forwards or backwards, at various angles, by twisting it with movements of the fingers and/or the wrist of the bowling hand. Spinning the ball makes it change direction after bouncing. The two main categories of spin-bowling are *wrist-spin* and *finger-spin*. There are various types of spinning deliveries: *leg-spinners, off-spinners, topspinners, backspinners (flippers)* and *wrong'uns* (googlies or bosies). Spinning also makes the ball *curve* uniformly or *drift* through the air before bouncing. Balls spinning from left to right (off-spin to the right-handed batsman) curve or drift from right to left; balls spinning from right to left (leg-spin to the right-hander) curve or drift from left to right.

spinning wicket. See *turning wicket*.

splice. The joint by which the handle of the *bat* is attached to the *blade*. The bottom of the handle ends in a narrow V-shaped tenon. A similar V-shaped mortise is cut in the middle of the top of the blade, and the handle tenon is wedged and glued into this mortise. The splice is usually covered by a label bearing the *maker's name* and insignia. (See also *sit on the splice*)

split field. In fielding, a split field is a divided *defensive field* placement, with five men on one side and four on the other. The division of fieldsmen (5/4 or 4/5) between off-side and leg-side suggests bowling inaccuracy and the bowlers' inability to direct their attack at one side of the wicket. Captains setting such fields adopt a defensive, each-way-bet attitude. (See also *bowl to one side of the wicket*; *packed field*)

In batting, to 'split the field' is to play a stroke which penetrates or 'splits' the cordon of fieldsmen positioned to restrict runs.

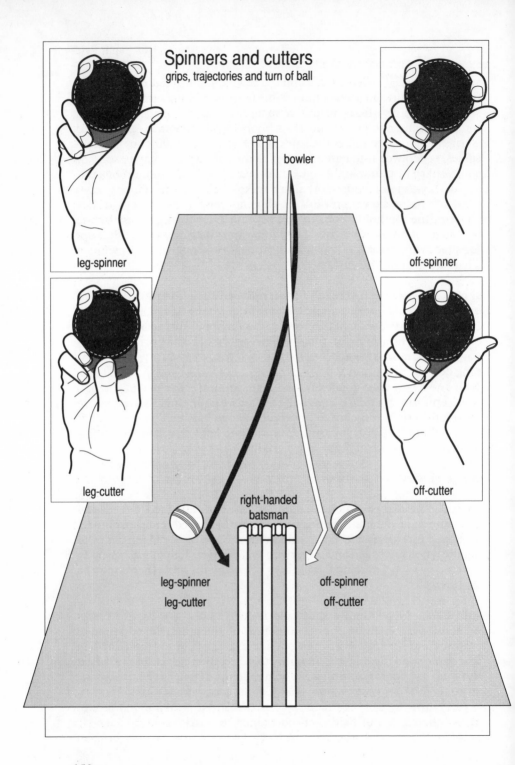

Spinners and cutters
grips, trajectories and turn of ball

bowler

leg-spinner

off-spinner

leg-cutter

off-cutter

right-handed batsman

leg-spinner
leg-cutter

off-spinner
off-cutter

sponsors. Supportive benefactors of cricket teams or competitions who donate money, equipment, clothing, goods and incentive prizes in return for advertising exposure on players' clothing and equipment, on the scoreboard, on fence hoardings, in cricket publications, and sometimes directly on television. The exposure of brandnames automatically entails media promotion for the company concerned when the teams and matches with which it is involved are televised. Major sponsors of national and first-class cricket are allocated corporate hospitality and viewing areas on grounds for the entertainment of their clients during important matches.

Sponsorship has been the lifeline of cricket in recent years: sponsors' support, particularly of *limited-over* cricket, has been the financial salvation of a fiscally foundering game. It is problematic, however, whether some sources of sponsorship can or should be maintained in the face of mounting popular and government opposition to the advertising of beer and cigarettes through the medium of sport.

sprigs. See *spikes.*

springs. Long thin strips of rubber or steel inserted between the glued cane components of the *bat* handle. The springs strengthen the handle and make it more flexible and resilient. Top-quality bats usually have three springs.

square. At right-angles to the line of the wicket or ball. A line drawn square of the batsman's wicket would join the *point* position to *square-leg*. A batsman who hits the ball square strikes it to those parts of the field. Fieldsmen stationed square of the wicket stand or move more towards point or square-leg than is usual in the position they occupy; for example, square-cover is the normal *cover* fielding position inclined towards point. Square fielding positions may be close to the batsman and pitch (short square-leg) or on the boundary (deep square-cover).

square (pitch area). A square or rectangular level area in the centre of the ground, from which the *pitches* are prepared. On large grounds, big squares give the *curator* a choice of a dozen wickets, allowing him to rotate his pitches day by day and week by week to prevent overuse and excessive wear. Some large grounds have more than one square. The objective always is a pitch which is level, will last, and will be fair to batsmen and the different types of bowlers.

The square is specifically constructed for its purpose; well-drained, with a base of permeable coarse stone, its soil becomes finer as it nears the surface. The topsoil is usually a black clay in Australia, and loam or marl in England. Squares are planted with both a couch grass to bind the subsoil, and a fine grass to give the surface a good finish. They are assiduously tended: watered, rolled, closely cut and maintained free of weeds.

In Australia, football is often played over a cricket square in the winter months, churning it into a morass of black mud and virtually necessitating its relaying before the cricket season. No winter sport dares to trespass on English squares; indeed, the person who as much as walks over a wet square incurs the groundsman's wrath.

square up. To move, while playing a stroke, into a position in which the chest faces directly down the wicket towards the bowler. This movement, sometimes referred to as *opening up* or playing chest-on, usually results in a *backlift towards third slip* and a swing of the bat *across the line* of the approaching ball towards the leg-side. The chances of the batsman hitting the delivery are reduced, particularly if the movement of the ball through the air and off the wicket is towards the off, i.e. in the opposite direction to that of the bat. (See also *side-on*)

square-cut. A stroke which deflects the ball on the off-side at right-angles (square of the wicket) towards the *point* position. It is a horizontal-bat stroke, usually off the back foot, to a delivery which is well wide of the off-stump and bounces above the level of the stumps to a height close to the batsman's waist. In the backlift the bat is raised behind the batsman's head as he steps *back and across* his wicket towards the off-side and into a position that brings him to an arm's length from the line of the ball. The batsman then hits down on the ball, using its pace to steer it away for runs. (See also *late-cut*)

square-drive. A front-foot or back-foot *drive* struck *square* of the wicket on the off-side towards *point*. It is played by opening the face of the bat and slicing the ball at right-angles to its flight. This involves the risk of playing *across the line* of the ball towards the off-side.

square-leg. Leg-side fieldsman, positioned in line with the *batting crease* and about 20 metres from the wicket. As a defensive fielder he stops any ball clipped or pushed off the batsman's toes square on the leg-side; he also attempts catches off balls lofted to that position.

One of the two *umpires* is usually stationed in this vicinity, and is known as the square-leg umpire.

stance. The way a batsman stands to receive a delivery and originate strokes. The orthodox stance involves the batsman taking up a *side-on* position at the *batting crease*. His feet are astride and parallel to the crease and his toes are directed towards point. His weight is evenly distributed between his two legs, which are relaxed and slightly bent at the knees. A right-handed batsman leads with his left shoulder, arm, elbow, side and leg down the pitch towards the anticipated line of the approaching delivery. His head is turned towards the bowler; head and eyes are level and steady.

In the unorthodox closed stance, the batsman prepares to receive the ball with his shoulder, arm, elbow, side and leg leading down the pitch towards mid-off rather than the anticipated line of the ball. Such a stance produces a *backlift towards fine-leg*, strong off-side strokes, but also a weakness on leg-stump. Each time a batsman plays forward from a closed stance, his leading leg automatically moves towards mid-off. To make contact with a full-length delivery moving in towards his leg-stump, he has to swing his bat in a semicircle around his front pad; this makes contact with the ball extremely unlikely. Australian opening batsman Kepler Wessels discovered the disadvantages of the closed stance against England's Bob Willis in 1982; the former South African was repeatedly bowled by what should have been innocuous half-volleys pitching on the leg-side blind spot created by his exaggeratedly closed stance.

The unorthodox open stance is the hallmark of a strong leg-side player. He awaits the ball with his body, chest and toes facing the bowler; his left leg is to the on-side of his right. Such a stance produces a *backlift towards third slip*, a tendency to hit *across the line* of the ball and a vulnerability against the delivery that swings, cuts, curves or spins away towards the off-side. It also places the batsman in danger when facing fast *bouncers*, since when he takes evasive action he ducks into rather than inside the line of the ball. Exponents of this stance have included England players Dennis Amiss and Peter Willey. (See also *take guard*)

stand. The joint and uninterrupted defiance of two batsmen in the face of opposing bowlers. A military term meaning defensive resistance after a series of reverses — hence a defensive *partnership*, often following a *collapse*. Stands, like partnerships, are measured in the number of runs they achieve or the number of minutes they occupy. In fact, 'stand' is often used as a loose synonym for 'partnership'.

stand back. The *wicketkeeper* stands back from the stumps to gather the deliveries of the faster bowlers which the batsman misses or allows to pass. The keeper stands back far enough to take the ball comfortably as it loses some of its speed and begins to drop, after bouncing and passing the batsman's wicket. He is expected to take snicked catches, and must run up to the wicket to take the throws from the fieldsmen every time the ball is hit into the *outfield*.

stand up to the stumps. The *wicketkeeper* stands up to the stumps to gather the deliveries of the slower bowlers which the batsman edges, misses or allows to pass. In this position the keeper always has the wicket within reach, so that, should the batsman leave his ground in attempting to hit the ball and missing it, he may put down the wicket and *stump* him. Standing up to the wicket, the keeper works in a semicircle behind the stumps, taking care never to contravene the laws by gathering the ball in front of the stumps — unless it has already hit the bat or the batsman's person.

stands. Elevated, covered seating accommodation, permanent or temporary, erected at vantage-points around cricket grounds to afford *spectators* a better view of a game in comfortable conditions. They are often multi-storeyed. On certain grounds specific stands are set aside for the sole use of club, association or county members — or for other privileged individuals. Other stands are open to the public at a price in excess of the general ground admission charge and seats in them may be reserved. Permanent stands on major grounds usually provide catering and bar facilities. Some grounds are surrounded by elevated land which affords passers-by a free view of proceedings on the oval. These areas are often dubbed the 'Scotsman's Stands'. (See also *pavilion*)

statistician. A chronicler of the numerical and factual details of cricket. His ambit is wider than that of the *scorer* since he enumerates, collates and records the achievements of individuals and teams in innings, matches, series, seasons and careers. All over the world individual statisticians and enthusiasts keep complete records of every first-class game played — either as a professional service to newspapers and journals or as a hobby. Some of them banded together to form the Society of Cricket Statisticians, with its headquarters in England. The scorer and record-keeper in the television and radio commentary positions is also referred to as the statistician.

steepler. A big hit and possible *catch* that reaches a great height — as high as a church steeple. Such catches are difficult to judge because they swirl around in the wind at high altitudes. Moreover, a steepler often descends out of the sun, and the time it spends in the air gives the fieldsman time to doubt his ability to take it. Humorists say that these are hard catches because they have snow on them when they come down!

sticky wicket. One of the most difficult *batting wickets* in cricket — hence the expression 'to be on a sticky wicket', denoting an extremely awkward situation. A wet wicket becomes 'sticky' when it dries quickly in the hot sun. A thin, dry crust forms on top of the sodden base. Sometimes this hard skin cracks and the edges of the cracks curl upwards. This is a convenient way of identifying a sticky wicket.

In England the *finger-spinner* exploits the 'sticky dog' best. His deliveries puncture the dry crust, then grip, *turn* and kick on the mud beneath. Spin and lift are spitefully wide, high and sudden, and there is little the batsman can do in self-defence. In tropical countries, captains generally rely on their quicker bowlers to wreak the damage, presumably because the faster-drying pitches take little away from the pace of the ball. Fast-bowlers under such conditions do not move the ball a long way sideways off the pitch, but their lift off the wicket is phenomenal.

stitches. The sewing that joins the quarters and halves of the exterior leather casing of a cricket *ball*. The six rows of coarse thread stitching, circling the ball completely and protruding from its surface, form the *seam*.

stock bowler. An extremely steady and accurate bowler, usually *medium-pace*, used by his captain to contain the scoring of the opposing batsmen and to frustrate them into unforced errors and dismissals.

stonewall. To *block* or defend the wicket, to the exclusion of every other consideration. A stonewalling batsman does not contemplate the possibility of attacking the bowling and scoring runs — he simply constructs a stone wall of defence in front of the stumps, and seeks only to survive. It is rumoured that the first stonewaller to make a tour of England came with the Roman team in AD 121/22 and was called Hadrian.

One of the most infamous stonewallers in cricket was the Nottinghamshire and England left-handed opener W.H. Scotton. In the Oval Test of 1886, Scotton crawled to 34 runs in three and three-quarter hours — and exasperated a *Punch* writer into penning these words:

> And the clock's slow hands go round.
> And you still keep up your sticks.
> But, oh, for the lift of a smiting hand,
> And the sound of a swipe for six.
>
> Block, block, block,
> At the foot of thy wickets, ah, do!
> But one hour of Grace or Walter Read
> Were worth a week of you!

straight. A hit or fielding position in line with the bowler or within an arc of a few degrees to his left or right. A batting stroke which is straight is hit back towards the bowler, or slightly to one side of or above him (see *straight-drive*). A fieldsman who is placed straight is posted closer to the line of the pitch than is normal for his position; thus, straight mid-on is to the bowler's right as he delivers the ball but closer to the pitch than the orthodox *mid-on*.

straight-bat strokes. Shots played with a vertical bat, off either the front or the back foot. Straight-bat strokes are offered in both defence and attack, when, because of the length and straightness of the delivery, the batsman may be bowled if he misses it. Consequently he seeks to cover as much of his wicket as possible with his bat in the execution of the shot. The area of the blade of the bat is about 550 square cm, and (when the bat is held vertically) can mask about one-third of the surface of the wicket, which measures approximately 1625 square cm. Straight-bat strokes include the *front-foot* and *back-foot defensive strokes* and the *drives*. (See also *cross-bat strokes*)

straight-drive. A front-foot or back-foot *drive* struck back towards the bowler's wicket. To get the ball past the bowler and score runs, this shot is often lofted over his head: a perfectly safe procedure, since fieldsmen are seldom placed behind the bowler to take catches. A hard straight-drive can compel the non-striking batsman to take sudden evasive action.

Charlie Macartney, Australian Test batsman of the World War I period, employed the straight-drive as a psychological weapon. 'The Governor-General' (as he was called) used to begin his innings by smashing fierce, head-high straight-drives back at the bowler — 'pour encourager les autres'.

stranded. The predicament of a batsman who finds himself far from the safety of his *batting crease* while trying to hit the ball or to run between the wickets. If a batsman jumps out of his crease to hit the ball but misses it, he may be stranded and *stumped*. If, in running between the wickets, a misunderstanding or *mix-up* occurs between the batsmen, one of them may find himself alone in the middle of the wicket, or at the same end as his partner: he is then far from home and the safety of his own ground when the wicketkeeper or a fieldsman takes off the bails to run him out. (See also *cross*; *run-out*)

strike. See *keep the strike*; *take strike*.

strike-rate. The frequency with which a bowler takes wickets and a batsman scores runs in a game of a specific competition. The benchmark adopted for the strike-rate is 100 balls. The fewer the balls required by a bowler to take a wicket, the more effective he is and the better his strike-rate. The greater the number of runs a batsman scores for every 100 deliveries he faces, the better his strike-rate. A batsman's strike-rate is calculated by dividing the number of balls faced into the number of runs scored and multiplying the result by 100. The calculation of the bowling strike-rate has become a complicated mathematical procedure which now measures other factors such as the bowler's economy. To have a strike-rate, a batsman must face and a bowler must bowl a minimum of 100 deliveries.

In some *limited-over* competitions, individuals who top the batting and bowling strike-rate tables receive substantial sponsored prizes.

striker. The batsman who hits or is about to hit a delivery. He is the batsman 'on strike'.

stroke. The act or result of hitting the ball with the bat. See *block*; *cut*; *defensive strokes*; *drive*; *hook*; *leg-glance*; *pull*; *sweep*.

stump-high. To get the ball stump-high is to make it bounce as high as the top of the wicket — i.e. 71.1cm. A fast-bowler's inability to do this indicates that the pitch is slow and lacks bounce. Such conditions favour batsmen, who are not then called on to make judgments about playing forward or back and can play off the front foot to practically every delivery.

stumped. A batsman is *out* stumped if, in receiving a fair ball, he is out of his batting crease, other than in attempting a run, and the wicket is put down by the wicketkeeper. A stumping commonly occurs when, in attempting to reach a delivery on the *full-toss* or *half-volley*, the batsman moves down the wicket out of his crease and, because of spin or his own misjudgment, misses the ball, which passes through to the waiting keeper.

Middlesex batsman R.W.V. 'Cock' Robins was well known for his impetuosity in *dancing down the wicket* to slow-bowlers. If he missed the ball, he never tried to regain his crease, but gave himself up as stumped and kept on walking to the pavilion. One day, while batting on an extremely wet wicket, he advanced to meet the spinner, missed, and as usual moved towards the exit. His partner, the waggish England batsman 'Patsy' Hendren, yelled 'Get back! The keeper's missed it!' Robins turned and dived back into his ground, full-length in the mud — only to be met by the amused glances of the close fielders and the stumper, who had long since removed the bails!

stumper. Old-fashioned term for the wicketkeeper.

157

stumps. The three wooden sticks which, together with the *bails*, make up the *wicket* at each end of the pitch. They are precision-fashioned, out of hardwood, and each stump stands 71.1cm high when implanted. The name derives from the fact that early cricketers used the stumps of trees as the bowler's target or wicket.

In Australia, 'stumps' is also used as an abbreviation for 'drawing stumps' or close of play.

substitute fieldsman. Fieldsman, usually the *twelfth man*, who acts for a player that has to leave the field because of illness or injury incurred during a game — or for some other reason wholly acceptable to the umpires and opposing captain. The latter cannot object to a substitute fieldsman, nor to the position in which he can field; but the substitute may not bowl or keep wicket, nor bat later.

A fieldsman leaving the field must obtain the consent of the umpire at the bowler's end. No substitute is allowed if a fieldsman leaves only to change his clothes. If a fieldsman leaves the field for more than 15 minutes, he is not permitted to bowl until he has been back for a period of playing time which equals that of his absence.

sucker hook. An obvious trap, set by a bowler to have a batsman caught *hooking* at *deep fine-leg*; it is so transparent that the batsman who falls into it is deemed a 'sucker'. The bowler positions two or three fieldsmen on the boundary between deep fine-leg and square-leg, before serving up a temptingly slow bouncer. Compulsive hookers automatically try to hook it; but they find it impossible to keep every stroke on the ground and are eventually caught. Australian opener Andrew Hilditch gained a reputation for himself as 'Botham's bunny' in the English summer of 1985, because of his failure to resist this hooking 'three-card trick'.

sundries. See *extras*.

super-sopper. A mechanized *roller*, used to remove surface water from the playing area after heavy rain. Also known as a whale, it resembles the normal heavy roller used for compacting the wicket; but its front and rear rollers are coated with absorbent sponge rubber. These rollers soak up water from the surface of the ground as they pass over it. At the rear of each roller is a wringing mechanism that squeezes the water from the absorbent sponge rubber and deposits it into a receptacle or trough, which is emptied into the *drains* as it becomes full. (See also *curator*; *drying the ground*)

Surrey cut. See *French cut*.

sweatbands. Bands of elasticized towelling, 5 mm to 8 mm wide, worn around the wrist or head to absorb perspiration rolling off the forehead or down the forearm. The cricketer is thus protected against salty sweat entering and irritating his eyes and impairing his vision. Sweatbands also prevent perspiration dampening the hands and making it difficult to grip the bat or ball; and are used to wipe sweat off the brow. They may be of any colour, but when a bowler wears a coloured sweatband around the wrist of his bowling hand, the batsman may request its removal to prevent being distracted by the flash of its colour in the swing of the bowling arm.

In India on one occasion, English players applied vaseline around their foreheads: they coated their eyebrows with the grease to prevent sweat flowing into their eyes. But the Indian players objected strenuously to this, claiming that the England bowlers were using the vaseline to impart *shine* to the ball and make it *swing* more.

sweater. Knitted woollen garment worn over the cricketer's shirt to keep him warm. Sweaters are usually white and may have long sleeves or be sleeveless, according to the desire of the player to keep his arms warm. On very cold days it is not uncommon for players to wear both a short- and a long-sleeved one. Sweaters maintain the body-warmth of a bowler after a spell, ensuring that he does not stiffen up. Batsmen often wear them, even on hot days, as extra defensive padding against the short-pitched delivery. Sweaters are usually banded with the player's team colours around the neckline and hem. Team badges and insignias are common on their fronts and *sponsors'* logos are also often found there. Invariably, cricket sweaters are knitted in cable-stitching; the reason for this tradition is a mystery.

sweep. A cross-bat, aggressive, leg-side stroke played against a slow-bowler's full-length delivery outside the line of the leg-stump and executed with the bat virtually sweeping the ground. The ball is also swept — towards or behind *square-leg*. As in all *cross-bat* shots, the striker lifts the bat back until it is in a horizontal position behind his head. He then advances his leading leg down the wicket, bending it and keeping it between the ball and the stumps as he lowers his rear knee to the ground. His head and eyes are just *inside the line* of the ball as he swings the bat down on the ball, keeping it parallel to the ground and scything the ball away towards square-leg.

English batsmen Denis Compton and Colin Cowdrey were masters of the sweep, placing it to perfection between the on-side fieldsmen and hitting it so late that they made contact with the ball after it had passed the body.

sweeper. Fieldsman who patrols the boundary, square on the off-side or leg-side, behind the *cover* or *mid-wicket* position. One of the fleetest members of the fielding side, usually blessed with a good throwing arm, he is the boundary rider who sweeps up the strokes that penetrate the inner ring of fieldsmen and seem certain to go for four. (See also *deep extra-cover; deep mid-wicket*)

swing. The movement of the ball in the air after release and before it bounces. Deviation from the off-side to the leg-side is *inswing*; movement from the leg-side to the off-side is *outswing*. The direction, degree and time at which swing occurs depend on the position of the *seam* at release, the seam's condition, the speed of the ball, and the smoothness or roughness of its respective hemispheres.

If the seam of the ball, when it is released, is vertical and pointing to the right towards fine-leg, it combines with the respective influences of its rough and smooth sides to produce less air-pressure on the right of the ball and inswing. If the seam is vertical and pointing to the left towards the slip fieldsmen, the result is less air-pressure on the left of the ball and outswing. The best speed at which swing occurs is approximately 110 km/h. A ball which initially travels down the pitch at more than this speed will not swing markedly; when it slows to the optimum pace for swing, it moves late in its flight, producing *late swing* — and embarrassment to the batsman if he is not able to adjust his stroke to the ball's late change in direction.

Experience says that the ball will move more in humid conditions; science does not. The probable explanation of this paradox is that the dampness in the atmosphere swells the stitching of the seam, magnifying its influence on the movement of the ball. A *new ball* at the beginning of an innings has a protruding seam, making it swing more; when it is older and the seam flatter, it moves less. The task of the opening batsmen is thus to see off the new ball, so that the later batsmen will find it easier to score off the older, flatter-seamed ball.

swinging conditions. Weather and wind conditions that assist the swing-bowler. A damp atmosphere raises the height of the *seam* and increases its aerodynamic influence on the movement of the ball; it also reduces the abrasive effects of the outfield and allows the bowler to retain the *shine* on the ball longer — and swing it for a greater number of overs. Wind direction can obviously assist the bowler. The breeze from the on-side helps the outswing bowler, whilst that from the off-side pushes the ball into the batsman. A bowler who bowls into the breeze can usually swing the ball both ways; one who has the wind at his back finds it difficult to move the ball in the air, since the ball is pushed through the air too quickly. (See also *swing*)

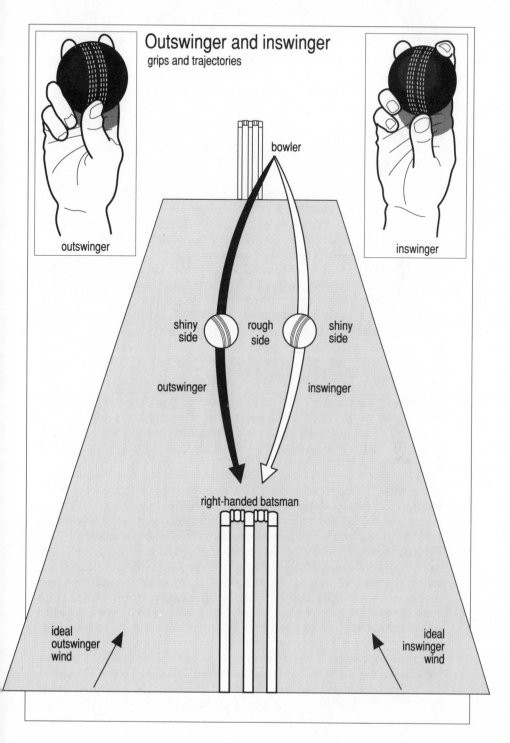

Outswinger and inswinger
grips and trajectories

outswinger

inswinger

bowler

shiny side

rough side

shiny side

outswinger

inswinger

right-handed batsman

ideal outswinger wind

ideal inswinger wind

t

tail-end Charlie. A *tail-ender*. In the slang of World War II, this was the name given to an aircraft's rear gunner, and to a plane or person bringing up the rear.

tail-ender. An unskilful batsman who bats at the tail or end of the *batting order*, from number 8 or 9 to number 11. He is also termed a *rabbit*, and no great expectations are held of his batting. Tail-end batsmen have performed some remarkable feats of achievement and non-achievement. By adept statistical manipulation the Australian touring side of England in 1953 ensured that tail-ender and bowler Bill Johnston ended the summer with a first-class *batting average* of over 100!

The record 10th-wicket partnership in first-class cricket was compiled by Alan Kippax and Hal Hooker of NSW, who scored a joint 307 against Victoria in 1928/29.

take a catch. To gather in, before it bounces, a ball hit into the air by a batsman, thus dismissing him. (See *catch*)

take a run for the throw. To take an additional run while an *outfielder*'s return is on its way back to the wicket, usually from a position near the boundary. This is a comparatively common procedure, since the time taken for a throw to travel approximately 100 metres is more than enough for batsmen to run 20.

take guard. A batsman takes guard to establish his normal preferred position in relation to the wicket he is defending and the bowler he is facing. He thus *knows where his off-stump is*, knows when he has to play at the ball to defend his stumps, and is aware when he can attack the ball. When he first goes to the wicket, he takes guard by placing the toe of his bat on the *batting crease* and holding it vertically in front of the wicket, asking the umpire to tell him when the middle-stump of the bowling wicket is aligned with both the bat and the stump of his choice (or a point between two stumps) of the batting wicket. Aligning the middle-stump at the bowler's end with the batsman's bat and his leg-stump is called 'leg-stump' or 'one-leg' guard; alignment with a point between his middle-stump and his leg-stump is called 'middle and leg' or 'two-leg' guard; alignment with his middle-stump is called 'centre', 'middle', 'centre to centre' or 'middle to middle' guard. Other guards, such as 'off-stump' or 'middle and off', are possible and permissible but rarely taken.

After a batsman has received guard from the umpire he usually makes a mark on or behind the batting crease with his boot sprigs or the toe of his bat, so that he will know, every time he takes his *stance*, where to place his bat to receive the ball.

take on a fieldsman. Term applied to the impudent action of a batsman in challenging a fieldsman who is about to gather the ball, return it to the keeper or bowler and run him out, before he can complete another risky run. The batsman relies on flustering his opponent and forcing him into a fielding error or an inaccurate throw.

take on the fielder's arm. To attempt to steal an extra run when a fieldsman, usually in the outfield, has already picked up the ball and is about to *return* it. The batsman risks being run out, but is relying on a weak or inaccurate throw from the fieldsman. Astute batsmen identify opposing fieldsmen with poor or weak arms and consequently are usually willing to challenge their returns.

take strike. To face the bowler. Before the *opening batsmen* go to the wicket, they decide who is going to take strike — i.e. who is going to face the first ball of the game. Each time a batsman is dismissed, the next man comes in and takes strike — unless the dismissal was a run-out in which the batsmen had crossed, in which case the next man in goes straight to the non-striker's end and the not-out batsman takes strike.

take the ball off the toes. To hit or *deflect* the ball off the line of the body, pads or toes. The policy of bowling a full length and attacking the leg-stump sometimes so cramps the batsman for space that he is unable to take a full swing at the ball. In such instances he can do no more than tuck his elbows close to the body, play close to the pads and hit the ball with a turn of the wrists to the leg-side for runs.

take the shine off the ball. A task of the *opening batsmen* which entails remaining at the wicket for a long period and continually hitting the ball into the ground, so than when and if the openers are dismissed, the *new ball* has lost its *shine*, has stopped swinging in the air, the opening fast-bowlers are tired, and much of the venom has been drained from the attack.

target. The number of runs or dismissals that a side must score or gain in order to win a match. In *limited-over* games, when the innings of the side batting second is curtailed by the weather, its target for victory is reassessed: the new target is calculated on the basis of the maximum number of overs possible before the expiration of the playing time, and the opposing team's highest possible total from that number of overs. Thus if a team, chasing 200 runs for victory in 50 overs, is prevented by *rain* from facing more than 35 overs, it can still win the match if its score, though less than 200, is greater than the aggregate of its opponents' 35 most productive overs. (See also *asking rate*; *run-rate*)

TCCB. See *administration*.

tea. Pause in play to allow players, officials and spectators to take tea. The tea *interval* is an institution in all grades of cricket. In games lasting a whole day or more, it takes place between the second and the third *session* of play and usually lasts for 20 minutes, although its start and duration can be varied according to the match and weather conditions, and by mutual agreement of the captains. In afternoon games, tea is taken in the interval between innings.

television commentary position. See *commentary-box end*.

Test. Short for Test match. A two-innings game played, usually over 5 days, between two representative national teams. The first Test was played between England and Australia on the Melbourne Cricket Ground on 15–19 March 1877, resulting in a win for Australia by 45 runs. Since that inaugural Test, more than 1100 'tests' of national cricketing strength have been played between teams representing England, Australia, the West Indies, India, Pakistan, South Africa, New Zealand and Sri Lanka. In the early 1990s, England, Australia and the West Indies led the winners' table, with over 230, 200 and 100 victories respectively. The term 'Test' was adoped by journalists in the 1880s. (See also *result*)

thick edge. A false stroke which, although not hit with the *meat of the bat*, still makes substantial contact with the ball, approximately 3 cm from the edge of the blade, and because of this 'thick' contact causes the ball to fly in an unintended direction. Thick edges often result in catches.

thigh-pad. Moulded pad of plastic, rubber or other material which is strapped or attached to the batsman's front leg beneath the trousers, above the *flap* of the *pad*. It protects the front of the leading leg against the delivery that rises above flap level. This type of protection is essential for batsmen who bowl: being hit on the thigh muscles of the front leg produces bruising and stiffness which can make a player strain a muscle when he begins to bowl.

thin edge. A stroke that makes only slight contact with the ball, approximately 10 mm from the edge of the blade of the bat, and because of this 'thin' contact causes the ball to fly in an unintended direction at an angle of 10° or less behind the wicket on either side. Thin edges may result in catches to the wicketkeeper, a slip or leg-slip.

third man. A fieldsman positioned on the boundary between *long-stop* and *point*. His role is to prevent deliveries deflected into this area by the batsman, either deliberately or off the edge of the bat, from reaching the boundary. Occasionally he is called upon to take catches off lofted edges or deflections.

three-card trick. An obvious trick or trap — usually one that has been set by a bowler.

through to the keeper. A delivery the batsman aims to hit but misses, or one he allows to pass without offering a shot, is said to go through to the keeper. The expression once caused a BBC commentator unintentionally to behead a batsman when, in reference to a fast-bowler's bouncer, he declared that the striker had 'ducked his head and it's gone through to the keeper'.

throw. See *return*; and also *backhand flip*; *cut-off relay return*; *flat throw*; *outfield throw*; *shy at the stumps*; *sidearm throw*; *underarm return*.

throwing or chucking. For a delivery to be fair it must be bowled not thrown. It must be delivered with the bowling arm straight throughout its swing. The bowler who throws straightens his arm, either wholly or partially, immediately before releasing the ball. He cuts the ball off the pitch more because he uses more wrist action. He also upsets the batsman's timing, since the striker swings his bat in the expectation of the bowling arm describing a complete arc before release of the ball. When that arc is curtailed, the ball arrives at the batting crease much earlier than expected. The umpire who is not entirely satisfied that the ball is bowled and not thrown should call and signal *no-ball*. (See also *bowling action*)

tickle. A *thin edge* sometimes resulting in a catch behind the wicket. To tickle is to edge finely.

tie. The *result* of match in which the scores of the two teams are equal at the conclusion of play and the side batting last has completed its innings.

timed out. If an incoming batsman wilfully takes more than 2 minutes to come in, he can be given *out* 'timed out' by the umpire at the bowler's end. The 2 minutes is timed from the moment the wicket falls until the new batsman steps on to the field of play. This comparatively new law was introduced into the 1980 code to prevent delaying tactics on the part of the batting side.

timekeeping. See *clock*.

tip and run. Children's game of cricket in which the batsman must run each time he hits the ball, no matter how gently or glancingly. In senior ranks, the term describes the tactics of batsmen who try to disconcert the fielding side by touching the ball and immediately running. Such a policy inevitably draws the fieldsmen closer to the pitch to save the *short single*, leaving gaps in the field through or over which the batsman can hit.

toecap. Front part of cricket footwear encasing the toes. Toecaps of conventional cricket *boots* are hardened by stiffeners: protection against the delivery that hits the batsman on the toe (see *sandshoe crusher*). Bowlers prefer soft toecaps, particularly for the leading foot in the delivery stride; this prevents injury to the toes and nails caused by friction with the hard toecap. Pace-bowlers who drag the rear foot in their delivery stride protect the toe of that boot with an external metal or synthetic toecap; this prevents the bowler wearing a hole in the leather toe of the boot.

togs. Cricket clothes.

Tom Mix. Rhyming slang for a *six*.

ton. Synonym for *century* or 100 runs. A batsman may score a ton; or an expensive bowler may have a ton against his name in the bowling analyses. Conservative cricket has not gone metric to the extent of adopting the term 'tonne'.

too far forward. One of an umpire's reasons for refusing to give a batsman out *lbw*. When a batsman, intending to hit the ball, steps forward well out of the *batting crease* with his front foot and is struck on the leading pad in front of his stumps, the umpire will turn down any subsequent lbw appeal. Under such circumstances, with the point of contact between pad and ball some 2 metres in front of the stumps, it would be pure conjecture to say that a delivery hitting the front pad would have carried on to hit them.

too high.   When an appeal for *lbw* is turned down because the ball was 'too high', this means that the ball hit the batsman too high on the pad and would have passed over the top of the stumps.

top edge.   The *outside edge* of the bat, when the batsman plays a *cross-bat stroke*; so called because the outside edge in that posture is the top edge of the bat, being the further from the ground. *Thin* top edges sometimes yield catches to the wicketkeeper or slip fieldsmen. *Thick* top edges usually fly above the heads of the slips or over the gloves of the keeper. The keeper's nightmare is to receive the ultimate in difficult catches: a thick deflection off the top edge while *standing up to the wicket* to a spinner; for this reason, good keepers await the ball with their gloves aligned with the top edge of the bat.

top-handed player.   A batsman whose top hand controls the swing of the bat in the execution of a stroke. This batsman *plays straight* and is usually a good off-side player.

topspinner.   A ball which is spun forward and turns neither from off nor from leg. The *finger-spin* bowler imparts topspin by pushing the first finger over the top of the ball towards the batsman. The *wrist-spin* bowler achieves the same result by thrusting the third finger forward over the top of the ball. The intention of the disguised delivery is to fool the batsman into thinking that the ball will turn, so that he makes allowance for the movement off the wicket and so misses the ball or edges it. In theory the topspinner should skid quickly towards the batsman's stumps after bouncing, because of its forward spin. But in fact it bounces more, since the bowler releases the ball earlier, giving it a looping flight. The higher trajectory of the ball makes it drop more steeply and bounce. One of the great dangers in playing the topspinner lies in not reaching the pitch of the ball before driving it. When this occurs, the resultant shot is inevitably lofted — often as a catch.

toss.   The spin of coin made by the home *captain* in the presence of the umpires and his rival skipper no later than 15 minutes before the beginning of the game. The visiting skipper calls 'heads' or 'tails' and, according to the result, is given or denied the choice of batting or bowling. The toss exercises a vital influence on the game, since it affords the side winning it the advantage of exploiting the nature and condition of the *wicket*. If, at the beginning of a match, the pitch is moist or *green*, the team bowling first will have the upper hand and will benefit later from the improvement of the surface as it dries out. Initially, a good firm pitch, with true and fast bounce, will favour the batting side, who will also have the advantage of exploiting a worn wicket when their opponents bat last. The accepted convention is to win the toss and bat first, since (theoretically) if the pitch has been well prepared it should favour batsmen when it is unworn. The age-old adage for captains is: 'If you win the toss, think about bowling, think again about bowling — then bat!'

It is said that the legendary Dr W.G. Grace, captain of England and Gloucestershire, rarely lost the toss. He always asked the opposing captain to spin the coin and invariably called 'the Lady'. Since the coins of his time bore the likeness of Britannia on one side and of Queen Victoria on the other, he was never wrong!

touch.   A very fine *edge*, the result usually being a catch to the wicket keeper.

track.   Familiar term for the *pitch*. Thus, a 'green track' is a green pitch or wicket.

trap.   To deceive and *dismiss* a batsman. A bowler may trap a batsman *lbw*, or he may trap him into hitting a catch to a fieldsman expressly positioned for a favourite, lofted stroke.

trimmer.   See *bail-trimmer*.

trinity.   The three *stumps* making up a wicket. To hit the trinity is to hit them with a delivery or throw.

triple-century.   A score of between 300 and 399 runs in a single innings. This feat is rare in first-class and Test cricket. The highest individual Test score is Sir Garfield Sobers's 365 not out against Pakistan at Kingston in 1957/58. Only a dozen-odd players have ever exceeded the 300 mark in a single Test innings.

trundler.   A mechanical and monotonous type of bowler who serves up deliveries of uniform *line and length*, but gives little thought to the subtleties of swing, curve, spin, cut, flight and variation in pace. The word is sometimes mistakenly used as a synonym for 'bowler'. To 'have a trundle' has also gained currency, and is synonymous with 'have a bowl'.

turn.   See *break*; *turning wicket*.

turn blind.   When a batsman, while running between the wickets, turns at the batting crease to embark on an additional run, he sometimes *grounds his bat* with his back to the ball and the fielding action. This fault, known as turning blind, prevents him from seeing any unexpected developments in the field and can lead to a *run-out*. (See also *change hands with the bat*)

turning (spinning) wicket. A pitch that, because of its characteristics, advantages the bowler who imparts *spin* or twist to the ball as he delivers it. These yielding or dusty wickets help the spinning ball to grip and change its original direction as it bounces. The speed of the ball's turn depends on the degree of dustiness or dampness of the pitch. There are three categories of turning wicket:

(1) The slow turner, an extremely wet wicket on which the ball spins only slowly and with little bounce. Normally batsmen have little difficulty in adjusting their strokes to such slow turn. But they experience problems when a *finger-spinner* pushes the ball quickly through the air, decreasing the degree of its deviation but hurrying the ball off the pitch. For the same reason, this is also the type of wicket that suits the medium-pace bowler of *cutters*.

(2) The *sticky wicket* or 'sticky dog', a sodden pitch drying quickly in the hot sun.

(3) The *crumbling wicket*, a worn pitch that provides quick bounce and turn for *wrist-spinners*.

If there is a lot of turn in a wicket, the spun ball deviates a long way after bouncing. If there is no turn in a 'plumb pitch', the ball *goes with the arm* after bouncing, in spite of the spin imparted to it.

tweaker. A slow ball which is spun by being tweaked with the fingers at the moment of delivery; also, the bowler who tweaks or spins the ball. A bowler who imparts a lot of spin to the ball is said to give it 'a big tweak'. The term is usually applied to *finger-spinners*.

twelfth man. Reserve player of a team. Selectors usually nominate twelve men in a side, leaving to the captain the responsibility of naming the final *eleven* just before the match. He determines the composition of his side, including an extra specialist fast-bowler or spinner or a supplementary batsman, according to the character of the wicket, the weather conditions and the strengths and weaknesses of the opposing team. The player omitted from the eleven becomes twelfth man. He may act as emergency or *substitute fieldsman* when a teammate has to leave the field through injury or some other unavoidable cause. On hot days he becomes the drink waiter, carrying cool *drinks* out to his teammates in the field. In the *dressing-room* he is the general factotum, catering to the creature comforts of the side: bringing meals for tired bowlers or batsmen who do not want to go to the dining-room, organizing the drying of clothes and the restudding of boots, etc.

Once a team has nominated its eleven, it may change its twelfth man at any stage of the match. In Test cricket, the man omitted from the national eleven may return to his state, province or county side for its next game, delegating his responsibilities to a junior player who is usually a specialist fieldsman; this person is then designated a substitute fieldsman.

u

umpires. Before the *toss*, two impartial umpires are appointed, one to each end of the wicket, to control the game according to the laws. Unless the *captains* approve, the umpires cannot be changed during the match.

Initially the umpires and captains jointly define the boundaries and any alterations to the numbers in the teams. The umpires then check that the wickets are correctly pitched, and that the equipment used is in strict accordance with the laws; they also indicate the *clock* to be used to time the game. On appeal they give a batsman *out* or not out, according to the ten possible methods of dismissal. They judge, signal and call *no-balls, dead balls, wides, short runs, byes, leg-byes*, and *boundaries*. They are the sole judges of fair and unfair play and of the fitness of the ground, the weather and the light. The umpires are in sole charge of a game; should they disagree about a decision, the status quo prevails. In a two-innings match they change ends after each team has batted once. They must consult with the *scorers* during and after a game, checking doubtful points and the correctness of the scores. They must report to the ground authority at least 30 minutes before the start of a day's play.

One umpire stands behind the bowler's wicket, as directed by the bowler and batsman. He must not impede the bowler or obstruct the batsman's view of the ball. His stance is comfortable. His head and eyes should be above and behind the middle-stump of the non-striker's wicket: the best position from which to judge possible *catches* behind the wicket and make *lbw* decisions. When the ball is struck, he moves to the side of the wicket to which it has travelled and stands in line with the *batting crease*. From there he can best return a verdict on *run-outs*, without impeding fieldsmen taking the return at the wicket or backing-up the throw.

The umpire at the batsman's end, also known as the square-leg umpire, stands in line with the batting crease, usually on the leg-side. If, however, his view of the line is obstructed by a fieldsman or a substitute runner, or if he finds it hard to see the crease because of light conditions (e.g. glare), he may move to the opposite side of the wicket, provided he first informs the fielding captain of his intention. He adjudicates on run-outs, *stumpings*, the *carry* of catches to fieldsmen such as the keeper and the slips, and (with the other umpire) on fair and unfair play.

In England, Test and other first-class matches are controlled by professional full-time umpires, usually former county players. Because of their extensive on-field experience they are widely regarded as the best in the world. In other countries, leading umpires at Test, province or state level are usually part-timers who owe their positions to their competence in club cricket and their knowledge of the laws. A few have played in the first-class game.

Umpires' behaviour and mannerisms around the cricketing world provide interesting contrasts. In England the 'ice-cream men' usually do not even bother going into the dressing-rooms to inform the teams that they are on the way to the middle; it is left to the *twelfth man* to convey that information to his captain. The 'cheats' stroll out to the pitch casually, totally out of step and sometimes metres apart. English touring teams are greatly diverted by the way Australian umpires enter their dressing-rooms to inform them officially that they are on their way to resume the game, before striding out to the pitch in two regimented columns at quick-march tempo, like uniformed Grenadier Guardsmen. (See also *referee*; *umpires' clothing and equipment*; *umpires, famous and amusing*; *umpires, origins of*; *umpires' signals*; *umpiring difficulties*)

umpires, famous and amusing. Theoretically, *umpires* should be faceless, unobtrusive individuals, handing out impartial decisions without becoming involved in the drama of human interaction which develops between two teams as a game progresses. Since, however, there are only two of them to control the match and govern the destinies of 22 players, they inevitably acquire an unwanted prominence: sometimes controversial because of their decisions, often funny because of their ability to see and express the humour in situations the involved combatants find deadly serious.

Famous early Australian umpires included R.W. Crockett and Jim Phillips, who gained notoriety in 1900 for no-balling the Lancashire fast-bowler Mold, for throwing. Between the wars, Frank Chester, a former Worcestershire player who lost an arm in France, was the doyen of English umpires. He was a law unto himself and no great lover of Australian players. After he had turned down a confident appeal for lbw from Lindwall in a Test of the 1948 series, he heard Lindy muttering an imprecation. 'What was that you said, Lindwall?' he demanded. 'Nothing, Mr Umpire,' replied the speedster. 'Just appealing to higher authority!'

Characters have abounded in the ranks of English county umpires. One such eccentric was Leicestershire fast-bowler and racing enthusiast Alec Skelding. He always ended the day's play by lifting the bails and declaring: 'And that, gentlemen, concludes the entertainment for to-day.' A close run-out decision often evoked the comment: 'A photo-finish, gennelm'n. But we haven't time to wait for the plates, so — not out!' It was he who, in his second year on the umpires' list, gave the Yorkshire bowler Horace Fisher his *hat-trick* of lbws against Somerset at Sheffield, saying, as he lifted his finger for the third time: 'As God is my judge, that's out!'

Television has brought universal recognition to England's Harold 'Dickie' Bird, the former Yorkshire and Leicestershire batsman who became a Test umpire in 1973. His flourishing signals, flat cap, short white coat, white shoes and dapper appearance made him instantly identifiable on television. Dickie always appeared to be in trouble: if a ball was struck back at the bowler, it usually contrived to hit him. He was once assaulted by an MCC member at Lord's for delaying the resumption of a Test!

The common attitude towards umpires was admirably epitomized by Australian Test arbiter Dick French, who described how, when he went to an official dinner, he was seated between an optometrist and a maker of artificial limbs! But whether he be as fiery-tempered as the aptly named Cec Pepper, or as laconic as his fellow Australian Bill Alley, every umpire has a great enthusiasm for the game. The most fanatical umpire in the annals of cricket was probably the man who insisted on being buried in his white umpire's coat. His family was instructed to erect above his grave a white granite tombstone in the shape of an index finger, raised in the signal of dismissal. The epitaph read: 'I'm out!'

umpires, origins of. Early cricket was conducted in an atmosphere of fair play which did not envisage disputes between sides and players. There was therefore no need for an arbiter of contested decisions. The text of the 1744 Laws suggests that any differences of opinion between the two teams necessitated a single 'odd man' to decide between contending parties: a man whose judgment was to be respected and accepted as final. The Middle English for such a person was 'noumpere', derived from the Old French *non* + *per* ('not a peer', 'not an equal'). By usage the 'n' was transferred to the indefinite article and 'an umpire' emerged.

Double-wicket cricket needed two umpires, and they were, judging from their dress in old prints, gentlemen of distinction. One stood at the bowler's end, while the other stationed himself at what would now be short-leg. Both umpires held a bat and 18th-century pre-match articles of conditions demanded that 'the batsmen, for every run they count, are to touch the umpire's stick'. (It is interesting to observe that when, in junior cricket, a member of the batting side substitutes for a missing square-leg umpire, he usually carries a bat.) It was not until the 1774 revision of the laws that the umpire at the bowler's end was required to give decisions on the leg-before-wicket rule.

It is untrue that 'umpire' is really derived from the French *non père* and signifies that the individual concerned does not have a father!

umpires' clothing and equipment. In the early days of the game, one recognized the umpire by the fact that he, like the batsmen, held a bat. The batsmen completed their runs by touching the bat of the umpire at the bowler's end or that of the umpire standing at what is now short-leg. Nowadays the umpire is more readily identified by his white coat. In England and New Zealand, this coat is long, and on cold days conceals other layers of insulation. In warmer climes such as Australia, a white jacket suffices; indeed, on extremely hot days umpires even dispense with their jackets and hand out their decisions in shirtsleeves.

The Australian umpire tends to be more uniform-conscious and *de rigueur* than his English counterpart. He always wears black trousers and the tie of his umpires' association, inevitably carries the badge of his state association or the Australian Cricket Board on his coat or shirt pocket, never fails to be shod in white shoes, and is without his white hat only when not acting in an official capacity. By contrast, English umpires indulge their own individual tastes in shoes, hats, shirts, trousers and ties. They would never march out abreast and in step to the centre of the ground as do the Australians; nor indeed do they signal in the same regimented fashion.

Though umpires differ in many respects from country to country, they do have one dependably uniform characteristic: they go on to the field equipped like quartermasters, carrying numerous items on their persons to expedite the conduct of the game. They have an accurate watch checked against the official ground clock; a counter to ensure that six balls are bowled in every over; and a light-meter to guarantee that equal visibility is afforded to each batting team. Naturally one of them carries a new ball to facilitate its taking when it becomes due; and often they will have a ball in roughly the same condition as the one being used, so that if the latter becomes damaged it can be replaced quickly. They also hold players' sweaters and caps. But they have much more. They carry spare shoelaces for players, bandaids for trivial cuts, scissors to snip broken fingernails or dangling threads off the ball. Sunburn block-out and zinc cream, vaseline, salt tablets and aspirin are not infrequently part of the chemist shops they maintain on their persons. They are a veritable treasure-trove of goods and equipment against any eventuality.

umpires' room. Separate changing-room for umpires. In club games umpires more often than not put on their white coats and hats in the same rooms as the teams. In first-class and Test matches, however, it is deemed desirable for umpires to remain apart from the teams, to avoid friction and unpleasant reactions to adverse decisions. After each *interval*, Australian umpires have to leave their room to go into the teams' changing-rooms to advise them that the game is about to resume.

umpires' signals. *Umpires* inform the *scorers* of events on the field by means of calls and visual signals. The scorers must acknowledge each signal before the game can proceed. The signals are as follows:
- Four-run boundary: waving the arm from side to side.
- Six-run boundary: raising both arms above the head.
- Bye: raising an open hand above the head.
- Dead ball: crossing and recrossing the wrists below the waist.
- Leg-bye: touching the raised knee with the hand.
- No-ball: extending one arm horizontally.
- Out: raising the index finger above the head. If the batsman is not out, the umpire calls 'Not out'.
- Short run: bending the arm upwards and touching the nearer shoulder with the tips of the fingers.
- Wide: extending both arms horizontally.
- Disregard the last signal: crossing the arms across the chest.

umpiring difficulties. Many of these stem from the amoral attitudes of players who seek to win at all costs, pursue a policy of non-cooperation towards *umpires* and stretch the laws to their limits. Questioning of decisions and abuse of umpires in junior cricket is common, making it increasingly difficult to recruit such officials. In senior ranks, some players make little or no attempt to help the umpires in their onerous task. Batsmen stand at the wicket, awaiting a decision, even though they know they have been caught; bowlers bowl intimidatory bouncers or full-tosses up to the maximum permissible; fielders *sledge* batsmen up to the brink of incommoding the striker.

Technical umpiring problems arise mainly in the areas of the *lbw* and *no-ball* laws. With the former, contentious issues centre mainly on the umpire's opinion as to where the ball pitched and whether it would have

Umpires' signals

no-ball

out

wide

short run

disregard last signal

bye

boundary 6

dead ball

leg-bye

boundary 4

175

gone on to hit the stumps. The difficulties of the front-foot no-ball law emanate not from its interpretation but from its consequences. A no-ball is called on the placement of the leading foot in relation to the batting crease, which necessitates the umpire keeping a close check on that foot. But since the grounding of the front foot in the bowling stride virtually coincides with the release of the ball, there is only a fraction of a second, while the ball is in flight, for the umpire to switch his attention from the bowler's front foot to the developments at the batsman's end; this can make it extremely hard for him to detect a catch behind the wicket or to rule on an lbw appeal.

unbeaten. Remaining *not out*; indicating that, at the termination of his side's innings, the batsman has not been beaten by the bowlers and dismissed. Thus, to score 'an unbeaten 75' is to be 75 not out at the end of an innings. (See also *red ink*)

undefeated. Remaining *not out*. (See also *unbeaten*)

underarm bowling. Projecting the ball at the batsman's wicket with a straight arm from below shoulder-level and generally alongside the legs. This was the only permissible way of bowling when cricket was first played, but it is never used in modern cricket. Simpson-Hayward was one of the last major underarm bowlers in England and he stopped bowling before World War I. Lob-bowling, as it is also called, was employed, however, on one notorious occasion, in the World Series Cup game between Australia and New Zealand in Melbourne in 1981. With New Zealand needing 6 runs off the last ball to tie the game, Australian captain Greg Chappell instructed his bowler and brother, Trevor, to bowl an underarm *grubber* along the ground: a tactic that effectively prevented the Kiwi batsman, McKechnie, from lofting the ball over the fence for the major boundary required. Since then, underarm bowling has been illegal in limited-over games.

underarm return. An underarm *throw* from a fieldsman to the wicket-keeper or to a man attending the bowler's wicket. The fieldsman stoops and picks up the ball with his throwing hand immediately in front of his rear foot; then, without rising, he steps forward towards the target wicket with his other foot. The return is carried out with the throwing arm pointing vertically towards the ground and almost brushing the leading leg. To ensure that the ball rises in its flight to the top of the stumps, the throwing elbow and wrist remain straight and rigid.

undercut. To cut the first finger of the bowling hand underneath the ball at the moment of delivery, imparting quick backspin and sidespin.

This is a technique used by *finger-spin* bowlers to make the ball skid on to the batsman in the manner of the wrist-spun *flipper*. Usually bowled with a slightly roundarm action, with less flight and at a faster pace, the undercut delivery hurries on to the batsman, creating problems of timing, especially if he is playing a cross-bat stroke.

unorthodox. Term denoting an unusual and more difficult way of performing a cricket skill. A batsman with an open, chest-on *stance* and technique stands and plays his stroke from a front-on position, minimizing his chances of lifting his bat back, and playing, straight. Unorthodox bowlers *bowl off the wrong foot* or devise idiosyncratic methods of swinging, cutting or spinning the ball. Unorthodox techniques sometimes give their exponents an advantage, enabling them to do certain things better than the more conventional players. A bowler who delivers off the wrong foot, for instance, can usually move his *inswinger* and *leg-cutter* far more than the orthodox bowler.

unsighted. An umpire, batsman, fieldsman or bowler is unsighted when his line of vision is blocked. The umpire at the bowler's wicket may be unsighted and unable to give an *lbw* or *caught-behind* decision if the bowler runs in front of him in his follow-through. The square-leg umpire may be unsighted when a fieldsman misfields and subsequently obscures the ball with his body: an occurrence which may lead to a batsman attempting an unrealistic run and being run out. A fieldsman or bowler may be unsighted by another player running across his line of vision, between him and the ball.

up saving one. The placement of a fieldsman who is instructed by his captain to come closer to the batsman in order to prevent his scoring a single by pushing the ball gently in the fielder's direction.

uppish. Slightly lofted into the air. The term describes a stroke which, while not offering a catch to a fieldsman, hits the ball into the air over a short distance.

use the feet. See *dance down the wicket*.

variation in pace. A subtly disguised change in the speed at which a ball is delivered. A fast-bowler usually varies his pace by bowling a slower ball, and a spin-bowler by producing a quicker delivery — both without any perceptible change in the action. The fast-bowler's slower ball results from the speedy removal of the hand from behind the ball at the moment of release, generally by means of bowling an *off-cutter* or *off-spinner*; thus the speed of the arm's movement is maintained, but the bowler's weight, power and effort pass around the side of the ball. The slower ball aims to evince a premature stroke from the batsman — to make him miss the ball completely or scoop it into the air for a catch. A bowler's faster ball should, ideally, be the product of a late and un-detectable use of the wrist rather than an obviously quicker movement of the arm. If the faster ball is pitched well up to the bat, preferably as a *yorker*, the batsman will be far too late in his stroke and may be bowled.

The Australian fast-bowler Fred Spofforth ('The Demon') was fa-mous for his wide range of pace and for what he termed his 'half-ball': a delivery in which he held half of the ball between forefinger and thumb and bowled with his hand passing around the right side of the ball. This produced a 'hanging' delivery — a startling contrast to the devastating and lightning-fast yorker that yielded Spofforth so many victims.

vice-captain. The *captain*'s deputy, who substitutes for him when he has to leave the field or is not available.

wagging tail. A situation in which *tail-end* batsmen score unexpected runs. The tail is then said to have 'wagged' — the way a happy dog's tail wags.

wagonwheel. See *scoring*.

walk. To give oneself *out* by walking from the wicket without waiting for the umpire's decision. Most batsmen walk when they are bowled or obviously caught, since there is little argument about their being out. No-one, however, surrenders when there may be doubt about the dis-missal. Appeals for close *run-outs*, *lbw* or disputed catches by the wicket-keeper or fieldsmen always find the batsman still at the crease awaiting the decision of the arbiter.

Some batsmen always await the umpire's decision, even though they are clearly out. To do less, they argue, would reflect adversely on the authority of the umpire. Moreover, they say, by staying at the wicket they establish a natural balance between wrong decisions in their favour and against them. Other batsmen always walk — even when only they know that they have edged a catch to the keeper. To do otherwise, they maintain, is unsportsmanlike and, in the case of professional cricket, unethical. The pro- and anti-walking camps are clearly defined and uncompromising: batsmen become known as walkers or non-walkers. Miscarriages of justice may occur when psychological stress at a crucial stage of a vital match causes a walker suddenly to change his policy!

walking in with the bowler. As the bowler runs in to bowl, all the fieldsmen in his side except those in *catching positions* move in with him towards the centre of the pitch. This ensures that they are in motion at the moment the ball is struck. They are thus able to approach, stop and retrieve it more quickly, by the simple — but sometimes unnecessary — expedient of a change in direction. Moving towards the pitch also makes it easier for the *cover* and *mid-wicket* fieldsmen to cut off the short single hit towards mid-off or mid-on.

warm-up. Players warm up by carrying out a series of gentle exercises for approximately 10 minutes before a game. The aim of these sub-maximal exercise routines is to raise the core temperature of the body and increase the flexibility of the muscles without tiring the athlete. The warm-up should be followed by stretching exercises to increase the range of movement in the limbs. Warm-ups eliminate stiffness in the muscles and prevent avoidable injuries.

warnings. First and second warnings are official reprimands issued by the umpires for violations of law 42 governing fair and unfair play. This law prevents the bowling of fast *short-pitched balls* and head-high *full-tosses*, time-wasting, and damaging of the pitch. (The warning procedure is outlined under *intimidatory bowling*.) Umpires frequently issue unofficial warnings to batsmen and bowlers when they appear likely to infringe a law. This occurs when bowlers come increasingly closer to bowling a *no-ball* or *running on the wicket*, when close fieldsmen trespass on to the cut wicket, when bowlers try to change the condition of the ball by lifting the *seam*, or when players incommode or obstruct opponents. (See also *penalties*)

water points. Recessed taps in the ground, usually found at the corners of big cricket *squares*, and covered by wooden lids to prevent players stumbling into them. They provide the water for the sprinkler systems around the ground and not infrequently are used by the fielding side as repositories for protective *helmets* when the close-in fieldsmen are not using them. In this way the fieldsmen avoid conceding the penalty of 5 runs incurred whenever a ball is stopped by an item of their equipment, such as a helmet lying on the ground.

watering the wicket. Sprinkling or dousing the playing surface with water. Watering a pitch binds the soil and promotes the growth of grass, and this is crucial in matches that extend over five days in warm climates. In these conditions enough water must soak down into the subsoil to compensate for the surface evaporation under a fierce sun. If insufficient water is applied, the pitch dries out too quickly, cracks, and disintegrates into a *dustbowl*. If the wicket is watered too heavily — or, importantly, too late — it will be too damp at the beginning of the game, giving an unfair advantage to the fast-bowlers of the side bowling first. No watering of the wicket is allowed during a game.

Usually in tropical countries, a Test wicket is watered heavily two or three days before the game is scheduled to begin. Then the *curator* can only pray that the weather will be fine in the days before the match, so that the pitch can firm up into a good dry stretch of turf. (See also *moisture*)

watermarks. Unimportant blemishes in a bat *blade*, caused by an excess of water trapped in the trunk of the willow tree from which the bat is made. Such marks are hardly noticeable because of the process of bleaching the wood from which the blades are turned.

weatherwatch station. Gimmick introduced in recent years on Australian television and consisting of a large visual display board incorporating a thermometer, barometer, and gauges for wind, humidity and ground moisture. These instruments are shown on the television screen, to give the viewer an idea of how hot it is on the ground, whether it will rain, and the direction and force of the wind — plus two pieces of esoteric information called 'ground moisture content' and 'player's comfort'!

well set. The condition of a batsman who has been at the wicket long enough to feel comfortable and ready to attack the bowling.

whale. See *super-sopper*.

wicket. Two wickets, each 22.86 cm wide and consisting of three wooden *stumps* with wooden *bails* on top, are used in cricket. The wickets are pitched opposite and parallel to each other in the middle of each *bowling crease*, with a distance of 20.12 metres between the centres of the middle-stumps. Each stump is 71.1 cm high and they are of a uniform thickness sufficient to prevent the ball passing between them. The tops of the stumps are domed and grooved for the placement of the bails.

The bowler, fieldsman and wicketkeeper aim to put down the wicket to dismiss the batsman, *bowled*, *stumped* or *run out*. A batsman may bring about his own downfall by hitting or kicking down his wicket in the execution of a stroke or in setting off to run. The *wicket is down* if the ball, or the striker's bat or person, completely removes either or both bails from the top of the stumps.

The word 'wicket' is derived from the old Saxon word *wican* ('to offer or yield the way through') applied to the movable sheep hurdle, consisting of two uprights and a crossbar, which was often used as a target in primitive cricket. The word is also commonly used to denote the pitch on which the game is played — see *pitch or wicket*; *wicket (playing surface)*.

wicket (playing surface). See *pitch or wicket*; and also *batting wicket*; *cracked wicket*; *crumbling (dusty) wicket*; *dead wicket*; *featherbed wicket*; *five-day wicket*; *green wicket*; *one-day wicket*; *seaming wicket*; *sticky wicket*; *turning (spinning) wicket*.

wicket is down. For the wicket to be down, it is sufficient for the ball, the striker's bat or his person or equipment to remove either *bail* from the top of the *stumps*. A member of the fielding side may put the wicket down by removing one bail with the hand or arm holding the ball. If both bails have already been knocked off, a fieldsman may subsequently put down the wicket by knocking or pulling one stump out of the ground with the hand holding the ball — or by replacing the bails and then knocking them off! (See also *out*)

wicket maiden. An *over* during which a bowler captures a wicket without conceding a run off the bat.

wicketkeeper. The fieldsman who attends the wicket at which the bowler is directing his attack. His duties include: (1) stopping balls that the batsman misses or refuses to hit; (2) accepting deflected catches off the edge of the bat; (3) stumping the batsman (putting down his wicket) when the batsman leaves his crease and misses the ball; (4) running out the batsman by putting down his wicket when he is out of his ground attempting a run and a fieldsman returns the ball; (5) taking fieldsmen's returns over the stumps, or running to the stumps to do so, to prevent or restrict the scoring of runs. A keeper's duties also include maintenance of the team's morale, and ensuring that all the fieldsmen keep on their toes.

The wicketkeeper takes up his stance and prepares to receive the ball by crouching just outside the off-stump. From that position he has a clear sight of the bowler in his run-up and action, and of the ball in its flight. He *stands up* to the stumps for the slower bowlers and *stands back* for the faster ones. He is aware of how far and how quickly he is able to move to his left or right to take balls sent down by the faster bowlers. He expects to take deflected catches within this arc and he does not permit any fieldsman, *slip* or *leg-slip*, to trespass on his domain.

The nature of the keeper's task necessitates his wearing protective equipment. This includes pads (sometimes abbreviated to increase mobility), padded *gloves*, and a protective *box*.

wide. A ball delivered by the bowler so wide or so high over the wicket that, in the opinion of the umpire, it passes out of the reach of the batsman standing in his normal guard position, and so prevents him from playing a stroke. The batting side is awarded a bonus run for the delivery. A batsman can be *out* from such a ball only if he hits his own wicket, is stumped, obstructs the field or handles the ball. The umpire signals a wide to the scorers by extending both arms at shoulder-level. The award of a wide may be revoked if the batsman moves from his guard position and comes within reach of the ball or hits it. A wide does not count in the over and an *extra* ball is bowled for it.

In *limited-over* cricket the definition of a wide ball is harder on the bowler but is left more to the discretion of the umpire, who has to determine whether a bowler is deliberately pursuing the negative policy of bowling wide to prevent the batsman from scoring. Accordingly, instructions are laid down that the umpire shall call and signal wide if the ball passes sufficiently wide of the batsman to make it impossible for him to play a normal cricket stroke. Even the *bouncer* is penalized in one-day cricket as a negative ploy designed to prevent run-scoring: some rules state that if the ball passes over head-height of the striker standing upright at the crease, the umpire shall call and signal wide. Certain competitions provide for wides to be designated *no-balls*, to reduce the number of ways the striker can be dismissed and to afford him a free hit at the delivery.

willow. *Bats* are manufactured from clefts, or wedge-shaped pieces, of open-barked willow wood. The bat is often referred to as the 'willow', and the sound of leather hitting willow is the 'sound of cricket'.

win by an innings. In a two-innings game, when one team not only wins *outright* but scores more runs in one completed innings than the opposing side does in its two completed innings, the side batting only once wins by the margin of an innings. (See also *result*)

Windies. Abbreviation, much in vogue in the media, for the West Indies team. A term disliked by the West Indians themselves because of its connotation of cowardice.

Wisden. Short for *Wisden Cricketers' Almanack*, a magazine founded by the former Sussex cricketer John Wisden in 1864 and produced annually ever since. The publication, now a fat but compact book, records cricketing activities and views from around the world each year. All noteworthy achievements of cricketers since the inception of the game are to be found in this 'Cricketer's Bible', whose pages abound in such eclectic items as families in Test cricket, the longest hit, the youngest and oldest players, matches of longest duration, the most balls bowled in a Test, the dates of the formation of clubs, and many, many other obscure, important and (to the enthusiast) fascinating facts. *Wisden* is recognized as the authoritative repository of the game's records and statistics. Notable editors have included the familial associations of C.F. and Sydney Pardon and Hubert and Norman Preston.

Wisden Trophy. The trophy awarded to the winners of a Test series between England and the West Indies. It was inaugurated in 1963 and donated by the publishers of the *Wisden Cricketer's Almanack*, to commemorate the hundredth birthday of the 'Cricketer's Bible'.

women's cricket. Matches between women's sides were reported as early as 1745 in the *Reading Mercury*. Sides have played under various titles, such as 'Married versus Single Ladies' and 'Ladies Light with Virtue against Those Heavy with Sin'. Selection for the latter game must have been a stormy affair! In 1926 the England Women's Cricket Association was founded. Representative games between regional teams from the North, South, East and West emerged in 1929 with the avowed aim of producing a national side which would tour Australia at the earliest possible date.

In Australia, the first public women's cricket match was played in 1874. The Victorian Ladies' Cricket Association organized various tours between itself and sides from Tasmania and New South Wales in the early 1900s. The Australian Women's Cricket Council was formed in 1931, the year that saw the inaugural and now annual interstate cricket carnival.

International women's cricket is now well established. England first toured Australia in 1933/34, and an Australian team first visited England in 1937. Women are now represented in the cricketing world by sides from England, Australia, New Zealand, South Africa, Holland, the West Indies, India, Ireland, Denmark, Canada, and Papua New Guinea. A World Cup is regularly competed for.

England has produced some notable women cricketers: Betty Archdale, wicketkeeper Betty Snowball, Molly Hide, Mollie Flaherty, and Rachel Heyhoe-Flint. It is said that when the former England and Worcestershire fast-bowler Reg Perks was asked in the 1950s who was the finest slow spin-bowler in his county, he unhesitatingly nominated Molly Hide! Australia's famous women cricketers have included Rosalie Deane (the first woman to be recorded in *Wisden* as having scored two centuries in one match), Betty Wilson, Peggy Antonio and Sharon Tredrea.

It should not be forgotten that it was a woman, Christina Willes, who introduced her brother and the game to the style of *overarm bowling* which John Willes later pioneered in the male domain.

work on the ball. To polish the ball (see *shine*) or *raise the seam* so that the bowler can make it swing through the air or seam off the wicket more. It is illegal to raise the seam to increase deviation off the pitch — but it is still done, usually under the pretence of cleaning it with the fingernails. To enhance shine is legal, and usually involves moistening the ball with sweat or saliva and then rubbing it vigorously on the cloth of the trousers or shirt. By agreement, the bowlers work on only one side of the ball, concentrating twice the work on half the surface area. Fielders are now also permitted to work on the ball. But it is illegal for anyone to use any polishing substances on it.

work the ball. In batting, to use the angle of a delivery, its trajectory and its movement through the air and off the pitch, to place the ball into the gaps between the fieldsmen and score runs. In bowling, to employ the wrist and fingers vigorously to impart *cut* or *spin* to the ball.

World Cup. International *limited-over* competition inaugurated in 1975 and contested every 4 years by all Test-playing nations plus one Associated International Cricket Council member side, chosen by a preliminary elimination series. Games are restricted to 60 overs. A round-robin of matches in two pools, each of four teams, selects the four semifinalists. The ultimate winner then knocks out its opponents in the semifinals and final. Provision is made for games to extend over two days should the weather intervene, and strict regulations restrict the number of players available for selection in each side.

The World Cup encompasses three weeks of intense competition in various venues, involves a great deal of travelling, and attracts immense spectator interest and national sporting kudos. When India won the final in 1983, the team returned home as national heroes. Presents, which included houses, were showered upon the victors!

worth a shout. Epithet applied to the possible dismissal of a batsman and meaning 'worth appealing for'. The umpire is called upon to decide whether or not the batsman is out; either way, the decision is close enough to have been worth the shout. (See also *appeal*)

wrap up the tail. To dismiss quickly the batsmen who go to the crease in the lower positions in the *batting order* — i.e. the tail, which is usually defined as the eighth and later batsmen to go in to bat.

wrist-spin. Sometimes known as 'over-the-wrist spin' or 'wrist leg-spin', wrist-spin is the twist imparted to the ball by a slow-bowler using a full anticlockwise rotation of the wrist and fingers of the bowling hand. This wrist rotation differentiates wrist-spin from *finger-spin*, in which the ball is spun with the fingers. Wrist-spin turns the ball a long way after it bounces — in the case of the right-handed bowler usually from leg to off. The bowler makes the ball rotate rapidly by twisting his wrist first inwards towards his body, then downwards towards the ground and finally outwards away from his body: the bowling hand arrives at the same position as the hand of a swimmer doing the Australian crawl and preparing to scoop the water behind his body. As he lets the ball go, the wrist-spinner imparts spin by flicking the third finger of his bowling hand forward and over the ball in the direction he wants the ball to turn: towards slip for leg-spin, towards the batsman for topspin, and towards leg-slip for the wrong'un.

Because he makes full use of both the wrist and the fingers of the bowling hand, the wrist-spinner turns the ball more than any other type of slow-bowler. But because there are more 'moving parts' in his spinning action, he needs experience and constant practice to be accurate. The ball is released before the hand reaches the highest point of the action, and this gives his deliveries the disadvantage of a higher trajectory than the finger-spinner's. Consequently they are slower through the air, allowing the batsman more time to use his feet to reach the pitch of the ball. Sluggish or wet pitches such as those found in England also penalize wrist-spinners, since their deliveries come off the wicket very slowly and do not bounce very much. On the hard pitches of hot countries, however, over-the-wrist bowlers are in their element, flighting the ball and eliciting the bounce that produces midfield and outfield catches, and turning the ball when the pitch becomes worn. No self-respecting Test team should dream of going into a match without a leg-spinner; he is the man who can buy the wickets of good batsmen and *wrap up the tail* with great expediency.

The right-handed wrist-spinner's stock ball is the *leg-spinner* and his variations on this theme include the *wrong'un*, the *flipper* and the *top-*

spinner. The left-handed wrist-spinner's leg-spinner (a ball that turns from the right-handed batsman's off-side into him) is known as the *chinaman*.

Wrist-spin was not fashionable in Test cricket before 1900. The successes of B.J.T. Bosanquet with his invention, the *bosie*, brought it into vogue in the early years of the century and its effectiveness at the highest levels of the game was ably demonstrated by the South African trio of Faulkner, Schwartz and Vogler just before World War I. Notable exponents of wrist-spin have included Australians Hordern, Mailey, Grimmett, Fleetwood-Smith and O'Reilly, and England's Freeman, Peebles and Wright. Sir Donald Bradman rates one of these — Bill O'Reilly — as the best bowler he ever faced.

wrong-foot the keeper. To make the wicketkeeper move away from the line of the ball as he prepares to gather a delivery. It is usually the outcome of a batsman unintentionally deflecting a ball off an outside or inside *edge*. The stumper moves towards the anticipated line of the ball to catch it; when that line suddenly and unpredictably changes, he finds it difficult to alter the direction of his initial movement. Only the most nimble keepers can gather the ball and take the catch after being wrong-footed.

wrong'un. Also *googly* or *bosie*. A slow, disguised, wrist-spun ball which appears to be a *leg-spinner*. The bowler bowls with the action and wrist-movement of a leg-spinner, but instead of the ball being spun out of the right side of the hand, the wrist is dropped so that the ball emerges from its left side, from behind the little finger and out of the back of the hand. Consequently the ball turns not like a leg-spinner from leg to off but from off to leg. The aim is to make the batsman play for the ball as if it were turning from leg, so that he leaves a gap between bat and pad and is bowled 'through the gate'. The wrong'un is the classical example of the bowler bamboozling the batsman by giving him the wrong clue about his intentions and then sending down a delivery precisely the opposite of what the batsman was expecting!

yorker. A delivery that bounces right on the batsman's *batting crease*. Since the batsman usually takes his stance with his leading foot in front of the crease and his rear foot behind, the ball may be described as pitching on a length level with the batsman's stance, thus causing him to 'hit over the ball' in attempting to *dig out the yorker*. If the ball is straight and bowls the striker, he is said to have been 'yorked'. The origin of the term is uncertain, but the word itself suggests that this ball could once have been the favourite delivery of a bowler hailing from the County of the Broad Acres. (See also *blockhole*; *sandshoe crusher*)